THE NEXUS OF PRACTICES

The Nexus of Practices: Connections, constellations, practitioners brings leading theorists of practice together to provide a fresh set of theoretical impulses for the surge of practice-focused studies currently sweeping across the social disciplines. The book addresses key issues facing practice theory, expands practice theory's conceptual repertoire, and explores new empirical terrain. With each intellectual move, it generates further opportunities for social research.

More specifically, the book's chapters offer new approaches to analysing connections within the nexus of practices, to exploring the dynamics and implications of the constellations that practices form, and to understanding people as practitioners that carry on practices. Topics examined include social change, language, power, affect, reflection, large social phenomena, and connectivity over time and space. Contributors thereby counter claims that practice theory cannot handle large phenomena and that it ignores people. The contributions also develop practice theoretical ideas in dialogue with other forms of social theory and in ways illustrated and informed by empirical cases and examples.

The Nexus of Practices will quickly become an important point of reference for future practice-focused research in the social sciences.

Allison Hui is an academic fellow in the Department of Sociology at Lancaster University, UK.

Theodore Schatzki is Senior Associate Dean and Professor of Philosophy and Geography at the College of Arts and Sciences, University of Kentucky, USA.

Elizabeth Shove is Professor of Sociology at Lancaster University, UK.

THE NEXUS OF PRACTICES

Connections, constellations, practitioners

Edited by Allison Hui, Theodore Schatzki and Elizabeth Shove

Routledge
Taylor & Francis Group

LONDON AND NEW YORK

First published 2017
by Routledge
2 Park Square, Milton Park, Abingdon, Oxon OX14 4RN

and by Routledge
711 Third Avenue, New York, NY 10017

Routledge is an imprint of the Taylor & Francis Group, an informa business

British Library Cataloguing in Publication Data
A catalogue record for this book is available from the British Library

Library of Congress Cataloguing in Publication Data
Names: Hui, Allison, editor. | Schatzki, Theodore R., editor. |
Shove, Elizabeth, 1959– editor.
Title: The nexus of practices : connections, constellations and
practitioners / edited by Allison Hui, Theodore Schatzki and Elizabeth Shove.
Description: 1 Edition. | New York : Routledge, 2017. |
Includes bibliographical references.
Identifiers: LCCN 2016028189| ISBN 9781138675148 (hbk) |
ISBN 9781138675155 (pbk) | ISBN 9781315560816 (ebk)
Subjects: LCSH: Sociology–Methodology. | Sociology–Research. |
Social sciences–Methodology. | Social sciences–Research.
Classification: LCC HM511 .N49 2017 | DDC 301.01–dc23
LC record available at https://lccn.loc.gov/2016028189

ISBN: 978-1-138-67514-8 (hbk)
ISBN: 978-1-138-67515-5 (pbk)
ISBN: 978-1-315-56081-6 (ebk)

Typeset in Bembo
by Out of House Publishing

CONTENTS

TABLE 1 Book organisation by themes (see the Introduction for elaboration)

	Suffusing	*Threading through*	*Largeness*	*Changing connections*	*Practitioners*
Alkemeyer and Buschmann (p.8)					■
Blue and Spurling (p.24)	■			■	
Gherardi (p.38)	■				■
Hui (p.52)		■			
Maller (p.68)				■	■
Morley (p.81)			■	■	
Nicolini (p.98)			■		
Reckwitz (p.114)	■	■			
Schatzki (p.126)	■	■	■		
Schmidt (p.141)			■		■
Shove (p.155)		■	■		
Watson (p.169)		■	■		
Welch and Warde (p.183)	■				

CONTRIBUTORS

Thomas Alkemeyer is professor of sociology and sociology of sport, and director of the research centre 'Genealogy of the Present', at the University of Oldenburg, Germany. His research foci are theories of practice, sociology of the body and practices of subjectivation.

Stanley Blue is a lecturer in sociology at Lancaster University, UK. His work traces the reproduction of everyday practices that matter for sustainability and health. His current research examines the temporal organisation of working practices in large institutions.

Nikolaus Buschmann was post-doc at the DFG (German Research Foundation) Research Training Group 'Self-Making. Practices of Subjectivation in Historical and Interdisciplinary Perspective' and is now member of the research centre 'Genealogy of the Present at the University of Oldenburg, Germany. His main areas of research are Modern German and European history, theories of practice and subjectivation, and the cultural history of politics.

Silvia Gherardi is senior professor of sociology of work and organisation at the Faculty of Sociology of the University of Trento, Italy, where she founded the Research Unit on Communication, Organizational Learning and Aesthetics (www.unitn.it/rucola).

Allison Hui is an academic fellow in sociology and a researcher within the DEMAND Centre at Lancaster University, UK. Her research examines transformations in everyday life in the context of changing global mobilities, focusing particularly on theorising social practices, consumption and travel.

Cecily Maller is a vice-chancellor's senior research fellow at RMIT University's Centre for Urban Research in Melbourne, Australia. As co-leader of the Beyond Behaviour Change Research Program, she researches human–environment interactions, health and sustainability in cities.

Janine Morley is a senior research associate in the DEMAND Centre at Lancaster University, UK. She is a sociologist who studies the relationships between everyday practices, infrastructures and resource-use, with particular interests in digital technologies, energy demand and social change.

Davide Nicolini is professor of organisation studies at Warwick Business School, UK. He co-directs the IKON Research Centre at Warwick Business School and the Warwick Institute of Health. His research interests include practice-based approaches to the study of knowing, learning and change in organisations and innovation process in healthcare and other complex environments.

Andreas Reckwitz is a professor of cultural sociology at European University Viadrina in Frankfurt (Oder), Germany. His research focuses on social theory and sociology of (late-)modern culture. His most recent publication is *The Invention of Creativity* (2016).

Theodore Schatzki is a dean and professor of philosophy and geography in the College of Arts and Sciences at the University of Kentucky, USA. Among his books are *Social Practices* (1996), *The Site of the Social* (2001) and *The Timespace of Human Activity* (2010).

Robert Schmidt is professor of process-oriented sociology at Catholic University Eichstätt-Ingolstadt, Germany. His research focuses on praxeology, praxeography and process-oriented methodology. His publications include *Sociology of Practices* (2012) and *Siting Praxeology: The Methodological Significance of 'Public' in Theories of Social Practices* (with Jörg Volbers, 2011).

Elizabeth Shove is professor of sociology at Lancaster University, UK and is co-director of the DEMAND Research Centre (Dynamics of Energy, Mobility and Demand). She has written about social practices, everyday life, and the changing demand for energy and mobility.

Nicola Spurling is lecturer in the Institute for Social Futures and sociology at Lancaster University, UK. Her research explores everyday futures and their implications, focussing on change in mobility, working and daily lives since 1950, theories of practice and futures methods.

Alan Warde is professor of sociology in the School of Social Sciences and professorial fellow of the Sustainable Consumption Institute at the University of

Manchester, UK. His research interests include the application of theories of practice to the sociological analysis of culture, consumption and food. He recently published *The Practice of Eating* (2016).

Matt Watson is senior lecturer at the University of Sheffield, UK. He is a human geographer with expertise on understanding the systemic relations between everyday practices, technologies, spaces and institutions to advance understandings of social change in relation to sustainability.

Daniel Welch is a research associate at the Sustainable Consumption Institute, University of Manchester, UK. His research interests focus on novel articulations between social theory, the sociology of consumption, sustainability, cultural economy and economic sociology, to inform socio-economic and socio-technical change.

PREFACE

This book is part of many histories. It catches and contributes to a rising tide of academic interest in theories of practice; as such it has a place in the ebb and flow of ideas and intellectual traditions. It also has a place in the lives and careers of each of its contributors and in the fields, debates and disciplines of which they are a part.

In knitting these various threads together, this volume is the tangible manifestation of a conjunction of practices linked via mediated forms of interaction otherwise known as writing, talking, revising and editing. Key moments in this sequence include a two-day meeting in Windermere in 2014, organised by the DEMAND (Dynamics of Energy, Mobility and Demand) Research Centre, where the idea of the book took hold. A second event, at Lancaster University in 2015 and again supported by DEMAND, brought contributing authors together to play floorball and to work through draft chapters, one by one.

This book is also part of many futures. Since practices like those of writing and reading are dynamic and generative, the ideas that are contained and carried in this collection move forward in, and as part of, an always changing nexus.

ACKNOWLEDGEMENTS

This work was supported by the Engineering and Physical Sciences Research Council (grant number EP/K011723/1) as part of the RCUK Energy Programme and by EDF as part of the R&D ECLEER Programme. Thanks to Emma Overmaat for administrative assistance in the production of the volume.

INTRODUCTION

Allison Hui, Theodore Schatzki and Elizabeth Shove

Social theorists have addressed the challenges of understanding and explaining social phenomena for the last two hundred years or more. During this time, different schools of thought have flourished and faded, and diverse conceptual schemes and frameworks have evolved. All ideas have histories, and those explored in this book relate to the school of thought that has come to be known as 'practice theory'. Ortner (1984) was one of the first to coin this term. It has since come to denote a body of ideas that, emerging since the 1970s against the background of the philosophical work of Wittgenstein and Heidegger, supposes that something called 'practice' is central to social life (Schatzki, Knorr Cetina and von Savigny, 2001; Reckwitz, 2002b).

This is an increasingly influential supposition, shared by people who, despite holding different ideas about society and how it works, uphold the following propositions: that practices consist in organised sets of actions, that practices link to form wider complexes and constellations – a nexus – and that this nexus forms the 'basic domain of study of the social sciences' (Giddens, 1984: 2). This set of ideas links such diverse theorists as Bourdieu (1977), Giddens (1979) and Lave (Lave and Wenger, 1991) – sometimes referred to as 'first generation' practice theorists – and second-generation proponents such as Schatzki (2002), Gherardi (2006), Reckwitz (2002b), Shove, Pantzar and Watson (2012) and Kemmis (Kemmis et al. 2014). It also forms the shared starting point for the contributions to this volume.

Individually, each chapter has something new to say about the nexus of practice and how it can be analysed and understood. Collectively, the contributions develop fresh approaches to important themes such as social change, language, power, people, reflection, large social phenomena and connectivity over time and space, treating these as aspects of or as rooted in the nexus of practices. In taking practice theory forward in these ways, the book counters certain often-heard criticisms. One is that practice theory applies best to small or local phenomena and poorly to larger, more expansive ones. According to this criticism, practice theory is useful for analysing activities like cooking, leisure pursuits or professional practices, but cannot handle 'big' topics including government alliances, international finance systems, religious institutions or power. Another pervasive objection is that practice theory neglects the individual. This criticism holds that practice theory is so fixated on practices and complexes thereof that it ignores the entities or practitioners whose actions compose and perpetuate practices and complexes. While practice theorists have given limited attention to these topics in the past, in this volume both are multiply addressed.

The volume also responds to a particular feature of the history of practice theory to date. In the last two decades, practice theoretical ways of thinking have been taken up in numerous fields including education, geography, history, art, sociology, political science and organisation studies and in the study of varied phenomena, including consumption, learning, teaching, professions, migration, organisations, international relations, sustainability and energy use. This rapid appropriation has not been matched by corresponding refinement in the theoretical ideas that are used to inform empirical research. This book responds to this situation by developing a richer repertoire of conceptual resources and directions for practice-theoretically inspired research.

Although the book is designed to inform future programmes of empirical enquiry, it is not a methodological handbook: accordingly, relatively little is said about issues of epistemology and methodology. Nor do contributors provide quick and easy recipes for those hoping for definitive instruction on what practice theory is about or how to apply it. Rather, chapters invite readers to venture into uncharted territory where debates have moved beyond familiar tropes such as micro/macro, agency/structure and process/product, and where the challenge is to explain how all social phenomena – including power, institutions, markets, change, organisations, science, religion, etc. – are aspects of, constellations of, or in some way rooted in the nexus of practices.

In exploring the nexus of practices, contributors address a wide range of issues. However, the approaches they take do not represent all possible strategies. 'Practice' is a rich polysemic word that, in addition to denoting organised arrays of action, also highlights the necessary embeddedness of human activity in social and material contexts and the relentlessly unfolding character of action and sequences of performances. Given these different meanings, it is perhaps not surprising that the range of 'practice approaches' has expanded and diversified over the past 30 years (Nicolini, 2012). This wider field encompasses not just the first and second generation practice theories mentioned above, but also so-called 'practice-based studies' that emphasise the concept of situated action (e.g. Gherardi, 2008), MacIntyrian conceptions that attribute internal goods to practices (MacIntyre, 1981), forms of discourse theory that focus on practices (e.g. Chouliaraki and Fairclough, 1999; Scollon, 2001) and traditions such as ethnomethodology that underline the processional quality of human social activity. Further afield, but not unrelated, lie endeavours such as social-cultural activity theory, actor-network theory and 'praxis' theory in the neo-Marxist tradition.

Only some versions of social-cultural activity theory, actor-network theory and praxis theory take practices as their central concern and can therefore be considered as 'practice' theories. In addition, important differences and incommensurabilities exist among practice theories (as defined above) and between them and the wider family of practice approaches. The contributors to this volume are not primarily concerned to detail compatibilities, incompatibilities and possible alliances or conflicts among these approaches. Instead, some draw practice theory together with other bodies of thought including theories of power and governmentality, actor-network theory, genetics, posthumanist and feminist theory in the course of working through specific questions about the nexus of practices. In taking this approach, various chapters develop and extend practice theoretical concepts alongside and in dialogue with other forms of social theory.

In confronting new and established topics, this book keeps practice theory moving, and with each move, new questions come into view. In this respect, the book is as much an exercise in setting agendas as in filling out or finally resolving well-worn debates. It is also, necessarily, partial: other themes could have been pursued, and those that we do tackle could be developed more comprehensively and in other ways. This volume nonetheless represents a concerted effort to think through the nexus of practices.

Guide for readers

As the book's subtitle suggests, its chapters offer new approaches to describing and analysing *connections* within the nexus of practices, to questioning the dynamics and implications of the complexes and *constellations* that practices form and to understanding the entities – the *practitioners* – that carry on or enact practices. Since individual chapters speak to more than one of these agendas, there is no one way of grouping them and thus no one way of reading the book. We have therefore taken the unusual step of presenting the chapters in alphabetical order, by author's surname. The resulting table of contents is complemented by a table which identifies themes that each chapter addresses (see p.vii).

Five significant themes are woven through the book, namely: suffusing, threading through, largeness, changing connections and practitioners. These themes did not arise by chance. Some authors, in tackling questions of largeness and in examining the roles of practitioners, respond to the prominent criticisms of practice theory mentioned above. Other authors concentrate on the problem of better understanding how practices hang together. The value of distinguishing between qualitatively different processes of interconnection (such as suffusing and threading through) emerged as the book took shape, as did an interest in characterising the dynamism, not of isolated practices, but of complexes and constellations of them. When read together, the chapters combine to provide new understandings of the nexus of practices and of its connections, constellations and practitioners.

The remainder of this introduction is designed to help readers navigate the collection as a whole. It describes the five cross-cutting themes, explains which chapters engage with each, and briefly comments on what the contributions have to offer.

Suffusing

The term 'suffusing' – which means to spread over or through as with a liquid or gas – suggests that certain phenomena can pervade practices and complexes thereof, providing a kind of atmosphere in which actions are performed and practices carried forward. Suffusing phenomena are often intangible in some sense, even though they are grasped by participants, expressed in doings and sayings and materialised in objects. Examples explored in this book include: affect, general understandings, linguistically articulated meaning and significance and certain forms of sociomateriality. For example, Reckwitz suggests that every social order, as a set of practices, is a specific order of affects. Welch and Warde argue that general understandings pervade practice complexes, developing this idea as an example of how culture can be conceptualised as a phenomenon of practices. Schatzki, who extends practice theoretical concepts to sayings and texts by working off ideas of prominent discourse theorists, discusses how the significance that is articulated in sayings and texts pervades the nexus of practices. And Gherardi draws attention to types of sociomaterial arrangements (e.g. involved in artificial nutrition or in emergency responses) that suffuse practices of ordering. As these chapters show, phenomena that suffuse individual practices and complexes of practice constitute diffuse but pervasive links among them. As well as revealing the subtlety of this particular form of connection, these chapters show how phenomena that are usually analysed aside from practice (affect, culture, etc.) are formed through multiple associations with multiple practices.

Threading through

The notion of 'threading through' captures the idea that things, for instance, an object or a practice, can move or advance through the nexus of practices, thereby linking the practices through which they pass or to which they are connected. Threading through differs from suffusing because it is characterised by identifiable trajectories and paths, particular links made and unmade and traceable, even concrete movement. By comparison, the presence and dissemination of affect, understanding and meaning is less distinct and more ethereal.

There are many variants of threading through, differing in spatial and temporal extent, the 'thickness' of threads and the density of the woven ties that result. For example, Shove considers things such as energy supplies, components, TVs, and houses as they thread through practices and as their status vis-à-vis different practices switches among the roles of resource, appliance and infrastructure. These threads form ties that span what are usually thought of as different 'scales'. Similarly, Hui writes about how things connect practices and about how different conjunctions represent sources of variation within the nexus of practices. Her method of following the ways in which things such as passports and funeral arrangements are threaded through practices enables consideration of simultaneously dynamic trajectories and interactions of practitioners, materials and social categories. Watson, whose chapter considers how practice theory can accommodate an analysis of power, examines objects that circulate among practice complexes and explains how this circulation affects the 'conduct of conduct' that Foucault called power.

Suffusing and threading through are not mutually exclusive forms. As well as exemplifying processes of suffusion, Schatzki's chapter shows how practice bundles connect through (and are partly composed by) the circulation of sayings and texts. Similarly, Reckwitz writes about how artefacts that circulate among practices can serve as 'affect generators'.

Largeness

In various ways, all sorts of practices connect. The resulting complexes are distributed across the spectrum of small to large, in the sense of spatial (temporal) extension. While many practice theoretical analyses of small-scale or local phenomena exist, comparatively few focus on large social phenomena (for exceptions, see Reckwitz, 2006; Jarzabkowski, Bednarek and Spee, 2015). This is something of a gap in that laypersons and scholars alike are often interested in large social matters, for example, markets, governments, international coalitions, football leagues and world religions.

Numerous chapters in this volume clear the ground for robust analyses of such phenomena (see also Schatzki, 2016b), examining processes involved in the construction of large phenomena or elements of their composition or workings. Understanding forms of interconnection, such as suffusing or threading through, also helps prepare this ground, but there is more to say about how large social phenomena form and change. For example, Watson's practice theoretical analysis of how power is exerted by institutions such as governments and corporations focuses on how some practices are capable of orchestrating, disciplining and shaping others. Likewise, in describing series of material relations that add up to more than the sum of the interconnected parts, Shove offers an account of the ongoing making of world trade and global energy demand. Morley similarly deals with material-practice relations, but concentrates on the implications of delegation and automation (for example to automated factories) for the constitution of large arrangements and how these change. Taking a different approach, Schmidt considers the role that reflection plays in the formation and transformation of practice bundles within contemporary football. And Nicolini takes stock of how practice approaches address issues of largeness, laying out options and possibilities for conceptualising this topic.

Changing connections

The chapters in this book repeatedly counter the claim that practice theory promulgates a static view of society. They share the assumption that the nexus of practices is constantly happening and continually changing in small and occasionally larger ways, although it is not, as theories of becoming aver, in constant flux. As several chapters demonstrate, focusing on connections within the nexus of practices has consequences for discussions of change. Two chapters suggest that interconnected systems of practice, as opposed to individual practices, are the locus of change, especially of changes that occur across decades or generations. Blue and Spurling discuss how changes in complexes of practices – in their case, those found in hospitals – are modulated by jurisdictional, temporal and material-spatial dynamics. Morley, meanwhile, considers the growing prevalence of automated machines, arguing that their operation in the absence of human bodies is crucial for understanding how systems of practice develop. These chapters suggest that the trajectories of both individual practices and complexes of them are in part outcomes of how multiple practices interconnect.

Maller's contribution takes a different tack, using epigenetic understandings of the heritability of embodied characteristics to highlight the importance of bodies as media of continuity and change that are connected to multiple practices. The idea that practices are carried across generations by human bodies is intriguing and challenging both for practice theories and for organisations and agencies that seek to direct or shape how practices change. It also raises further questions about the roles of practitioners in theories of practice.

Practitioners

The final cross-cutting theme concerns people as participants in practices, a topic about which practice theories have historically said relatively little (but see Dreier, 2008; Alkemeyer, 2013). The book's chapters explore people as entities that become participants and who subsequently perpetuate and transform practices through their actions. Alkemeyer and Buschmann extend practice theoretical approaches to the study of learning, scrutinising the bodily and mental-cum-bodily formation of practitioners through their participation in practices and through the intertwined processes of becoming-a-subject and becoming-subject-to the normative organisations of practices. Reckwitz writes about how individuals' affects and motivations are tied to the regimes of affect that suffuse practices, while Maller enquires into the possible epigenetic effects of engaging in specific practices. Gherardi likewise considers the shaping of practitioners' bodies, in particular the bodily molding that results from their incorporation into the sociomaterial (à la Barad) regimes of particular practices. Finally, Schmidt's chapter shows that from a practice theory perspective, phenomena traditionally considered to be mental and individualist in character, namely, thinking and reflection, are really features of activity-in-practices, and that it is in this form that they contribute to the transformation of practices over time.

Unfinished business

This book makes important strides towards conceptualising and understanding the nexus of practices, highlighting themes of connection, constellations and practitioners. However, much more work still needs to be done. For example, although the book shows how practice theoretical analyses of large phenomena might proceed, such analyses are not developed in any detail. Similarly, there is clearly more to be said about power, language, learning, practitioners, connectivity and their dynamics. Reading through the chapters, other areas of unfinished business come into view. For example, if practice theories aim to conceptualise and analyse social phenomena in terms of the nexus of practices, what types of social scientific enquiry should be devised, what kinds of knowledge should be produced, and with which tools and methods? We hope this book will inspire researchers to engage with these questions and with others that clearly remain on the practice theory agenda.

1

LEARNING IN AND ACROSS PRACTICES

Enablement as subjectivation

Thomas Alkemeyer and Nikolaus Buschmann
(Translated by Robert Mitchell and Kristina Brümmer)

Practice theorists have a vested interest in studying how social order emerges via the interplay of things, artefacts and bodies. However, they rarely reflect upon how the people involved in order-making come to be or, indeed, put themselves in the position to be able to participate as competent 'players'.[1] One reason for this oversight, from our perspective, is that practice theoretical discussions still mostly operate within the framework of familiar alternatives, namely, whether social structures constitute social action and its actors, or whether the structures are constituted by activities within the bounds of preformed agency. Accordingly, two – oversimplified – perspectives can be differentiated by the relationship they propose between praxis[2] and participants. If praxis is seen as pre-structured, i.e. as practice, then participants are mere dependent variables keeping routinised action 'going'. If, on the other hand, praxis is conceived as a contingent accomplishment, then participants become autonomous actors with stores of practical knowledge that enable them to deal with the contingency of practice in a skilful and creative manner. These differences notwithstanding, the perspectives both pay very little attention to how playability[3] arises. Furthermore, within the framework of their respective conceptions of praxis, the participants are conceived of in one way or another as pretty much 'play-able' out of the box, so to speak. In contrast, we understand play-ability not to be an always given property of individuals, but rather to be formed within the framework of 'distributed agency' (Rammert and Schulz-Schaeffer, 2002): things, artefacts and bodies mutually enable one another in their play-ability and, by doing so, bring forth a specific reflexivity of praxis.

In this chapter, we reconstruct how play-ability arises qua learning through participation in shared practices. We do this in connection with our thesis that practice theories need to be complemented by theories of subjectivation if they are to resolve the issues of both how practices are transmitted and reproduced and how they are accomplished in situated praxis. Against this background, we conceptualise subjectivation as a process inherently embedded in praxis, in which the ability intelligently to orient one's own action towards practice-specific requirements is continually being formed and in which the process of doing can also entail the critique and transcendence of these requirements. Learning cannot be understood as the passive acquisition of operational skills. Instead, people (trans)form themselves via their engagement as recognisable subjects and cultivate their play-ability by learning to comply with the normative standards unfolding in praxis.

In this context, we utilise the processual and relational category of *en-ablement*.[4] This term indicates that people only become carriers of specific abilities through participation in practices. It also suggests that the status of a participant is dependent upon mutual recognition. We assume that 'our participation in ... practices enables us to become the agents we are through our mutual accountability to the possibilities those practices make available and to what is thereby at stake for us in how we respond to those possibilities' (Rouse, 2007b: 53). Accordingly, we introduce the idea of en-ablement as subjectivation in order to incorporate activity alongside passivity, adaptation and defiance, routine and reflexivity, which are all involved in the formation of play-ability.

By conceiving of the unfolding of practices and the formation of play-ability as co-constitutive and co-extensive, we attempt to do justice to the ultimate, not yet fulfilled aim of abandoning the traditional contrast between methodological holism and methodological individualism. In pursuit of this aim, we try to grasp the emergence of play-ability within a practice theoretical framework without succumbing to old habits of either attributing deterministic power to practices over the activities of participants or presupposing fully formed actors who are ready for action.

In taking this approach, we enter a research field that is usually dominated by such terms as learning or education. Hence, the first section discusses how these terms are conceptualised within the framework of practice theories. Subsequently, the second section argues that a practice theoretical perspective must seek to reconstruct the processes in which play-ability emerges in praxis. The following section portrays the development of competent participation as a process in which specific knowledge, identity and social membership are formed, thus embedding learning within power relations and conflict. The section thereafter shows that the process of becoming a 'player' cannot be reduced to a purely mental interaction with the world, but rather emerges as part of one's bodily being and acting in the world. The chapter concludes by shedding light on the relationships between normativity, enablement and subjectivation.

Practice theories and learning

Within the 'family' of practice theories, research in the field of learning and education addresses concepts of socialisation, habitualisation and embodiment (Hillebrandt, 2014: 67). These concepts have the advantage of bringing often neglected bodily, pre-reflexive and non-linguistic processes to the fore (Alkemeyer and Brümmer, 2016), thereby avoiding the reduction of learning and education to cognitive processes and the acquisition of propositional knowledge. However, they portray participants mostly as passive embodied receptacles of practice-specific stores of knowledge (Shove *et al.*, 2012: 63–79). By assuming a fit between field and practice-specific orders and participatory competences, they focus primarily on what participants have to (be able) to do in order for practices to continue their routine course (Brake, 2016: 97). To put it succinctly: the position that teachers hitherto occupied in mechanistic theories of learning has been filled in these approaches by practices, which teach participants a specific way of perceiving (Reckwitz, 2015: 448) and practical know-how. Learning appears foremost as adaptation to the status quo and the issue of the acquisition and the constant (re)creation of play-ability in praxis never emerges (Nicolini, 2012: 78).

The neglect of these issues in some of the currently most discussed practice theoretical approaches in sociology[5] is the consequence of studying practices as quasi-automatically succeeding 'choreographies' within which participants' actions interlock frictionlessly, as if following a hidden rhythm or magical hand.[6] This view on practices is an artefact of observation which owes its existence to the overview inherent to a 'theatrical perspective' on the social world; how this world presents itself to participants remains invisible (Alkemeyer and Buschmann, 2016).

As a consequence of this perspective, these approaches neglect, first, the many different requirements for engaged participation that arise from the uncertainty of practical accomplishments. In the flow of praxis, participants must always be able to adjust to situational necessities and possibilities. There is always a 'potential of the situation' (Jullien, 1999: 33ff) and scope for transformative interventions of participants. Second, these approaches overlook the point that learning requires disposition and activity from participants who must be amenable to being taken in by or to engage with practices. Due to their tendency to extrapolate from practice-specific orders to participatory competences, we learn very little about how people mindfully, actively and purposefully partake in their formation as participants (Brümmer, 2015: 72). Third and related, the status of materialities such as things, artefacts and bodies also appears in a different light. In a functionalist perspective, which primarily considers how practices succeed, materialities are viewed as 'proposals for being' whose potentials in general are fulfilled in the successful practical connection with other participants. However, the verily important finding that things as warrants of their usage 'thicken' the contingency of practical accomplishments (Schmidt, 2012: 55) should not hide the trouble and resistance which emanate in situ both from the things and artefacts as well as from embodied habits. For example, which 'affordances' (Gibson, 1979) artefacts invoke within learning processes and to what extent they become meaningful objects therein, presenting and delivering practice-specific knowledge, cannot be ascertained at the outset. This is instead an empirical matter which must be investigated in each socio-material constellation in connection with the practices performed within it.

These, in a common functionalist perspective neglected, aspects are much more strongly represented in currently less noticed practice theoretical concepts as post-Marxist approaches or the New Pragmatism of Boltanski and Thévenot (Boltanski and Thévenot, 2011), which emphasise the multi-positionality, multi-perspectivity and power asymmetry of praxis, and which evoke the conflictuality and instability of practices (Schäfer, 2013). In this view, performing a practice 'not only leads to stability through habituation but also to diversity, brought by the unstable structure of practices themselves' (Gherardi, 2012b: 228). The research focus then lies on the processual, relational and therefore interactive construction of social order. Consequentially, these approaches are concerned with making empirically visible the diverse methods, strategies, competences, activities and activity forms utilised in the practical creation of a specific intelligible social reality (Garfinkel, 1967; Nicolini, 2012: 134–61). Attention, consequently, shifts to participants' coping strategies. The pendant to the 'flow' of praxis is the improvisation of participants from whose perspectives the practical accomplishment-in-the-moment appears as a never completely predictable sequence of responses to situations. Each one of these situations presents participants with a specific task. The necessity for continual learning becomes obvious when we recognise the often conflictual demands and situationally specific requirements with which participants are confronted: learning is not only required in order to form practice-specific habits and routines, but also to be able to deal with conflicts, ambivalence and uncertainty.

It is only when open-endedness, fragility and unpredictability are taken into account alongside the prefiguration and structuration of praxis that we catch sight of the bodily, mental and cognitive resources that participants bring to bear in the collective accomplishment of all practices (Barnes, 2001). This applies even when the diverse elements of a practice routinely harmonise, as appears to be the case when, for example, soldiers march in formation: what may appear from the theatrical perspective as a '*continuity of form*' (Giddens, 1979: 216, original emphasis), becomes tangible from the participants' perspectives as an uncertain string of events in which every single soldier must invest effort – e.g. in breathing (Lande, 2002) – in order to be 'recruited' by the practice of marching in the first place (Brümmer and Mitchell, 2014: 159ff).

Thus, practice theory cannot stop at viewing the emergence of play-ability as a mere fitting into extant orders, nor should it succumb to the individualistic myopia of reducing learning to an internal process within solipsistic individuals. Rather, it must attend to the reciprocal production of social order and play-ability. Only then can it provide a plausible account of how skills are acquired and made available via participation in practices and of how this allows for participants not only to make routine contributions to the workings of a practice but also to intervene creatively in events and therefore be a transformative force in praxis. Accordingly, the approach presented here emphasises that it is participants who produce the social regularity in praxis as an empirically concrete structuration. In doing so, participants undergo a transformation themselves: they become able to adjust and improve their participation in the context of not just one practice but many similar practices in a process of learning self-structuration. By laying 'focus on the trajectories of learners as they change' (Lave, 1996: 128) through active engagement in and across practices, people appear as increasingly competent carriers of specific abilities, including critical competences. As such, they become enabled via the interplay with other participants to not automatically reproducing the social order, but also to reflectively modifying and critically transcending it.[7]

At this juncture, and in summary, our approach sheds light on the fundamental heteronomy of the acquisition of participatory competences. We stress that candidates for participation reciprocally initiate themselves as and make themselves into participants by equipping one another, with the collaboration of things and artefacts, with situational possibilities of action and, at the same time, delimiting them. Being enabled therefore means simultaneously to be put and to put oneself in the position to fulfil the requirements (or rather what is recognized as a requirement) of a practice. Thus, learning comes into view as a process encompassing both active and passive elements, opening up new realms of possibility and entailing moments of resistance and limitations, hence implying the necessity to find new or different forms of organisation within the relations of praxis.

Learning as a precondition and form of social membership

By understanding learning as a process of self-(trans)formation within practices, it is no longer sufficient to focus on the transfer of propositional knowledge in societally cordoned-off areas of learning and teaching. Rather, learning knows no bounds: it occurs in explicitly educational forms such as drills, exercises and training as well as in games, rituals or competitions and even in the 'implicit pedagogy' (Bourdieu, 1977: 94) of everyday life. This means that it can pertain to all kinds of practices and that different kinds of practices imply their own techniques and contents of learning. Therefore, all situations should be taken into account in which embodied agents transform themselves by interacting in the context of a shared practice with one another as well as with the things and artefacts involved.[8]

This is also the main idea behind the concept of 'situated learning' (Lave and Wenger, 1991), which aims to avoid any reification of learning as a distinct activity. Understood as an ongoing process potentially taking place in any practice, learning is disconnected from explicit pedagogical intent. It is not defined as a top-down process driven by experts, but as an interactive event, with varied positions that participants can occupy vis-à-vis others' doings in a shared practice. Learning is conceived of as a process of participating in practices in which, alongside practical and propositional knowledge, identity and social membership are formed. Thus, learning and social membership are co-dependent: learning appears as a precondition as well as 'an evolving form of membership' (Lave and Wenger, 1991: 51) in a 'community of practice' (Wenger, 1998). It requires involvement and simultaneously contributes to the development and transformation of practices. Therefore, learning processes do not merely bring out practice-specific participatory competences, but can themselves transform what is learned (Hager, Lee and Reich, 2012: 9–11).

In this view, learning is located in interactions of praxis that bring novices to possess collectively shared knowledge that is created in these very same interactions. Within an interplay of socialising acts, they learn by taking the perspectives not only of the senior members or designated instructors, but also of other novices, as they constantly correct themselves, recognise room to manoeuvre in and, thus, keep within the order at hand: *all* participants teach themselves and each other theoretical and practical knowledge. They reciprocally determine one another's becoming, converging on a collective practice and, in doing so, gain a specific position within the collective, which itself is constituted as a community of practice within this process.

From this perspective, learning is a socially structured process of positioning and equipping participants with different resources and possibilities. Thus, it always takes place in historical contexts shaped by power relations (Nicolini, 2012: 79): both the historical and social structure of a practice as well as the power relations that define a specific regime of participation determine possibilities of learning and the learning trajectories of novices (Dreier, 2003; Nielsen, 2008). Since every practice provides different social positions, which come with varying amount(s) of power and influence, the responsibility for the 'product' of a shared practice is distributed and attributed differently. The insight that power relations and normative orders unfolding in praxis define conditions of learning illuminates why learning is associated with conflicts and disagreements (Elkjaer, 2009: 87). The established members of a community of practice are at once forced to impart their knowledge to novices and obliged to maintain their positions of power which are based on this knowledge. Novices, on the other hand, sometimes try to do things differently in order to gain independence and to claim originality for themselves. Conceived in this way, learning leads to the imitating repetition of what already exists as well as to an active negotiation of interests, interpretations and knowledge, which contains moments of critical reflexivity about established hierarchies and practice-specific requirements.

By analysing learning as embedded in social (power-)relations, this approach brings to light, first, how learning actually takes place, how techniques, knowledge and know-how are passed on between generations. Sharing socially dispersed knowledge arises through participation in a community of practitioners; learning proceeds through interactions between novices and more established members as well as among novices (Hara, 2009: 118). Second, Lave and Wenger point out that passing on knowledge involves conflicts, the setting up of boundaries of and divisions between memberships and the attribution of identities within power relations. This makes apparent that the development of competent participation is inherently connected with the reproduction and transformation of the social structures in which the learning processes are located. Third and last, Lave and Wenger notice that learning also includes the norms that are established within a practice. Participants, especially novices, not only acquire necessary skills, but also learn how one does something correctly. Seeing this clearly brings the 'immanent didactics' (Schindler, 2011) of every practice into view: participants show each other what is to be done and how it should be done to be recognised as correct, situationally adequate and proper.

By acknowledging informal ways of learning and highlighting the co-emergence of skills and participation (Evans, 2009: 137), the concept of situated learning offers diverse starting points for conducting practice theoretical studies of exactly how play-ability is developed (Gherardi and Nicolini, 2002; Hager *et al.*, 2012). However, just as with Bourdieu's concept of habitus (see below), the situated-learning approach provides a more persuasive account of persistence and perpetuation than of change and innovation.

This situation reflects a preference for describing the success and finality of learning processes: since their empirical material is mostly drawn from areas of trade, Lave and Wenger emphasise the *common sense* constituted within a community of practice, which arises through reciprocal engagement, working on a shared object, a shared pool of resources and a shared history of learning. Conflicts are primarily located in conflicts *between* generations with*in* a community. This account thus neglects other conflicts resulting from the internal multi-perspectivity, polyphony and differentiation present in all praxis (Warde, 2005) as well as from the external differentiation of practices emanating from different social fields.

As a consequence, a practice theoretical approach to learning must pay closer attention to the fact that every practice distributes its practitioners into different positions with distinct perspectives, thus differentiating them (Nicolini, 2012: 94) and inevitably pitting them against one another. Neither linguistic communication nor co-operation can bring these disparate perspectives and interests into complete harmony (Boltanski and Honneth, 2009: 101). Moreover, the simultaneity of disparate perspectives unfolding in praxis 'produces dissonance rather than a canon' (Gherardi and Nicolini, 2002: 429ff). Given a specific socio-spatial positioning and biographically determined personal situatedness, every participant finds him or herself confronted with specific expectations, limitations and possibilities. Learning consequently involves acquiring the ability to identify and differentiate various perspectives, gradually to see and to correct oneself from one's own perspective with others' eyes and to abide by the shared conventions of the practice.

It thus becomes clear that the norms defining 'good', 'correct' or 'proper' actions depend on the participants' different perspectives. Working on a shared object by no means inevitably produces consensus. Being 'a much richer notion than mere rule following or rigid adherence to standard procedures' (Hager, 2012: 28), the normativity of learning emerges as a contested product in the continuous process of self- and other-positioning and struggle in praxis. It follows that learning has a *political* dimension; it is not enough to do something in a merely functional, technically correct manner. Rather, actions must be performed appropriately. Appropriateness emerges in praxis, understood as an ongoing attunement of different participants, which is likely to imply conflict and the potential to fail.

Practice, learning and embodied reflexivity

From a practice theoretical perspective, learning means to come to participate in a practice by acquiring and performing the skills and the knowledge required of acceptable participation. In this perspective, not only practical but also propositional knowledge is learned by performing practices in interaction with other participants, involving bodily perceptions and doings like movements, attitudes and gestures within the socio-material arrangements of different 'sites of the social' (Schatzki, 2002) – for example driving a bobtail, playing the piano or proving a mathematical theorem: one has to operate the steering wheel, move one's fingers over the keyboard or write while sitting at a desk. Even when performing an allegedly purely 'inner' activity, one is bodily situated and thus has to adopt a posture that constitutes a specific attentiveness and 'inner' attitudes of absorption and thoughtfulness.

The irreducible bodily existence of people in the world has at least two consequences for their participation in practices: first, it means that in a situation (as a momentary configuration of participants in the course of a practice), two or more participants can never occupy the same socio-material position. Therefore, each of them has his or her unique perspective on the shared practice related to the position they occupy in this situation. It is this multi-perspectivity that introduces difference into all practices (Boltanski, 2010: 95ff). As the relational positioning of bodies hangs together with the functional requirements as well as the normative demands and power inequalities of a practice (Alkemeyer, Brümmer and Pille, forthcoming), the conflictual character of praxis is manifoldly over-determined. Second, people act and learn both *with* their bodies and *as* bodies. From birth onwards, babies stretch their limbs towards things that they encounter as 'affordances' (Gibson, 1979) in their environment and to which they respond by fingering, touching and grasping. Gradually, things also come to encounter them as restive objects, challenging them to cope with emerging difficulties *in praxis*, e.g. fighting with a 'rebellious' parka while dressing (Bröskamp, 2015).

Bodily situatedness always corresponds to mental and affective situatedness (Holzkamp, 1995: 258ff). It implies the constitution of context-sensitive perceptions, awareness and ways of thinking. These respond to the (position-specific) demands of the practice or the resistance of the things involved as they are given to the participant in his or her lived experience. Moreover, this experience not only depends on a participant's *actual* bodily and mental situatedness in a practice, but is also informed by a 'personal situatedness' (Holzkamp, 1995: 263ff) that is defined by his or her position in the social space of a given society and in the trajectory of his or her life.

This means that while jointly performing a practice, participants interact with one another from various positions that differ in multiple dimensions. In order to play along while at the same time pursuing their particular position-specific interests, they have to orient their doings and sayings not only to the rules and 'teleoaffective structures' (Schatzki, 2002), which themselves evolve in the shared praxis, but also to the affordances of other human and non-human participants, as well as to situationally specific opportunities for intervening in the flow of praxis. Similar to a surfer who has to be constantly attentive to the next advantageous wave, human participants attend both to the right moment for intervening and to suitable ways of acting. On only a few occasions is it adequate just to reel off automatic or routine responses. Even routines have to be continuously tuned to situational demands and possible courses of action on the basis of an ongoing attentiveness.

As studies of sports practices demonstrate, such attention is the affair not of an isolated mind, but of an embodied agent in its sensual-material interplay with a concrete world. The body is not only an extended 'thing' (*res extensa*) with clear, visible outlines, but also a *lived body* that is exposed to the world, that can be affected *in* (e.g. Riedel, 2012) and *by* (Lindemann, 2017) concrete situations and that responds to those situations by 'incorporating' other participants into its 'space of muscular sensation' (Wittgenstein, as quoted in Gebauer, 2009: 64) on the basis of its kinaesthetic experience (Noland, 2009) and sensorimotor skills (e.g. Christensen, Sutton and McIlwain, 2016). Understood as a lived body, the human body comes to the fore not only as 'raw material' (Moore and Kosut, 2010: 1) that is shaped in social processes, but also as an 'unexceedable mode of human experience' (Bedorf, 2015: 139) orienting and guiding people's acting in the world. In this sense, it is passive and active, a *patiens* and an *agens* at the same time.

The lived body is studied in the philosophical tradition of phenomenology (e.g. Merleau-Ponty, 1966). Here, the bodily sensorium is considered a fundamental, a priori (i.e. pre-social, pre-practical) source of access to the world and any kind of knowledge. However, from a practice theoretical perspective which tries to overcome every kind of methodological individualism, such a fundamentalist understanding that traces back acts of perceiving and acting to the 'zero-point' of the body is insufficient. From this perspective, the 'twofold social genesis' (Wacquant, 1992: 22) of an embodied capacity to play along and the objectivity of the social world has to be taken into account. In the field of practice theory, it was particularly Bourdieu who investigated the capabilities of the lived body not as a priori universals, but as empirical variables that develop first and foremost in the social relations of praxis. For him (Bordieu, 2000: 134), the receptive human organism develops a set of continuously transforming dispositions (i.e. habitus) comprising tendencies and schemata of perception, feeling, cognition and evaluation which absorb all (further) carnal experiences and structure them. From this perspective, the sensitivity of the lived body is a historical and 'social sensitivity' (Ostrow, 1990), which is cemented in flesh and blood through experience, thus ensuring the instantaneous differentiation of objects of experience, stimuli and demands towards which behaviour can be oriented (cf. Wacquant, 1996: 42, n.35).

According to Bourdieu (e.g. 1990), the embodiment of a 'practical sense' has contradictory effects: on the one hand, it usually enables the agent to produce acts spontaneously and creatively that match the demands of a situation. On the other hand, it constrains the possible courses of action and ensures – as a social 'sense of one's place' (Goffman) – that the agent actively reproduces the social structures of inequality to which he or she is subjected. Indeed, Bourdieu's concept of the incorporation of the social has been often criticised for being able to explain the reproduction of structures but not structural changes (e.g. Reckwitz, 2000b: 337–9), because it reduces learning to a mere adjustment of bodily and mental structures to socially 'structured possibilities for individual action in the world' (Lave, 1997: 147) and thus views agents as mere executors of external orders (see also King, 2000). Bourdieu, however, conceptualises incorporation not as a social or cultural imprint, but as an active acquisition of the social world through mimetic re-enactment of the move-ments, attitudes and gestures of other agents (e.g. Bourdieu, 1977: 87ff) as well as through trying things out, copying and responding to situational affordances or demands by 'regulated improvisation' (Bourdieu, 1990: 57). Since meaning, cultural orders, beliefs and value systems only exist, according to Bourdieu, within the per-formances of social praxis, this acquisition cannot be conceived in any other way than as *experience*, which is made in interaction with other agents and in a concrete environment (Krais and Gebauer, 2002: 61),[9] i.e. as learning in the sense of a rela-tional, social process.

However, the micro-logic of habitus (trans)formation by learning remains a black box in Bourdieu's work. An attempt to rectify this is Wacquant's (2004) auto-ethnographic study of his own becoming a boxer. Using Bourdieu's theoretical vocabulary, Wacquant describes how, through the arduous and often painful process of an 'implicit and collective pedagogy' (Wacquant, 2004: 99–126), not only his physique, but also his ways of perceiving, sensing and feeling were transformed so thoroughly that his whole being gradually transformed with regard both to the functional requirements of movements as well as to the moral and affective order of boxing in the context of a gym in a Chicago ghetto.[10] Wacquant's empirical obser-vations clarify that risky agonistic practices like boxing require a permanent bodily, sensorial and mental tenseness, a constant alertness and attentiveness for the move-ments, gestures and glances of the opponent as moments of an outright practice-oriented 'sensual cognition' (Holzkamp, 1978) and 'empractical' awareness which orient action in practice in a pre-theoretical manner (Caysa, 2016).[11] This kind of cognition and awareness is entirely incorporated in the sensual-material interac-tions of praxis and enables the agent to adjust his or her doings (also strategically) to rapidly changing and therefore profoundly uncertain conditions in the flow of praxis itself.

Already Wittgenstein, as a precursor of recent practice theory, conceived of thinking (cognition) not as an internal mental operation of a separate mind, but as a dimension of an agent's sensual-material interplay with the concrete, material world. According to Wittgenstein, things in an agent's environment that are identi-fied as relevant for acting are not perceived in terms of their abstract features but with regard to their concrete 'qualities of handling' ('Umgangsqualitäten', Gebauer, 2009: 64). Using the concept of a 'language game' ('Sprachspiel'), he argues that all things, including their verbal denomination, acquire meaning only through agents' practical engagement in the social world. In this respect, learning a language game goes hand in hand with a corresponding formation of bodily performances, motor skills and the lived body's sensorium. In his interpretation of Wittgenstein's anthro-pology, Gebauer (2009) calls a body attuned to a language game a 'handling body' ('Umgangskörper').[12] This body warrants an agent's intelligibility within a speech community and serves as the carrier of a practical knowledge adequate for a specific language game. Seen in this light, all actions in social games are based on the ability of an adequately trained and shaped body to deal with the world. For Wittgenstein, 'training brings about "spontaneous" reactions which serve as anchors in human life around which motivated and complex behaviours develop' and makes possible 'both the acquisition of knowledge and participation in practices' (Schatzki, 2016c).

For the purpose of theoretically differentiating the concept of 'handling body', we suggest analysing the 'order' of the body that appears and is constituted in praxis as a 'lived-body-in-accomplishment' ('Vollzugskörper'; cf. Alkemeyer and Michaeler, 2013). This concept reflects that both the physical body and the sensorium of the lived body become attuned to the requirements of a practice through concretely situated practical accomplishments.[13] As can be shown in detailed analyses of training practices in sports, it is not only the body's movements, but also its receptiveness, attentiveness, senses and readiness for acting that are shaped according to the demands of the practice it is engaged and engaging in: at earlier stages of training processes – e.g. in acrobatics – direct manipulation and touching by the trainer or by other experienced athletes help the exercising novice bring his or her movements into proper shape. At the same time, touching allows the trainer to check and qualify the tension of the athlete's body and to direct his or her attention to specific parts of the lived body which are crucial for the performance of an acrobatic figure. An embodied reflection is thus cultivated which enables the athlete to join a (collective) practice. At later stages of exercise, gestural and verbal pointing replaces direct manipulation and touch. Pointing in this sense constitutes an intermediate step between direct intervention and the fully developed capability of kinesthetic self-organisation (Brümmer and Alkemeyer, forthcoming).

This capability indicates that praxis is characterised by a permanent interplay and transition between 'outer' bodily or motor activities and 'inner' phenomena such as perception, consciousness, thinking and reflection as both obtain a consistent structure and shared orientation in praxis (Leontjew, 1979). In a practice theoretical perspective, the joint orientation of outer and inner activities has to be explained in methodological respects as an integral part of the 'teleoaffective structure' of the practice the participants are engaged in and to whose unfolding they contribute by acting.

Enablement as subjectivation

Learning can be conceived of as the successive acquisition and embodiment of a repertoire of heterogeneous dispositions or habits,[14] understood as mutable potentials (movements, skills, body techniques, preferences, desires, etc.). These can be selectively called upon for diverse operations in different practices and situational configurations of bodies, things and artefacts, thus ensuring competent, knowledgeable participation (Alkemeyer and Michaeler, 2013). For whatever happens in one practice could either be or become part of other practices elsewhere; there are cross-contextual and trans-situational connections between practices.[15] Dispositions and habits can be both picked up through and actualised by actions in different practices in diverse social domains with their particular material arrangements and infrastructures. By moving along those trajectories, people also develop the capability to establish connections and disconnections in and among practices: they learn to direct and adjust their doings and sayings, their bodily and mental activities to the requirements of specific contexts.

The way in which acquired habits take shape in recognisable and competent behaviour not only depends on functional requirements aiming at the fulfilment of certain targets or results, but also on normative expectations and aesthetic criteria of style. The phenomenon of learning is therefore 'intimately tied to the augmentation of operability' (Schatzki, 2016c), on the one hand, and to the adjustment to norms that organise the individual performances in the context of a practice on the other. Violation of these norms can imply that a performance is unintelligible and hence not recognisable as a competent way of acting by other participants. This can be illustrated by simple examples. Leontjew (1973), for instance, describes how the hand movement of a child learning to use a spoon gradually succumbs to the 'objective logic of usage' of this tool. With learning, the child transforms 'necessarily reflective' movements into object-adequate skilled moves with tool character (Leontjew, 1973: 239). In doing so, it explores the 'material-social object meaning' (Holzkamp, 1995: 282) of the spoon and gradually is enabled to eat independently. However, acceptable spoon usage does not derive simply from the normative standards given by object structures. A spoon can be swung with great vigour to one's mouth in a generous movement or take the shortest, most economic route from plate to mouth. It is other participants such as parents who through demonstration, admonitions, manipulation, corrections and sanctions contribute to bringing the movement into specific forms. Violations of these normativised forms 'elicit not just expressions of disapproval, condemnation and disapprobation but also questions such as, What is he doing? How does that action fit in with her projects and ends? and How can she be doing that?' (Schatzki, 2016a: 26). Alongside *what* one is learning, one also must learn *how* to act to be recognisable as a competent participant.

In this context, recognition is not to be understood as a positive affirmation of attributes, which an already pre-extant subject seems to possess as for example in Honneth's approach (Honneth, 1992), but rather, in a continuation of Bourdieu's and Butler's works (Butler, 1997; Düttmann, 1997), as a powerful performative act of instituting someone *as* an intelligible subject which can also take the form of failure, degradation or contempt. Since one is always recognised as a specific someone, recognition implies an element of submission under or insertion in established, historically contingent orders of recognition and suitable behaviour.

In practice theoretical terms, recognition is to be analysed as a specific dimension of the interactions unfolding a practice 'step by step' and 'move by move' (Scheffer, 2008). This unfolding is a reflexive process insofar as the connection of single acts does not proceed automatically as in sequences of stimulus and response, but instead presupposes a connectivity of these acts as intelligible and accountable contributions to the shared practice.[16] Consequently, by practically relating to one another, participants not only keep the practice going, but also mutually appraise each other with regard to practice-specific (cultural, social, institutional) frames, which guide the perception and interpretation of what is going on (Goffman, 1974) and provide for normative criteria of appropriateness and correctness. Yet, participants neither need nor can fully explicate these criteria (Loenhoff, 2012: 18) since they are imparted through cultural ways of living, institutions and practices are predominantly part of a tacit know-how. Therefore, the tacit terms in which actions are evaluated, also in response to previous actions, are mediated by these frames. They are involved in the sequence of interactions and interpreted and transformed in ways that reflect situational configurations. This means that in order to be considered worthy of recognition, every act must carry a 'fingerprint' of the particular frame in which it is formed: by demonstrating to each other what and how something is to be done and by correcting, criticising and sanctioning each other accordingly, participants performatively develop the normativity and 'teleoaffective structure' of the practice they are engaged in and orient their acts toward these.

In current debates, the issue of recognition and recognisability is raised mainly within educational science and the sociology of education, which up to now have focused primarily on discursively articulated norms of recognisability and linguistic positioning (e.g. Balzer, 2014; Reh and Ricken, 2012; Schäfer and Thompson, 2010). Hence, the prefiguration of interactions by material arrangements and the bodily situatedness of participants in those arrangements remains overlooked. For example, a pupil who has to solve an arithmetic problem on the blackboard in front of his or her classmates is exposed to their linguistic and gestural comments like a performer on a theatre stage. This example makes clear that each position within a concrete socio-material arrangement is connected with particular normative demands that open up and close off certain possibilities. It also points to the fact that the evaluation embedded in any response to the acts of another participant is often implicit and subtle, with minimal bodily hand or head movements, a briefly raised eyebrow, changes in prosody, speed or intonation. In this context, participants' bodies not only exist as 'displays' (Goffman, 1979), from which a wide range of information (about intentions, attitudes, emotional states, etc.) can be discerned, but also as intelligent (i.e. sensitive to failure, or deviations) 'lived bodies-in-accomplishment', whose ways of perceiving, sensing and feeling are reflexively oriented to the frames, 'teleoaffective structures' and situational requirements of the practice they are engaged in. Thus, the evaluative dimension of participants' affective reactions to one another (either anger, eagerness, inattention, antipathy or pleasure, attraction, sympathy, etc.) are mediated both by these frames and the participants' 'habitus' (Bourdieu) as well as their bodily and personal situatedness in the here and now of ongoing praxis: they are a matter of a 'mediated immediacy' (Plessner, 1975) or of 'second nature' à la Marx.

In reacting and responding to each other, participants construct an 'implicit pedagogy' (Bourdieu, 1977) and 'didactics' (Schindler, 2011) of practice which unfolds as participants socialise one another into practices and position one another in them. We describe this process as *en-ablement*. We use this processual, relational category to analyse the power-laden explicit and tacit addressings that happen in interactions, through which participants both endow each other with possibilities for further action and delimit each other's room for manoeuvre. The term underlines the fundamental heteronomy of the imparting, acquisition, and performance of competences and emphasises that people only become recognisable as competent participants by engaging and addressing each other in praxis.

This also means that en-ablement not only is the attribution of a general ability to act, but implies a mutual commitment of the participants to specific positions, identities and relational possibilities. In an empirical study of the physical dimensions of recognition in school practices, we reconstructed how pupils assigned one another particular 'class-identities' such as 'model pupil' or 'class clown', which have their own distinct history as school-typical ideas. One observable effect of these assignments was that pupils gradually adjusted their doings and sayings to fit those identities and performed even formal school practices like solving an arithmetic problem on the blackboard in a style of the 'model pupil' or 'class clown'. Meeting increasingly well-established expectations related to the respective 'class-identity' turned out to be an easy way for pupils to be recognised as a 'co-player' not only by classmates but also by teachers – with unforeseeable consequences for the official assessment of their school performances (Pille and Alkemeyer, 2016).

In short, pupils attained play-ability by adjusting their style of acting to normative expectations that had been performatively established in the course of school praxis with respect to the frames and 'teleoaffective structures' of the shared practices. In poststructuralist approaches in the tradition of Althusser, Foucault and Butler, the recognition of someone as a competent and accountable 'co-player' is analysed as subjection or subjectivation (e.g. Reckwitz, 2006). In contrast to a 'classical' understanding of a pre-social given, autonomous subjectivity, this concept highlights the social processes in which people become recognised as subjects. In addition to a discourse analytical perspective, analysing subjectivation as a process of en-ablement *in praxis* implies that it does not only depend on discourse formations, but always takes shape in situated performances of practices (Alkemeyer, 2013).

The acquisition of play-ability and agency happens in a mesh of heterogeneous practices and always involves the acceptance and embodiment of practical norms. It is only by adopting norms in praxis that a subjectivity emerges that is recognised as capable of acting and therefore en-abled to reflect on the social conditions to which it owes its own existence. As various practices of different social domains boast diverse power-relations, norms and codifications, the emergence of subjectivity is a conflictual process in and between practices. It allows people to attain a generalised, i.e. 'relatively autonomous', standpoint *across* practices. This standpoint not only makes them 'capable of mediating their overall participation across contexts' (Lave, 1997: 149), but is at the same time the condition for them to develop a 'sense of possibility' (Musil, 1987: 16).

Conclusion

In addition to practice theoretical approaches that either dissolve agents in practices or tacitly presuppose participants' capability to perform practice-adequate acts, it was our concern to pursue the question of how this capability is formed in practices. For this purpose, we recommend, first, investigating learning as a process in which people are en-abled to participate in practices and, thus, to keep practices going, and second, analysing en-ablement as subjectivation. According to these concepts, learning is not to be analysed as a mere adjustment of participants to given social structures, but as a process in which a subjectivity comes into being, which allows for people to realise situationally emerging potentials that transcend the given structures of reality. It is the practices themselves that generate these potentials and at the same time establish the context for the formation of a subjectivity which is en-abled to recognise, capture and evoke them. Subjectivity is thus not pre-practically given, but emerges in and across practices as a capacity to engage with the reality of practices by reproducing and transforming it.

Notes

1 *Translator's note*: 'player' is used here to translate 'Mitspieler', which not only refers to the player of a (in this case: socially constructed) game, but also to the entanglement of one player 'with' others ('Mit').

2 In this chapter, 'praxis' and 'practice' denote two different but connected matters. By 'praxis', we mean the contingent *unfolding* of events, whereas 'practice' refers to typified and socially intelligible bundles of non-verbal and verbal activities.

3 *Translator's note*: the hyphen in 'play-ability' signifies the abilities that enable agents to participate competently in a (socially constructed) game.

4 *Translator's note*: 'en-ablement' is used as the German word 'Befähigung' is used in the original manuscript of this chapter to denote not only abilities and competences (the normal translation of 'Befähigung'), but also the process through which they are constantly acquired. Being en-abled means to become and to be able to meet the requirements of a practice. The term is ambiguous regarding whether competences 'really' belong to the participants or are only ascribed by the authorised others.

5 In contrast, action theory, pragmatic and activity theory traditions have played a less prominent part in these discussions (cf. Nicolini, 2012; Alkemeyer, Schürmann and Volbers, 2015).

6 See, for example, Schmidt's (2012: 9ff) representation of coordinated masses of people in a subway station.

7 Thus, critique comes into view as a component of all practices. Its consequences are empirically open-ended, but it is always transformative in praxis: even in the case that a practice, which has become precarious, is stabilised by adapting elements of the critique, this still means that a transformation has taken place.

8 Note that explicit learning could be studied as a particular type of practice in which specific subjects of learning are formed. Then the question would be how this form of learning relates to the practices or contexts for which the learning aims to prepare.

9 According to Bourdieu, it is only from this socialisation process of the body that individuation ensues: the singularity of the 'I' is formed in and through societal relations (Bourdieu, 2000: 134). Similar to John Dewey's pragmatic approach, it is experience in this model that has the function of constituting the subject and not presupposing it (Nassehi, 2003: 228). The subject appears *with* the experience it has as *its* subject (Volbers, 2015).

10 In such training processes, membership becomes noticeable in a direct sensory manner through 'social motor skills' (Gebauer, 1998), understood as movements and gestures shaped through learning and characterised by 'family resemblances' (Wittgenstein). This is observable in diverse communities of practice such as skilled trades, sports teams (e.g. Brümmer, 2015) or school classes (Alkemeyer, 2006; Pille, 2013). According to McNeill (1997), shared (rhythmical) movement in dance or drill, for example, produce a 'muscular

bonding' which is at the same time a social bonding: it modifies human emotions and feelings, thus consolidating social solidarity.

11 Insofar as Wacquant's ethnography reveals the fundamental necessity of an ongoing sensual cognition and awareness, it points beyond Bourdieu's understanding of the relation between praxis and thinking (reflecting). Bourdieu, like many others (cf. Schatzki, 2016a) conceives of reflection as a response to disruptions of normally unconscious embodied routines. Therefore, he himself tends to reproduce the body-mind dualism he claims to overcome.

12 'Umgang' is the German word for practical handling, for dealing and acting with other humans or objects.

13 This means that the lived body-in-accomplishment is not the natural or biological basis of the historic and cultural existence of the human being, but the concrete performed and performing reality ('Vollzugswirklichkeit') of a historically, socially and culturally shaped and cultivated body.

14 While according to Elgin (forthcoming) material objects can also have dispositions, she conceives habits as dispositions which can only be formed by human agents and are 'to some extent under their control'.

15 Schatzki (1996) therefore draws a distinction between what he calls 'integrative' and 'dispersed' practices. Integrative practices are 'the more complex practices found in and constitutive of particular domains of social life' (Schatzki, 1996: 98), e.g. cooking, farming or business. By contrast, 'dispersed practices' include 'describing … explaining, questioning, reporting, examining and imagining' (Schatzki, 1996: 91) and can take place within and across different social domains.

16 This means that reflexivity emerges in the performance of a practice between the human and non-human participants.

2

QUALITIES OF CONNECTIVE TISSUE IN HOSPITAL LIFE

How complexes of practices change

Stanley Blue and Nicola Spurling

> The design of the pavilion hospital was, of course, closely connected with the expression of a specific theory of disease – the miasmic theory of disease. Within the terms of this theory the essential elements of a hospital architecture are to be found in such features as the spaces between patients, the flow of air through the wards and the patterns of ventilation between wards … one of the greatest advocates of such design was Florence Nightingale, whose *Notes on Hospitals* (Nightingale, 1859) is inscribed in the very discourse of a zymotic theory of disease.
>
> *(Prior, 1988: 94)*

> It sounds obvious, but hospital environments with access to views, light and greenery can improve patient recovery and outcomes, acting as healing balms to the body and mind. In the old Alder Hey … with its 18-bed Nightingale wards and unrelenting corridors, often the only panoramas were of dispiriting brick courtyards.
>
> *(Slessor, 2015: 5)*

Introduction

In many ways, 'hospital life' has changed dramatically in the last 150 years. In other ways it has remained remarkably the same. These changes (and lack of changes) can be seen in the design of the New Alder Hey Children's Hospital in Liverpool. While architects and hospital planners have done away with the traditional, department – connecting central corridor, the New Alder Hey maintains many of the now essential features of hospital design that were advocated by Florence Nightingale in the 1850s, including the spacing between patient beds and the use of verandas for patient access to daylight and fresh air (Prior, 1988). Moreover, it has been designed in such a way as to facilitate a whole host of practices that would have been completely out of place in the old pavilion style hospital, but that are now essential to hospital design, including socialising and shopping. 'Resembling a more salubrious version of an airport concourse, the internal street [of the New Alder Hey] is the entry point and social condenser, colonised with shops, café, specially designed furniture and a giant, conical structure containing a multi-faith space' (Slessor, 2015: 6). Hospital life is made up of different combinations of activities at different points in history.

But how do these combinations of activities change? And why do they stay the same? These are our starting questions in exploring how hospital life has changed over time. In order to tackle these questions, we begin with complexes of practices and not 'a practice'. This starting point reflects other contributions in this volume and echoes recent developments in theories of practice that are moving away from a focus on the constitution and trajectories of specific practices to an emphasis on the interdependencies, connections and configurations that are central to the constitution, reproduction and transformation of social life.

Conceptual headway regarding how practices hang together has been made on several fronts. Steps that have been taken include recognising that practices become organised in time in different ways (Southerton, 2006); practices gather around particular places (Shove *et al.*, 2012: 84); and that practices compete and collaborate for time (Schatzki, 2010b). Multi-practice configurations have been described as bundles, complexes, constellations and systems in order to capture issues of scale, fixity, flexibility and structuration in connection. While these ways of conceptualising complexes of practices are useful for understanding how one practice is connected to another, they are of less value in helping us understand relationships between the connections that hold practices together. To date, much less has been said about how different types of connection impact on and matter for each other. For example, how are we to understand the changing material-spatial organisation of practices in hospitals and how those changes are affected by and shape the temporal sequencing of activities that take place within and beyond the hospital?

In what follows, we propose that in order to understand how complexes of practices change, we need to consider the multiple ways in which practices hang together and to show how these different types of connection matter for one another and ultimately for the reproduction of the complex itself. Our ambition is to build the foundations of a theory of practice (and of change) that is concerned from the outset with relationships between connections (*inter*connections). In our schema, new elements of practice are not the source of change. Rather trajectories of change are an expression of the ways in which practice complexes *inter*connect. In our description of these *inter*connections we put forward an understanding of complexes of practices as held together by a connective tissue that is itself an essential feature of practices.

We develop and illustrate this idea through a discussion of the transformations of complexes of practices that make up hospital life. A hospital is an intriguing site in which multiple activities necessarily combine and coordinate in routine and observable ways. What seem to be outwardly static structures have changed radically over the past century, meaning that any one hospital is constituted by historically specific complexes of practices. So how has that happened? The multiple activities that go on in a hospital and their orchestration to make an institution that functions 24 hours a day, 365 days a year, means that hospitals are sites in which temporal aspects of connection are especially visible. Hospitals have multiple socio-temporal peaks, sites and cycles and they have been studied as such (Zerubavel, 1979). But they also vary in terms of the kinds of infrastructure, built environment and technology which constitute them and the past design and implementation of these material arrangements is obviously important for contemporary hospital life. As such, hospitals provide a revealing setting in which to pursue our goal of understanding change as an outcome of the constitution of practice complexes.

Drawing from more recent developments in theories of practice (e.g. Shove *et al.*, 2012; Schatzki, 2010a; Schatzki, 2010b; Shove, Watson and Spurling, 2015), as well as from established ideas in social theory (e.g. Zerubavel, 1979; Abbott, 1988; Prior, 1988), we develop the beginnings of a conceptual scheme that can better account for changes in the complexes of practices that make up hospital life from the 1850s to 2015, as described in the two architectural accounts of hospital design introduced at the start of the chapter. Analysing the organisation of activity in architectural designs has been proposed by others (Prior, 1988; Shove *et al.*, 2012). For example, Shove, Pantzar and Watson write: 'Since buildings represent sites in which practices are contained, separated and combined, the history of domestic architecture provides a telling record of how daily life is organised and how this changes' (2012: 84).

We recognise that activity cannot be explained in full from building design alone, and indeed that is one of our central arguments. We claim that the architecture and layout of hospital buildings, such as the newly built Alder Hey Children's Hospital in Liverpool, is not simply the outcome of design trends, but represents one facet of multiple registers of transformation in institutional life. Others include: vast advances in medical science and in theories of infection and disease; a reconfigured and extended system of health professions, with their altered, emergent and redundant jurisdictions and areas of expertise; cultural shifts in social categories like children and childhood, social class, gender and age, all of which have implications for ideas of good hospital care; along with changed schedules and rotas of staff and patients associated with new forms of training, departmental opening hours, and different kinds of treatment, therapy and surveillance.

Given these multiple registers of transformation, it seems obvious that changes in hospital life cannot be revealed only through a story of developments in architectural design and professional planning, nor through a narrative of changing medical knowledge and professional organisation, nor through an understanding of the temporal organisation of the hospital. Instead, what is required is an account that reveals the dynamic interplay between these registers and their historical development. Such an account would get at changes in configurations of complexes of practices. What is needed is a method of understanding how different types of connection between practices matter for each other and how these connections matter for the reproduction of complexes of practices over time. Our original contribution is to focus on the different qualities of what we call the connective tissue (Shove et al., 2012)[1] of complexes of practices, and the *inter*connections within the connective tissue, in order to understand how the combinations of activities that make up routine and everyday hospital life have changed and how they have stayed the same.

We begin by briefly mapping some of the ways in which theorists of practice have dealt with connections between practices in order to situate our notion of connective tissue. In the subsequent sections, we develop three qualities of connective tissue in more detail, namely jurisdictional qualities, temporal qualities and material-spatial qualities. In the final section we focus on *inter*connections among these three qualities to show how such a focus helps to understand better how complexes of practices change and stay the same.

(*Inter*)connections in complexes of practices

Work that has looked at complexes of practices has, for the most part, focussed on singular dimensions of connectivity (e.g. temporal, material) without accounting for how that connection is itself related to other types of connection (e.g. Southerton, 2006; Shove et al., 2012). Similarly, this work has yet to account for how connections have shaped complexes of practices in the past and in ways that influence present and future connections and configurations. As a result, theories of practice tend to describe one dimension of connection when accounting for how practices hang together in the present. We argue that we need a more precise account of how multiple forms of connectivity between practices have come to be and how they matter for future iterations of a given complex of practices.

One example of recent writing on connections is Southerton's examination of the temporal organisation of practices. Southerton tells us that '[t]he temporal organisation of the day can be characterised as being constituted by practices that have a fixed position within schedules' (2006: 451). This fixed position is a result of various features of a given practice, for example, that it involves co-participation with others, that it requires a high degree of obligation to others or a significant degree of personal commitment and a relatively long duration. These features of a given practice are understood in terms of tempo, periodicity, duration, coordination and synchronisation. Practices that 'have' different temporal features have a more or less malleable position within sequences of activity that make up the day. This description of how practices connect in time is important because it shows us that certain features of a practice matter for the ways in which it can link with others. However, from this account it remains unclear how a given practice came to have these features in the first place. How did it come to require a high degree of obligation to others, or personal commitment, or co-ordination with others? Why does a certain practice have a particular tempo, duration or periodicity?

Place has also been considered as a significant dimension of ordering, organising and connecting practices. For example, different combinations of practices happen at home as compared to those that happen at work, facilitated by various spatial and material topographies. Shove, Pantzar and Watson write that:

> … there are various ways in which spatial arrangements constitute and underpin potentially important patterns of association. Some have to do with physical location of material elements. For example, practices requiring good supplies of running water converge around taps and drains.
>
> *(2012: 84)*

Technological infrastructures also bring practices together in ways that allow their mutual influence. Shove *et al.* (2012) go on to draw on an example from De Wit, Van den Ende, Schot and van Oost (2002), who write about the office as an innovation junction. Their argument is that spatial and material arrangements are important for the re-structuring of administrative practice. In this explanation, it is the emergence of a new technology, the typewriter, that allows a new kind of practice to emerge, typing, and for the re-combining of different practices in office life, such as filing, storing, etc. As Shove, Pantzar and Watson explain, this demonstrates that 'the office' as a space, and the typewriter as a technology, facilitate new linkages between practices. Although historical comparison shows that these spatial and material arrangements have changed over time, De Wit *et al.*'s account is driven by a narrative of technological innovation and does not comment on further qualities of connectivity. It is unclear in what ways (and if at all) the temporal features (i.e. the periodicity, tempo, duration, etc.) of typing and its fixity in the working day were affected by the material and spatial reconfiguration of practices in the office. Indeed, each of these accounts gives an example of a single kind of connection, temporal or material-spatial, without addressing the relationship between them.

Building from these arguments, our aim is to develop an explanation that both accounts for the multiple ways in which practices connect and that shows how relationships between connections have come to be. To do this, we propose a method of conceptualising practices not as entities that have external and singular connections, but as being held together by a connective tissue which has multiple qualities. We make the case that as qualities of connection interact, they change the shape of the complex of practices and therefore potential future connections that practices are able to make.

In the following sections we give examples of three different qualities of connective tissue,[2] namely temporal, material-spatial[3] and jurisdictional. In each section we begin by drawing out important and useful ways of thinking about how practices hang together and then build from these ideas to show how the jurisdictional, temporal and material-spatial qualities of the connective tissue *inter*connect to form enduring, morphing practice complexes across time.

Jurisdictional qualities

The division of expertise and labour in a hospital offers a useful starting point for understanding how practices of hospital life hang together. Hospitals typically have departments that serve different functions, such as cardiology or ophthalmology, and draw on professions with different knowledges and skills including nursing and prosthetics. These divisions are important for connections between practices in hospital life and for how professions depend on each other. For instance, doctors rely on radiologists to provide X-rays and scans that are vital in diagnosing patients (see Abbott, 1988). Although jurisdictions and their related forms of connection are important, they are not the whole story. The constitution of hospital life depends on the *inter*connection of jurisdictional qualities with temporal and material-spatial qualities too, and in the subsequent sections we discuss why this is so.

For Abbott (1988), jurisdiction is a concept that is useful for analysing how the division of expert labour is reproduced over time and how it changes. Jurisdictions are the categories of social problems around which expert tasks are organised. These categories include the (re)framing of the social problem itself, tools and equipment and natural objects and facts. To give an example of each in turn, alcoholism might be (re)framed as a medical, psychological or moral condition, respectively, placing it within the jurisdiction of doctors, psychologists or the clergy. Expertise might develop around specific skills or technologies. In a hospital we might think of the radiology profession, and the kinds of previously non-existent expertise that have emerged around different ways of looking inside the body, including X-ray, computed tomography, magnetic resonance imaging and ultrasound. Also common in health-related professions is the organisation of expert knowledge around 'natural'[4] objects and facts such as podiatry, dermatology and ophthalmology, which are respectively concerned with feet, skin and eyes, and paediatrics, midwifery and geriatric medicine, which have formed around 'natural' facts of life course and gender.

For Abbott, the complexes of practices that make up hospital life and how these change are explained through shifting jurisdictions and the relations between them. Patterns of interdependence are observable in key processes such as those of diagnosis and treatment. Assembling a picture of the patient involves identifying which experts are and are not relevant to them, and the order in which they should be seen. It is through everyday activities like this that the organisation's map of jurisdictions is both revealed and reproduced. Abbott also accounts for historical change in interrelated jurisdictions, pointing out that social problems are reframed (e.g. if experts are unsuccessful), that new technologies and associated knowledges develop while others wane and that illness and disease itself changes.

These are valuable insights. We agree with Abbott that the categorisations of expert knowledge and actions, and the dynamics of power between such groups are very important for the organisation of practice complexes in hospital life. However, since Abbott is concerned to analyse professions in general, his account cuts across institutions and specific sites of action producing an analysis which is 'systemic' and fractal. He has little to say about the day-to-day goings on of hospital life and their material and temporal qualities.

As noted at the beginning of this chapter, a Victorian hospital provides a very different material-spatial infrastructure of practice than a newly designed facility. This has implications for the spatial organisation of experts within a hospital, potentially complicating the abstract system of professions that Abbott describes, and resulting in a variety of distinctions and patterns on the ground, as layouts vary and are used in different ways. Such spatial arrangements have implications for temporal patterns of hospital life too – the relative location of departments and experts affects patterns of time within the working day – a fact that might result in ideal sequences of diagnosis being adapted to local settings.

Jurisdictions, that is, the abstract organisation of expert tasks, play a vital part in the organisation, reproduction and transformation of what is done in hospital life. Put another way, they form a vital quality of connective tissue within complexes of practices. However, to argue against Abbott, any moment of performance does not simply reproduce a jurisdictional map. Rather, moments of performance reproduce practice complexes: phenomena that are an outcome of jurisdictional qualities *inter*connecting with temporal and material-spatial qualities.

Temporal qualities

Practices are clearly linked together through a range of temporal connections. For example, Shove *et al.* (2012: 87) make reference to Zerubavel's (1979) work to show that practices in hospital life hang together by virtue of their connection across a number of temporal scales. They explain that the timing of an operation depends only in part on the patient's condition; it depends significantly more on the scheduling and co-ordination of parallel practices that themselves depend on shift patterns, the day of the week, the time of the year and various stages of career training. In this account, the position of a practice within the socio-temporal order is less a result of the seemingly essential features of the practice itself and much more about the organisation of patterns of practices and hence time in the hospital as a whole.

Beyond this, Zerubavel's work highlights a relationship between temporal and jurisdictional connections. In Zerubavel's account, it is the temporal order of activities in the hospital that solidifies group boundaries and that defines the organisation of everyday activity – who works where, when and with whom. A hospital's schedule of activities does not only reflect the social structure of the organisation, but actively establishes and consolidates social boundaries. He writes: '... the temporal structure of hospital life confirms the definition of group boundaries within the hospital...' (1979: 63). In his account jurisdictions are (re)produced through temporal patterns of working activity.

We find three problems with this position. First, it implies that temporal connections define group boundaries. It therefore fails to give a more nuanced and balanced account of how changes in jurisdictions matter for the reproduction of the socio-temporal order. Second, this account of the socio-temporal ordering of practices says rather little regarding the material-spatial connections between activities in the hospital, including the production of space and equipment, the built environment and objects. Finally, it side-lines analysis of how socio-temporal orders (or complexes of practice) become established, how the temporal organisation of activity is contested and therefore how jurisdictions and temporal orders change over time.

Schatzki's position developed in *The timespace of human activity* (2010b) helps us develop a more persuasive account of how complexes of practice form and change. In that work he argues that the dimensions of practices that orient activity within a sequence represent one means through which practices hold together. These sequences constitute activity timespaces that are multiple and interwoven. This activity timespace forms a kind of backbone or temporal-spatial landscape that orders social phenomena. He writes: '… interwoven timespaces form an infrastructure that runs through and is essential to social affairs' (2010b: 65).

The notion of a landscape or infrastructure of temporal-spatial connections that underpins or runs through complexes of practices is a powerful one. It helps to get across the ideas that practices are not free to connect with just any other practices and that it is not easy for them to be reproduced in different places, different times or by different groups. But, moving on a step from Zerubavel's (1979) account, it also helps to explain that changes in practices matter for the organisation of activity timespaces that run through social affairs.

However, this conceptualisation is not without its problems. First, it positions the dimensions or features of a practice that orient activity as intrinsic to the practice. Second, it extracts activity timespace as the landscape or infrastructure of temporal-spatial connections and sets it apart from the complex of practices itself. Finally, because it combines temporal-spatial connections, it forges an analysis of how temporal connections matter for spatial ones and vice versa, privileging the temporal-spatial over other types of connection.

Building on these positions, we need an account of how different connective qualities impact on each other. A first step is to recognise that individual practices do not have intrinsic dimensions, features or temporal qualities. Instead, they are always bound up with other activity. What look like features of a practice are rather outcomes of a practice's positioning within a complex. Telos/teleology, the future dimension of practice, for example, is not an inherent aspect of an individual practice itself, but a product of interacting, changing and metamorphosing complexes of practices. Similarly, the temporal qualities of practices that Southerton (2006) describes such as periodicity, tempo, synchronisation and coordination, duration and sequence are not the property of an individual practice, but an outcome of the practice complex, which is itself formed and connected in various ways beyond the temporal.

In other words, it is not that '[t]he organization, regularities and settings of a practice engender a net of interwoven timespaces …' (Schatzki, 2009: 40). Instead, it is the landscape of the complex of practices itself and its *inter*connections that define sequences, periodicities, durations and its telos. More than that, all of these temporal qualities depend upon and shape a variety of other qualities of connection including the jurisdictional and, as we discuss in the next section, the material-spatial.

Material-spatial qualities[5]

Materiality has been conceptualised in various ways by different theorists of practice. While 'things' barely feature in the writings of Bourdieu and Giddens, science and technology scholars have demonstrated that physical objects and technologies are mobilised in the doing of practices and are vital to their existence and perpetuation. Shove, Pantzar and Watson's self-described 'slimline interpretation of practice theory' (2012: 119) positions materials as one of three constitutive elements of practice (alongside meanings and competencies) in order to emphasise the importance of the material in action. Positioning materiality as a key component of practices, however, does not quite capture the connective quality of materials such as infrastructures and built environments which cut across and connect multiple practices at once (a quality that we argue belongs to technologies and artefacts as well). Indeed, conceptualising the built environment and networked infrastructure as constitutive materials of practice arguably sidelines their spatial and spatialising properties.

Schatzki's concept of 'material arrangements' (2002) provides a better representation of the spatial quality of material connections between practices. He writes:

> Human coexistence is inherently tied, not just to practices, but also to material arrangements. Indeed, social life, as indicated, always transpires as part of a mesh of practices and arrangements: practices are carried on amid and determinative of, while also dependent on and altered by, material arrangements. I call the practice-arrangement nexuses, as inherently part of which human coexistence transpires, sites of the social.
>
> *(Schatzki, 2010b: 130)*

The 'hanging together of people's lives' depends in part on interconnected material entities, that is the material arrangements amidst which practices are enacted. Materiality for Schatzki connects human activity. However, conceptualising 'material arrangements' in this way as somehow 'outside of practices' loses something of the constitutive property of materiality as described by Shove *et al.* (2012). So while Shove, Pantzar and Watson position materials as constitutive of practice and Schatzki positions material entities as part of separate arrangements that connect practices, in our notion of connective tissue we want to capture both the constitutive and connective features of materiality, by positioning it as a material-spatial quality of connective tissue.

Shove *et al.*'s recent (2015) account of infrastructures moves a step closer to our position. These authors recognise that '… practices are partly constituted by and always embedded in material arrangements…' (2015: 1) and use this position to advance the argument that infrastructures are both shaped by and shaping of complexes of practices. In their examples, road networks and journeys connect emerging complexes of car-dependent practices, distributed in time and space. As they explain, car dependence has become integral to a number of practices including shopping, commuting and getting to school, and through an iterative process involving transport and town planning, infrastructural development and emerging patterns of daily life, material-spatial arrangements and complexes of practice come to reflect one another.

These are useful ideas in thinking about material-spatial changes in the complexes of practices that make up hospital life. We share the central premise that 'things' both constitute and connect practices, but rather than attributing the spatialising properties of 'things' (that is the ways in which objects connect activities) to either constitutive elements of individual practices or to external 'material arrangements', we attribute this material-spatial quality to the connective tissue that holds the practice complex together.

By way of example, we might consider hospital plans and layouts as historical records of the ways in which practices have connected and disconnected. Prior's (1988) account of the design of children's wards from the early 1850s to the present demonstrates how ward layouts reflect changing theories of illness and disease as well as the changing practices of nursing, pedagogy, play and doctoring that characterise different periods in the history of treating sick children. These changing theories, jurisdictions, definitions and practices were materialised in 1900 wards, which used glass partitions to isolate child patients from one another and from physical contact with parents; that had the sisters' office in a centralised panoptic location; and that had only the bed and no other kinds of furniture in the room. All of these material-spatial qualities reflect and serve to maintain a particular patient-professional relationship and set of medical, nursing and patient practices on the ward.

While Prior's (1988) work is limited in an analysis of plans, and designs cannot reveal patterns of use, it nevertheless points us in the direction of two key ideas. First, materials are clearly constitutive of practices on the ward. Isolation chambers matter for what patients and staff do. Isolation chambers with a single bed mean that children cannot play together, while playrooms mean that they can. But beyond this, it shows that materials enable and disable different types of connections between multiple activities. The redesign of the built environment is part and parcel of a change in complexes of practices which are also changing in other ways: in response to changing theories of disease, in response to changing professional jurisdictions, in response to changing medical practices and the timings of those practices.

In science and technology studies, the case has been made that the built environment pervades and orders daily life, establishing more and less obdurate patterns of social activity (Hommels, 2005). This is just one form of structuring and other qualities of connection such as the temporal and the jurisdictional are no less or no more obdurate or flexible. Indeed, each of these qualities (and there could be others depending on the empirical site and question) form a historical layering of connections which holds practice complexes together. Material-spatial forms consequently exist alongside and in overlaying and fluctuating relationships with jurisdictional and temporal connections. No one form prefigures or dominates another, rather, each exists in relation to one another and all are mutually shaping.

Connective tissue: a method for understanding how complexes of practice change over time

Having argued that complexes of practices are held together by forms of connection that are multiply interlinked (by connective tissue) and that have various qualities, we now consider how complexes of practices change. Our starting question was this: how can we account for the changes (and lack of changes) over the last 150 years in the complexes of practices that make up hospital life? To answer this, we need to account for changing complexes over time and for changes in how these complexes are constituted. One response is to suggest that the connective tissue of a given complex of practices, its qualities of connection and relationships between the different types of connection, has a history. What we mean is that past *inter*connections shape qualities of contemporary complexes of practices that matter for the kinds of connections they make and enable in the present and the future. Understanding, in these terms, the connective tissue that holds complexes of practices together allows us to consider the significance of past and present *inter*connections. These lines of enquiry offer an alternative, sociological way of thinking about how past activity matters for present and future social action.

Prior (1988) provides a more classical historical account of the development of the design of children's wards. She demonstrates that the design of children's wards is both shaped by and shapes changing medical knowledge. She describes that in 1852 (when the first children's ward in an English hospital was opened) there were no special design requirements in that both adult and child medicine were underpinned by a miasmic theory of disease (the idea that prominent diseases of the time were spread by 'bad' or stagnant air). The pavilion plan of the hospital, advocated by Florence Nightingale (1859), was designed to facilitate the dissipation of miasma and allow the flow of fresh air. 'Space in the pavilion hospital is necessarily, then, full of light and air. The use of verandas, to which patients can be expelled during the hours of daylight, facilitates the circulation of air…' (Prior, 1988: 95). The architectural features of openness that allow the flow of air and light are repeated in contemporary hospital design despite medical knowledge having moved on from this theory of disease. The design director for the New Alder Hey Children's Hospital writes: 'The sense of openness extends to the clinical areas… to optimise observation and daylight. In the Critical Care Unit this approach has produced an innovative layout with patient bays curved around a central staff base and a rooflight that floods the eight-bed cluster with daylight' (Zucchi, 2015: 13).

While medical knowledge, and with it the organisation of medical, nursing and administrative practices, has clearly progressed significantly in the last 150 years, many design features remain. According to Prior '… it is essential to underline the fact that these features of physical environment were woven into entirely different discourses on disease and medical practice' (Prior, 1988: 101). To understand why some features of hospital life remain the same, while others have changed, we need to turn not just to aspects of knowledge and design, but to a more subtle account of the organisation and hanging together of hospital life.

The shift in medical knowledge from the miasmic theory of disease to 'germ theory' is important, but knowledge is only one aspect of the connective tissue that holds complexes of practices together. Instead of viewing architectural features (the isolation cubicle or glass doors to restrict the flow of air and germs) as a material expression of changes in medical knowledge, we would see these developments as part and parcel of changing jurisdictions that connect nursing with practices of sanitation and isolation and that disconnects it from practices involving socialisation and interaction. We would see that these changing jurisdictions matter for the temporal organisation of activity on the ward (so that nurses spend less time interacting with patients and more time cleaning up, etc.) and beyond. These changing jurisdictional and temporal qualities of how practices on the ward hang together matter for and are shaped by the material-spatial qualities imposed by isolated beds and separate wards.

Similarly, jurisdictional qualities change as practices of education, socialisation and recreation fall under the medical and nursing remit and, as they do so, temporal qualities change as play and interaction, and not just observation, become fixed practices in nursing schedules. Visiting hours become more flexible as children are no longer isolated from their parents. Instead, parents are encouraged to be with their children to lessen the 'emotional shock of a hospital visit'. The inclusion of 'mother's divans' and 'playrooms' in wards connects medical and nursing practices to practices of parenting and socialising. And as all these examples show, material-spatial qualities do more than just reflect changes in other domains.

The contemporary design of the large glass-sliding doors to patient's rooms in the newly built Alder Hey Children's Hospital embody and reproduce this multiple layering of historical *inter*connections. The doors can be closed completely and blinds pulled down to isolate and facilitate patient privacy. They can be closed and transparent to enable observation and they can be fully drawn back to open the patient's room into the ward to assist socialisation and interaction with staff and other patients.

Our point is that past *inter*connections shape features of contemporary practices that matter for the connective tissue, its qualities and *inter*connections in the present. The design of the hospital does not simply reflect changes in the complex of practices that make up hospital life, rather, the spatial organisation of the hospital is in a recursive relationship with the organisation of activity, but so too is the temporal organisation of the hospital and the organisation of jurisdictions within it. In connecting through the built environment, through patterns of time and through systems of professional responsibility, those multiple *inter*connections become features or characteristics of the complex of practices, the connective tissue that holds practices together.

Finally, while this historical layering of *inter*connections, and the development of connective tissue, appears structuring and directive, we stress that human activity remains indeterminate and that past connections and *inter*connections do not directly determine present activity or what will happen in the future. That current activities are indeterminate does not mean that they have no relation to the past. We follow Schatzki when he writes: '… past phenomena circumscribe, induce-orient, and underwrite the public manifestation of – but do not cause or antecedently pin down – present activity' (Schatzki, 2010b: x).

In any specific instance, the relation of the past to the present and the influence of past *inter*connections (of the connective tissue) in current complexes of practices is an empirical question. Our aim has been to lay some foundations from which to begin investigations of these relations and thus of how practices hang together.

Conclusion

We are calling for a version of practice theory which begins with complexes of practices and not 'a practice' and that focuses on relationships between connections and on how different types of connection matter for each other. We have developed an approach which is concerned from the outset with how complexes of practices hang together. Central to our framework is the idea of a connective tissue that both holds complexes of practices together and that is itself an essential feature of the practices involved. With this idea in place, it is possible to focus on the different qualities of connective tissue, and the *inter*connections between those qualities, to understand changing complexes of practices over time.

Taking the *inter*connections of connective tissue as a starting point is significantly different to focussing on the constitution and trajectories of specific practices. It also contrasts with work that has focussed on singular dimensions of connectivity. Instead, we have sought to account for multiple registers of change at the same time. We consequently argue against the conceptualisation of connective qualities as either background or as part of a practice, instead we contend that they are both. Finally, we suggest that no particular *inter*connection should have ontological privilege, but rather, that understanding the character of *inter*connection is a question for empirical research.

These ideas point to new ways of thinking about the relationship of the past to the present. In viewing the present as an outcome of intersecting registers of reproduction and change, we challenge the view that the past somehow causes the present and the view that future trajectories can be anticipated by extrapolating from the past. Providing an exhaustive catalogue of processes by which past *inter*connections influence present shapes or forms of connective tissue is beyond the scope of this chapter. However, we hope to have demonstrated the potential of such an approach and given some clues as to how it might be developed.

Notes

1   We build on and extend the notion of connective tissue as developed by Shove, Pantzar and Watson in *The dynamics of social practice* (2012).
2   Of course there will be other identifiable qualities of connection. These will depend on empirical questions and sites of enquiry. We give these three as examples because we think they are the three most pertinent to hospital life.

3 We have separated out temporal and spatial qualities not because we consider them as somehow separate. Instead, we want to explore actively how the layering of spatial and temporal relationships works and how temporal-spatial qualities shape and are shaped by other kinds of connections/qualities.

4 Abbott is referring to categories like 'the body' when he uses the term 'natural', though we note that natural facts are social constructs or outcomes of scientific interventions.

5 In this section, we take the material-spatial qualities of connection to be a category that encompasses all kinds of physical-spatial connections between practices, including objects, technologies, the built environment and the physical landscape. We are not attempting to demonstrate a particular relationship between the material and the spatial so that we might then analyse the relationship between the material and the temporal, the material and the jurisdictional. Instead, we distinguish between our own position and Schatzki's notion of timespace, that positions timespace as necessarily immaterial. We argue that the physical environment, artefacts and tools form part of the 'technological infrastructure' of place that connects practices together. The term 'material-spatial' signifies the physicality of space and includes the range of equipment that might be found in that place.

3

SOCIOMATERIALITY IN POSTHUMAN PRACTICE THEORY

Silvia Gherardi

Introduction

The literature that has produced and consolidated the turn to practice and put in motion the 'bandwagon of practice-based studies' (Corradi, Gherardi and Verzelloni, 2010) is now in need of better understanding of the differences among approaches to practice. Since the beginning of what has been called a re-turn to practice (Miettinen, Samra-Fredericks and Yanow, 2009), it has been stressed that a unified theory of practice does not exist and 'disagreements reign about the nature of embodiment, the pertinence of thematizing it when analyzing practices, the sorts of entities that mediate activity, and whether these entities are relevant to practices as more than mere intermediaries among humans' (Schatzki, 2001a: 11).

At the beginning of the practice turn, much work was devoted to identifying the elements of a practice and some models were named 'element-based practice theory' (Morley, this volume). The elements of a practice were defined by Reckwitz (2002b) as bodily and mental activities, objects or materials and shared competences, knowledge and skills; Shove *et al.* (2012) identified them in competencies, meanings and materials; Warde (2005) pointed to understandings, procedures and engagements, moreover, for Warde (2005: 134), 'practical activity and its representation' are components of practice. According to Schatzki (2006), the elements that comprise a practice are linked to each other through five main mechanisms: practical understanding, rules, teleoaffective structure, general understanding and social memories. It is evident that the identification of the elements within a practice varies from author to author; nevertheless – according to Guzman (2013) – a momentary agreement regarding the identification of elements is apparently in place. Nevertheless, the issue is not whether or not materiality matters within practice theory; rather, it is whether materiality merely mediates human activities – as in human-centred theories – or is constitutive of practice, as in posthuman practice theories. The term 'sociomateriality' enters this debate without resolving the tension between a substantialist ontology that assumes that the social and the material, human beings and things, exist as separate entities that interact and impact on each other and a relational ontology that assumes the constitutive entanglement of the social and the material.

At present, the debate on the sociomateriality of practices is still in a precarious equilibrium between the social and the material, on the edge of interpreting practice as an object of change (privileging humans) or an agent of change (privileging its agency vis-à-vis humans). I would point out that one of the reasons for a re-turn to practice theory was to move beyond problematic dualisms (Schatzki, 2001a: 10) and for this reason, I want to explore how the dualism between the social and the material may be overcome with a concept of sociomateriality in which it is the 'glue' that connects all the elements of a practice. Jones (2014), who conducted a literature review of the 140 journal articles published since 2007 in which sociomateriality appeared, distinguished a strong and a weak sociomateriality. Strong sociomateriality addresses all the concepts that Orlikowski (2010) suggests are entailed in sociomateriality – materiality, inseparability, relationality, performativity and practices – while the weak version employs only some of these concepts selectively. I shall take a strong sociomaterial approach to practice.

I shall use the term 'posthumanist' better to qualify an approach to practice (Gherardi, 2015) in which relational materialism is the assumed epistemology that differentiates it from human-centred practice theories (for an articulation of the difference, see Monteiro and Nicolini, 2015). A posthumanist practice theory has its roots in the sociology of translation (Latour, 1992; 2005), in the principle of symmetry between humans and non-humans and in a relational epistemology (Law, 1994; Law and Hassard, 1999). In order to stress how within a relational epistemology both the idea of performative accomplishment and becoming are central, I propose to leave aside for the moment current definitions of practices as arrays of activities (human, non-human or intertwined) and to focus on the image of a practice 'as a mode, relatively stable in time and socially recognised, of ordering heterogeneous items into a coherent set' (Gherardi, 2006: 36). Practice is thus seen as a mode of ordering, rather than an ordered product, an epistemology rather than an empirical phenomenon. In fact, considering practice as epistemology 'enables scholars to theorize the dynamic constitution of dualities and, thus, to avoid the twin fallacies of "objectivist reification" on the one hand and "subjectivist reduction" on the other' (Feldman and Orlikoswki, 2011: 1242).

In this chapter I shall use three examples to ground the concept of sociomateriality in bodily practices such as fathering, in organisational and working practices such as caring for the elderly, and in the aftermath of Hurricane Katrina that made visible the interdependencies of the practices that had constituted New Orleans over time. The rationale for choosing examples ranging from male bodies in fathering practices, through caring discourses situated in changing technological practices, to the co-dependencies of the practices producing a territory, is to show how sociomateriality overcomes also another classical dualism, that between 'micro' and 'macro' analysis. In fact, as Welch and Warde (2015: 84) note, this dualism creates an analytic problem whose clarification and resolution would enhance the power of practice theories, since it concerns the relationship between the minutiae of everyday performances of practices and the macro-institutional context.

The chapter will open by positioning the concept of sociomateriality within ongoing conversations in organisation studies and their connections with new feminist materialisms. I shall then offer three examples to illustrate the '*viscous porosity*' in between entangled practice elements.

Exploring the concept of sociomateriality

Sociomateriality, with or without a hyphen, is a key topic of research in organisational and working practices, following the tradition of sociotechnical literature in which the social and the technological are inextricably linked. Similarly, the concept of sociomateriality has a long history in the study of working practices connected to information systems (Cecez-Kecmanovic, Galliers, Henfridsson and Vidgen, 2014). Within these fields of research, 'the material' in sociomateriality is mainly technological but not solely so, since the technological effects in social life and in epistemic practices have been considered.

The term 'sociomateriality', without a hyphen and in reference to the feminist onto-epistemology of Barad (2003), has been introduced into organisation studies by Wanda Orlikowski (2006; 2007; 2010) together with Susan Scott (Orlikowski and Scott, 2008; Scott and Orlikowski, 2014). The term 'entanglement' or 'generative entanglement' is present in their work together with a relational ontology and an acknowledgement of relational materialism discussed by Law (1994) and performativity from actor network theory. These terms refer to the fact that within a practice, meaning and matter, the social and the technological, are inseparable and they do not have inherently determinate boundaries and properties; rather, they are constituted as relational effects performed in a texture[1] of situated practices.

Donna Haraway (1991; 1997), who has also deleted the hyphen (in sociomateriality), proposes to talk of natureculture as a unity, a universe rich in material-semiotic actors and metaphors, like the cyborg, the OncoMouse, the multispecies crowd and otherworldly conversation. Her questions revolve around what 'nature' means in the complex practices of our contemporary society. The image of the cyborg is based on a science fiction imagination, but a woman taking contraceptive pills is already a cyborg, a hybrid of nature (body) and technology. The OncoMouse, manufactured in scientific laboratories and not born, is another example of artificially produced nature. An oncogene, the gene that produces breast cancer, has been transplanted into it, so that the OncoMouse is the techno-body *par excellence* and at the same time the mammal rescuing other mammals.

Haraway's work dislocates the centrality of the human in favour of the in/non/posthuman and of bio-centred egalitarianism. In fact, what we call a 'body' is a multispecies crowd if we consider that human genomes can be found in only about 10 per cent of cells, while the other 90 per cent of the cells are filled with the genomes of bacteria, fungi and other tiny messmates. And she concludes by saying that 'to be one is always to become with many' (Haraway, 2008b: 3). The image of the companion species (Haraway, 2008b) links to the idea of otherworldly conversation (Haraway, 2008a), in which various non-human entities participate as subjects. Her work 'calls for a renewed kinship system, radicalized by concretely affectionate ties to nonhuman "others"' (Braidotti, 2006: 199). And in fact, Braidotti (2013) proposes using the term 'more-than-human' instead of 'non-human' to overcome the human/non-human dichotomy.

Karen Barad again removes the hyphen between the social and the material and with her work, the term 'sociomateriality' has entered the debate on technology as a social practice (Orlikowski, 2010; Suchman, 2007a; 2007b; 2011). Barad's (2007; 2013) work defines her epistemological position as agential realism. In order to understand what she means with this term, we must bear in mind that her book begins with a conversation between Heisenberg and Bohr on the so-called particle-wave duality paradox. For the former, quantum theory represents an epistemological concern and the particle-wave duality demonstrates that we can only make probabilistic predictions (uncertainty principle); for the latter it is an ontological issue, since particles do not have determinate values of position and momentum simultaneously (indeterminacy principle). Barad uses the term 'intra-action' to denote the Bohrian ontological inseparability of all words (culture) and all things (nature). Rather, culture and nature are entangled, since Barad seeks to avoid the issue of representationalism, so that 'realism' is not 'about representations of an independent reality but about the real consequences, interventions, creative possibilities and responsibilities of intra-acting within and as part of our world' (2007: 37). Reality is defined as things-in-phenomena and not as things-in-themselves. In fact, 'phenomena' are considered as the primary ontological units, recalling Bohr's definition of them as observations under specific circumstances, including an account of the whole experimental arrangement. Both Haraway's and Barad's work are reflections on epistemic practices and both talk of a way of knowing in which the knower is not external to, or pre-existing the world. Rather, the knower and the 'things' do not pre-exist their interactions, but emerge through and as part of their entangled intra-relating. This assumption allows us to reformulate the notion of agency and to transcend the duality of social versus material agency, human versus more-than-human agency, material versus discursive. From these points of view, the idea of engagement with sociomateriality requires an onto-epistemology that does not separate nature from culture.

Building on these ideas, the challenge is to develop appropriate methodologies for the empirical study of sociomaterial practices. My first step is to consider methods of analysing the sociomateriality of the body.

Sociomateriality and bodily practices

The concept of sociomaterial practices implies not only that the social and the material are co-constituted, but also that nature and culture are entangled. It has a methodological corollary that entails studying how, within a practice, bodies, matter and discourses are expressions of the same sociomaterial world. The term 'embodiment' expresses how the nature/culture divide is blurred in the materiality of bodies encountering a material-semiotic environment. When we study working practices empirically, we focus on how practical knowledge is embodied and how practitioners rely on sensible knowledge in order to bring a practice forward (Gherardi, 2012a). The centrality of bodies in approaching practices is self-evident, yet it has been overlooked even when humans are considered the carriers of practices. One reason for this may be the Cartesian and idealist tradition in Western culture that undervalues the sociomateriality of human bodies and the other-than-human bodies with which human bodies meet.

But what is a body? Do we 'have' bodies or 'are' we bodies? From Merleau-Ponty's (1962) widely cited concept of 'body subjects', ideas of the indivisibility of mind and body and of human beings as embodied social agents spread into the sociology of the body (Crossley, 1995), feminist theorising on embodiment (Howson and Inglis, 2001; Fotaki, Metcalfe and Harding, 2014), and corporeal ethics within organisation studies (Pullen and Rhodes, 2015b).

Human perception is intrinsically embodied for Merleau-Ponty: 'we are in the world through our body, and… we perceive that world within our body' (1962: 206). He argues that to be a body is to be tied to a certain world; the perception of the world is always embodied and the perceiving mind is an incarnate mind. Moreover, embodiment is bidirectional in that the body is sentient and sensible: it sees and is seen, hears and is heard, touches and is touched. Thus, embodiment is neither idea nor matter, neither subject nor object, but both at the same time.

Merlau-Ponty's concept of embodiment enables us to see how sensible knowing is enacted in situated practices and how aesthetic judgements sustain working practices (Strati, 1999; Gherardi and Strati, 2012). Moreover, Dale (2005) sees in this conceptualisation of the embodied subject a tool for understanding the negotiation of the material and the social (that she keeps in interaction as mutually enacted), the organisational and the subjective, the everyday relationship of the individual with organisational control systems.

Embodiment is a concept present in practice theories. Reich and Hager (2014) consider it one of the six threads of the literature on practice (the others being: knowing-in-practice, sociomateriality of practices, relationality, historical and social shaping of practices, emergent nature of practices). In fact, it is now widely accepted within the social sciences that selfhood is not only social, but also embodied. Nevertheless, the collapse of the mind/body and psyche/soma dichotomies originated from many different sources. Here, I shall mention only a few that may be relevant to a discussion of sociomaterial bodies.

A telling example of the intra-connection of space as both symbolic and material, is the liminal space of in-betweenness aptly described by Ettinger (2006) as 'matrixial', in the sense of uterine, with reference to the pregnant body and to the permeable membrane between the body of the mother and that of the foetus. The concept of matrixial space as a space of non-separation and non-distinction has been taken up in organisation studies by Kenny and Fotaki (2015), because the concept of the co-emergence of partial subject (the mother and the baby) with the matrixial borderspace provides the image of an emerging subjectivity in a sociomaterial encounter. The authors argue that Ettinger's work provides a fruitful new direction for the study of corporeal ethics within organisation theory. The idea of corporeal ethics draws on Diprose's (2002) notion of an ethics grounded in embodied experience.

When we consider subjects as embodied subjects and the body as 'neither brute nor passive' (Grosz, 2011: 18) but as 'agential intra-activity in its becoming' (Barad, 2003: 818), we can consider practices as embodied and emplaced (Ingold, 2000), since the issue is not the body *per se*, but the shifting sociomaterial intra-actions of bodies and matter across time and space.

By emphasising the notion of 'emplacement', Elisabeth Hsu (2007) adds another aspect to the body-mind paradigm, since emplacement implies a body-mind-environment interrelationship. Drawing examples from Chinese medicine, she illustrates how body concepts derive from ecological experiences and she illustrates the relationality of the body and its composition in diverse networks of desire, practices and habits. Our understanding of a 'body' is changed into a 'body-assemblage', a series of affective and relational becomings. At the same time, Hsu also suggests that space ought to be understood as a dimension of social relationships, a site where capacities can be enacted.

A good exemplification of what I consider the entanglement of a body-mind-environment is provided by Doucet's (2013) research on the practice of fathering. She considers parent-child relations as processes of 'intra-active becoming' (Barad, 2007: 146) or 'generative becoming' (Bennett, 2010: 3). In her research on breadwinning mothers and care-giving fathers, she stresses the recurring invisibility of the body in studies of parental care-giving and especially the invisibility of male embodiment. The embodied relations of parents and children are issues of 'matter':

> [P]eople – mothers, fathers, babies, children, others – are in a perpetual state of becoming, and this 'becoming' posits the fundamental units of analysis, not as things or words, or subjects or objects, but as dynamic phenomena that are constituted by and through entangled and shifting forms of agency.
>
> (*Doucet, 2013: 295*)

When we take 'becoming' as the unit of analysis – as Doucet does – we may see not only how embodiment is the entanglement of a body-mind-environment, but also how its meaning changes in time and within 'a choreography of becomings'. Doucet gives a full description of the *agencements*[2] of entangled elements in fathering:

> The meanings of fathers and infant care have also been gradually changing, partly through the constitutive intertwining of sociocultural practices, ideologies, and embodied subjects (via workplace policies and cultures, state policies, popular culture, media, and social media, including the burgeoning of daddy blogs), but also through women's rising employment, men's slow take-up of parental leave, and the social acceptance of that leave.
>
> *(Doucet, 2013: 295)*

We can see how fathering as a sociomaterial practice is embedded in a wider texture of practices connecting the situated and everyday encounters of embodiments to the macro-institutional context. Therefore, gender becomes not a fixed biological identity, but a social practice (Poggio, 2006), a performance playfully and cannily enacted, that changes from context to context and from day to day, as men and women adjust their ideas of themselves to fit changing sociomaterial circumstances.

The title of Doucet's article – *A choreography of becoming* – is inspired by Coole and Frost's (2010: 10) expression, where the issue is 'that matter becomes', rather than that 'matter is'. The same expression may be extended to Nick Hopwood's (2014; 2015) work on parental embodiment in care as the enactment of a texture of practices through the four dimensions of times, spaces, bodies and things. Similarly, Maller (2015) in health settings research assumes a posthumanist approach, illustrating how health and wellbeing are outcomes of participation in a set of social practices mutually constructed by the materiality of everyday life.

The physical 'matter' of the body, its material-discursive production, its sensible knowing, its choreography of becoming, are all instances of embodiment as irreducibly material, social and emplaced in practices. By implication, a posthuman practice theory can inform a research programme that takes serious account of the concepts of both entanglement to undermine oppositional dualism, and intra-action to explore how practice components intra-act.

I offer another example of sociomateriality, drawn from my own research, to discuss working practices in relation to discourses on ethics.

The sociomateriality of caring in the practice of artificial nutrition and its discourses

Caring as a situated practice indicates a collective emergent capacity to take care of, and take care for, a knowing-in-practice accomplished as ongoing, adaptive, open-ended responses to care needs.

In the empirical setting of nursing homes, we (Gherardi and Rodeschini, 2016) illustrate the *agencement* that the changing practice of nutrition is bringing into the way that care practices are accomplished. Besides forms of feeding by mouth, recent years have seen the increasingly frequent use of artificial feeding, a practice which a few years ago was almost unknown in the long-term care of the elderly (Rodeschini, 2013). With the presence of increasingly elderly and increasingly sick residents, artificial feeding is used to a significant extent in almost every nursing home. The practice raises numerous ethical issues, since it is often the last resort in the case of residents with particularly severe malnutrition or ones no longer able to take nourishment by mouth. At the same time, it interferes in the 'natural' end of life and in the public discourses about life and death.

As soon as a patient presents severe nutritional problems, the medical staff usually proposes the application of a percutaneous endoscopic gastrostomy (PEG) or a nasogastric intubation (NGI) to the family. Since the decision on artificial feeding is so emotionally and legally charged and because it is involved in different sociomaterial relations, it enacts quite different discursive practices in different settings, since matter and meaning intra-act differently within the same *agencement*.

In principle, the resident should be the subject who has the choice to accept or refuse the connection between his/her body and the technological device that is in principle removable but in fact once inserted is not removed and becomes part of the techno-body. The following episode illustrates the intra-action between subject/object in the process of objectivation:

> I [Giulia Rodeschini] was with the nursing coordinator in Mr Marco's room. She told him that if he did not start eating again immediately, she would be forced to put him on PEG or NGI. He shook his head [he cannot speak but communicates with a chalkboard] and wrote "no" on the chalkboard … When we left the room, the nursing coordinator told the doctor that if Marco continued not to eat and refused PEG, they would have to insert a NGI, and she advised the doctor to talk to Marco's sister.

The relatives are connected within a complex system of inter-corporeality and intra-corporeality: care is an affective and sociomaterial practice that is embodied as body work (work done with the body on other bodies), mainly in nursing but also in medical work, that is not only shared, but also coproduced with the bodies and the emotions of the relatives. Care is an embodied, collective, knowledgeable doing that relies on bodily sensible knowledge (touch, smell, sight and hearing), individual and collective, symbolic and material.

Artificial nutrition severs old connections: food becomes no longer food with aesthetics and emotional properties, but simply nutrition. The emotional bonds of feeding are removed, since nurses do not spend the same amount of time at the bed of the patient. The value of 'good nursing' is conveyed by the words of this daughter of a resident, when she mentions a nurse who was particularly concerned in caring: "when she inserted my mother's feeding tube, she also gave her a caress … It was impossible for her not to caress my mother". At the same time, what is implied by this sentence is that the practice of artificial nutrition changes how bodies relate to each other, how body work is done and how emotional labour is carried out.

The *agencement* of the practice 'artificial nutrition' also takes on material-discursive elements in the form of the medical discourse at the moment of choice, of the relatives' discourses on their choice and of the nursing staff's discourse (that cannot be voiced aloud and is expressed only within their professional community). I give a short extract concerning each element in order to communicate the atmosphere of a non-communicative plurivocal exchange of multiple viewpoints:

> Doctor, talking with the daughter of a resident: I can't tell you what to do, the decision is yours. I can only tell you that if we don't do something, your mother will gradually waste away, but with PEG the situation would certainly improve, but the decision on what's best is up to you.
>
> Daughter of a resident: I'm speaking from my personal experience … you're not prepared for it … We arrived there [at the hospital] and I said 'yes'. It was one July afternoon and I was in the hospital courtyard crying because I didn't know what to do … I felt an enormous sense of guilt, and I said 'could I really make her die of hunger and thirst?' Later, I understood that it's not true. It's not true because when persons live in great pain they have the right … I stress they really have the right, to rest in peace.
>
> Care assistant coordinator: They [doctors] put this person on PEG when he was ninety-nine years old … This is what we can't understand … it's a sort of therapeutic obstinacy. Why? What sense does it have? What quality of life can you give a person in this way?

The choice of artificial feeding therefore weaves together several material-discursive practices in a process whereby the doctors are exonerated (or exonerate themselves) from taking decisions, because of the ethical and legal complexity of those decisions in professional and organisational accountability terms. This 'non decision-making' by the doctors affects the residents, their relatives and the non-medical personnel. It shifts the responsibility to the relatives, who, without experience in this difficult choice, often agree to artificial feeding because they do not want their loved one 'to die of hunger and thirst'. This triggers vicious connections in the practice that may lead to consequences not previously imagined by people without personal or professional experience in this care domain and who are also closely involved emotionally. The non-decision by the doctor, moreover, reverberates on the non-decision concerning removal of the PEG and thereby makes it definitive.

We witness the emergence of an ethical dimension in the practice of artificial nutrition that is characterised by the difficulty or impossibility of saying 'no' to life-extending interventions, without questioning the meaning and the boundaries between life and death.

Without entering into a long discussion on the ethics of care in feminist theory (Gilligan, 1982), nor on the logic of care versus the logic of choice (Mol, 2008), I wish to stress how ethics is a material-discursive component of an *agencement* of a practice. I shall introduce the concept of corporeal ethics in order to highlight how ethics and politics intra-act within it.

The concept of corporeal ethics was developed by Rosalyn Diprose (2002), an Australian feminist philosopher, and it has been taken up in organisation studies by Pullen and Rhodes (2014; 2015a). For Diprose, the body, and its interaction with, and dependence on, other bodies makes for the 'system of intercorporeality' (Diprose, 2002: 90, quoted in Pullen and Rhodes, 2014: 787) where ethics begins. In Diprose's thinking, ethics is a pre-reflective embodied interaction arising from openness and generosity towards the other as a form of hospitality in which the other is welcome in her/his difference, rather than being the institutionalisation of a set of conditions and values guiding ethical behaviour. In organisation studies, a 'corporeal ethics' may inform people's behaviours in the context of, and in resistance to, the dominant organisational power relations in which they find themselves. Such an ethics has been elaborated as a practice and as an ethico-politics of resistance (Pullen and Rhodes, 2015a; 2015b).

In summing up, I wish to underline the intra-acting of all the entangled practice components within 'a choreography of becomings': subjectivities-objectivities, embodied matter, techno-bodies, intercorporeality, affect and emotions, situated material-discursive elements, medical discourses and ethical-political discourses about life and death. All these elements, in their entangled heterogeneity, assume agency and perform the capacity for care and caring (not for the simple provision of a service).

A situated practice – like artificial nutrition – is always enmeshed in a texture of connections in action (past and future). When we consider the methodological implications of doing empirical research on organisational and working practices, we can say that following the traces from one *agencement* to another, we may be able to track the connections from one practice to the next. This methodology has been called 'ethnography of the object(s)' (Bruni, 2005; Bruni, Gherardi and Parolin, 2007), since instead of being focused on humans and their practices, it follows objects and their becomings with humans. It may be the guiding principle on which to describe the entanglement of sociomaterial practices where neither the humans nor the more-than-humans are privileged.

Another example of sociomaterial entanglements connecting practices from the past to actual practices disrupted by a natural disaster (partly also a man-made disaster) is the case of Hurricane Katrina. The connectivity of a texture of practices became more evident when an event severed the links holding the social and the material together.

Katrina, viscous porosity and situational entanglements

Tuana (2008: 188) takes what she calls an interactionist approach to construe 'the rich interactions between beings through which subjects are constituted out of relationality'. She offers Hurricane Katrina's case study to demonstrate the 'urgency of embracing an ontology that *rematerializes the social and takes seriously the agency of the natural*' (Tuana, 2008: 188, emphasis in original). Katrina is emblematic of the viscous porosity between humans and the environment, between social practices and natural phenomena. The metaphor of viscous porosity – rather than fluidity – offers an image where viscosity is neither fluid nor solid and the attention to the *porosity* of interactions helps to undermine the notion that distinctions signify a natural or unchanging boundary of some kind. Moreover, viscosity retains an emphasis on resistance to changing form, which helps to find sites of resistance and opposition in the complex ways in which material agency is involved.

Katrina made New Orleans visible as a complex material-semiotic site. Historically, in order to create usable land, water was pumped out of the area, which in turn caused the ground to sink even lower. The sediment from the Mississippi created areas of 'natural levees' that transformed the local geology and hydrology. Local geology and hydrology emerge from complex social vectors: human consumption and refuse practices resulted in altered flora habitats, which in turn altered human interests. Material agency in its heterogeneous forms interacted in complex ways and the agency in all these instances emerged from the situated interactions and was not antecedent to them. The viscous porosity between human and non-humans happened also at more intimate levels, since Katrina left New Orleans flooded in a 'toxic soup' when water reached some toxic waste sites in a corridor named 'Cancer Alley', where many types of industry clustered and their location had been favoured by governmental policies. Tuana goes on to describe the viscous porosity between plastic industries – namely polyvinyl chloride (PVC) – and 'my flesh and the flesh of the world' (2008: 199).

The flesh that Katrina made visible – and that Tuana interprets as materialisation of ignorance[3] – was the flesh of the poverty, the racialised world, the disability that suddenly appeared in the media and had hitherto been cancelled or denied. In the breakdown of the texture of practices that had historically materialised New Orleans and made their hidden inequalities visible in the aftermath of Katrina, also the epistemic practices of researchers were involved in performing Katrina as a sociomaterial phenomenon. Tuana (2008: 196) advises that 'our epistemic practices must thus be attuned to this manifold agency and emergent interplay, which means that we cannot be epistemically responsible and divide the humanities from the sciences or the study of culture from the study of nature'. Her use of the concept of epistemic responsibility comes from Lorraine Code (1987), who persuasively argues that epistemic analysis cannot be separated from ethical analysis, since we must be responsive to how the distinctions we embrace construct our experiences, as well as how these distinctions are enacted in social practices in what they conceal as well as what they reveal.

While viscous porosity interprets the connections between sociomaterial elements in interaction, another interpretation of Katrina describes how these elements are entangled. Amanda Porter (2013) investigates the emergence of organisation and technology at a city shelter not far from New Orleans, where Katrina evacuees sought refuge in the days prior to and following the disaster.

Emergence is defined as an empirical phenomenon, affecting and affected by the use of technology, and emergent organisations are defined as those with both new structures and non-regular tasks. At the shelter, emergence occurred as the situational entanglements of three main elements: salient moments in time, key actors and boundary-making practices. The first salient moment occurred during the initial hours of the response when volunteers experienced significant pressure and uncertainty at the shelter. The second salient moment occurred around the second day of the response, when volunteers experienced the failure of the technologies they had initially designed.

These two salient moments then triggered key actors' boundary-making practices. In fact, some volunteers responded quickly to situational demands with the design and deployment of responsive technologies, while other volunteers waited to take action. These boundary-making practices enacted distinction and dependency between key actors. First, a distinction was enacted between the volunteers and technologies at the shelter that were responsive versus those volunteers and technologies that were reactive to the initial extraordinary demands. Second, a dependency was enacted between volunteers and responsive technologies at the shelter, resulting in a divided organisation. On the one hand, responsive volunteers and technologies co-emerged to gain control of the situation at the shelter, becoming defining actors. On the other hand, reactive volunteers became exterior to the developing situation at the shelter and soon became isolated actors.

Porter's work (2013: 11) 'articulates the *situation* (emphasis in original) as the focal point for selecting and discerning which agencies matter in emergence'. Moreover, in order to study emergence with a situational focal point, she theorises relationships between agencies specifically as situational boundary-making. She argues that 'the boundary-making focus extends existing theory on emergence in organizational technology studies by showing how emergence occurs through the *(in)determinacy of meaning*' (2013: 26). In other words, meanings are the making of boundaries – through the subtle dynamics of power and control – through response practices in time, rather than being inherent to an actor or resulting from a single purposeful act. Inclusion and determinacy of meaning are always accompanied by exclusion and indeterminacy of meaning (Barad, 2007) and in Porter's work, we can see the sociomateriality of meanings through the articulation of practices of inclusion and exclusion on the basis of meanings situationally enacted.

Conclusions

In this chapter, I have stressed how the concept of sociomateriality is at the very heart of a posthumanist practice theory. The diffusion of Karen Barad's work and vocabulary outside feminist theory can be considered the beginning of a conversation among separate fields of research. In writing about the shift from 'inter' to intra-thinking, John Shotter (2013: 41) notes that 'small changes in words can provide big changes in our orientations'. In fact, sociomateriality has already become the symbol for the disappearance of the hyphen that connects but separates oppositional dualisms.

The chapter has offered a selective immersion in the concept of sociomateriality and argued that it enriches the study of practices with special consideration of the materiality of bodies, technologies, discourses, meanings and material-institutional contexts of interconnected practices. This argument has been illustrated with references to empirical research projects, since the problem of how to craft a methodology for the empirical study of the entanglement of sociomateriality within the practices under scrutiny is still open and crucial.

While a humanist approach to practice assumes the centrality of humans as sites of embodied understandings and then proceeds to analysis of humans and their practices, a posthumanist approach instead interrogates how all the elements within a practice hold together and acquire agency in being entangled. In the latter case, 'sociomateriality' may be considered an attribute of any practice, and 'sociomaterial' an adjective that stresses how a practice is constituted by matter and culture. Moreover, on considering sociomaterial practices, the situatedness of a practice being practised in a contingent space and time is linked to other sociomaterial practices that sustain and allow the situated performance of that practice.

In this chapter, on considering the male body in the social practices of fathering, we could consider at the same time how fathering practices are linked to institutional contexts, to women's work, to social regulations on parental leaves and many other practices in which the social and the material are entangled. Similarly, in looking at a working practice like artificial nutrition in a nursing home, we could trace how the sociomateriality of bodies no longer able to take food, their nursing, medical practices and family care become entangled with ethical discourses on life and death as sociomaterial issues. In the last example of the sociomateriality of a territory – New Orleans – disrupted by a so-called natural event, we could see the social practices deriving from the past and shaping the territory in the way that a hurricane impacted on it with such violence. In all the three cases, the materialities of bodies, technologies, discourses could not be separated from the society that formed them and vice versa, the social was not external or separate from materialities. My argument is therefore constructed around the evidence that, in the three cases, both ethics and politics are sociomaterial and are part of the *agencement* of the heterogeneous elements in the becoming of a practice.

A final consideration concerns how the practices of representation of the topic of study (practice in our context) are linked to the concept of epistemic responsibility (Code, 1987). Not only are we – as researchers – internal to the object of study, but also our epistemic practices cannot be separated from ethical analysis. Hence, as researchers, we should be responsive to how the distinctions that we embrace construct our experiences and how these distinctions conceal as well as reveal what we research in the practices that we study.

Acknowledgements

I would like to express my great appreciation to all the other colleagues who took part in the discussion of the first drafts of the chapters of the book and especially to the three editors who generously took care of the whole process. Moreover, I wish to thank Marie Manidis for the long email conversations over the chapter and for her warm friendship.

Notes

1   The term 'texture of practices' (Gherardi, 2006) denotes 'connectedness in action'. This term brings out the definitive feature of texture, its endless series of relationships which continually move into each other. Texture is a strongly evocative concept which recalls the intricacies of networking, but at the same time allows for an analytical, qualitative framework (Strati, 2000).

2   I have proposed elsewhere (Gherardi, 2016) to resume the original French word *agencement* instead of its loose English translation as 'assemblage'. *Agencement* has been used as a philosophical term by Deleuze and Guattari (1987) with the sense of 'in connection with', which gives a first good approximation of the term. The problem, however, is that its translation into English as 'assemblage' has changed the original meaning. The French term in fact has a processual connotation – the idea of establishing or forming an assemblage. It focuses on process and on the dynamic character of the interacting between the heterogeneous elements of the phenomenon. While a certain use of the term 'assemblage' risks rigidifying the concept into the thingness of final or stable states, the French term *agencement* works as an evocation of emergence and heterogeneity. The term *agencement* is the key to connecting with the vocabulary of becoming and with the temporality of practice as it unfolds.

3   Ignorance is a phenomenon often overlooked in epistemological scholarship. Feminist epistemologies of ignorance (Tuana and Sullivan, 2006: vii) were born from the realisation that we cannot understand complex practices of knowledge production without understanding the practices that account for not knowing. In fact, the persistence of controversies is often not the consequence of imperfect knowledge, but a political consequence of conflicting interests and structural apathies.

4

VARIATION AND THE INTERSECTION OF PRACTICES

Allison Hui

Variation is an extremely common feature of social life – we expect to study different school subjects, meet with different clients, develop different skills and become interested in different leisure pursuits over time. Yet despite this prevalence, there are limited conceptual resources for articulating variation within theories of practice. Many established categories exist for discussing variations between people – for example, those related to gender, race and class. A vocabulary for articulating how *practices* vary is, however, comparatively underdeveloped. This chapter extends this nascent discussion – distinguishing variation within practices from variations in relation to the wider nexus of practices and identifying further differences within each of these categories.

To develop an account of how practices vary, I draw upon a range of previous writing. For contemporary theories of practice, as developed by authors such as Giddens, Bourdieu, Schatzki, Shove and Reckwitz, 'the social is a field of embodied, materially interwoven practices' (Schatzki, 2001a: 3) that is 'ordered across space and time' (Giddens, 1984: 2). Multiple practices come together as a nexus with diverse links and relationships that contribute to the production of variation within the social field or plane. Some research traditions resist the move to name and codify practices within this field – as in actor network theory's hesitancy to use summary categories outside the specific empirical contexts in which phenomena have been observed and enacted. However, I follow Schatzki (1996; 2002), Shove (Shove *et al.*, 2012) and Reckwitz in identifying and discussing specific practices – *Praktiken* (Reckwitz, 2002b: 249) – that can be recognised as patterns created through the bringing together of a set of activities, materials, understandings and skills. Links and relationships therefore exist between both the components within a practice and between practices themselves.

The dimension of variation best addressed in previous work has been that between different performances of one practice. Since a practice is 'a pattern which can be filled out by a multitude of single and often unique actions' (Reckwitz, 2002b: 250), each time it is performed, different elements are brought together. Close empirical consideration of such processes has highlighted that the same set of activities can never be enacted in exactly the same way, making even 'routine' practices the site of ongoing reproduction and change (see discussion below). Empirical studies have also considered how variations emerge through the circulation of practices to new countries (Shove and Pantzar, 2005a; Wang and Shove, 2008). The ensuing discussion of variation *within* practices consequently focuses on how even a recognisably patterned activity can be internally varied.

Although variation *within* practices has been discussed both theoretically and in relation to empirical cases, much remains to be explored about variation *between* multiple practices – differences that exist between, and are apparent within the connections of, different practices. Concepts that name different types of connected practices – including bundles, complexes or nets (Schatzki, 2002: 154–5; Shove *et al.*, 2012: chap. 5) – have so far received relatively limited discussion and empirical investigation. Yet as this chapter argues, dimensions of variation become intelligible in different ways when considering the nexus of multiple practices.

In order to identify variation, some grounding in a plane of potential similarity is required. That is, the potential to recognise either variation or similarity only ever exists in relation to particular categories that serve as shared points of reference. Ham and hummus can be considered varied in relation to the category of 'sandwich fillings', but not in relation to differentiations between 'protein and non-protein sources' or 'edible or non-edible items'. Within the plane of practices, identifying referents for gauging similarity and difference, and hence variation, could be approached in many ways.

I argue that the intersections between practices are crucial for developing analytic approaches and vocabularies more attuned to variation within a specific nexus of practices. Dimensions of intersection are overlaps and commonalities between practices that may be either material (e.g. a laptop used for leisure and for work) or abstract (a shared category or understanding such as clock time). They are therefore enacted by and exist in multiple material and non-material forms and are points wherein the consideration or performance of one practice might pivot into consideration or performance of another. Theoretical discussions have already supported the existence of such 'shared' aspects or summary units of diverse social practices and this discussion further develops implications for understanding variation. Considering different types of intersection within the plane of practices provides reference points for identifying and discovering similarities and differences among practices.

The main aim of this chapter is to highlight variations within and between *practices* rather than focusing on things that are themselves *situated in between practices*. I therefore use the general terms 'intersection' and 'crossing points' in order to leave open specific forms of interdependence, power and positioning that characterise intersections themselves. That is, variation in types of intersection is not taken up as a central focus. In this chapter, intersections and relations between practices are highlighted in order to acknowledge that while variation may be identified in various forms and through various means, a better understanding is needed of how variation between practices relates to their interconnections and interdependence. As a result, variations within the nexus of practices are summarised in relation to properties that are shared by multiple practices.

This approach may evoke comparisons to Star and Griesemer's (1989) discussion of 'boundary objects' that mediate between intersecting social worlds. In their example of museum workers, abstract or concrete boundary objects such as specimens, field notes or maps adapt to the different worlds that they are a part of – changing meanings and being managed to maintain at least some common identity that facilitates coherence and translation across worlds (Star and Griesemer, 1989: 393). While this chapter similarly takes intersections to be adaptable – with for instance objects or meanings taking on varied forms in different practices – it also makes several key departures from this work. First, Star and Griesemer emphasise how boundary objects are created in order to work at the boundaries of social worlds – thus presuming the pre-existence of different social worlds and the resulting need to create objects that can inhabit more than one (1989: 408). By contrast, I do not presume that bounded practices necessarily precede intersections. It is possible that what will serve as intersections – for instance understandings of spatial or temporal categories (e.g. an objective geographical location or clock time) – pre-exist the emergence of practices that are eventually seen to share them. Second, although Star and Griesemer suggest that boundary objects are actively constructed to span worlds, some intersections between practices may not have been purposely or intentionally forged and may be of comparatively little consequence. While field notes can be written with the explicit intention of translating and circulating knowledge from the person collecting a natural specimen to a museum curator or archivist, all three participants in such an exercise might use objects such as pens or mobile devices without these being actively created as devices to conjoin their practices. Not all objects involved in multiple practices are thus actively enacted to cross boundaries in the sense that Star and Griesemer discuss – and as Nicolini, Mengis and Swam demonstrate (2012). Third, the case of natural history practices leads the authors to focus upon how 'boundary objects are produced when sponsors, theorists and amateurs collaborate to produce representations of nature' (1989: 408). By contrast, I do not take intersections to be necessarily tied to representations. This creates room to investigate how people are enrolled in multiple practices, as well as how particular meanings or spatio-temporal dimensions that have a myriad of representations can be understood as constituting intersections between practices. Finally, and most obviously, while Star and Griesemer's discussion, and related expansions upon it (Nicolini et al., 2012), emerges from an interest in discussing collaboration and cooperation, this chapter is concerned with expanding understandings of variation and its treatment of intersections is shaped by this aim.

The rest of the chapter is divided into two main sections focusing upon variation within practices and variation in relation to the nexus of practices. Each introduces several forms of variation and illustrates these in relation to examples from four cases: birdwatching, eating, identity verification practices and funerals.

Variation within practices

As noted above, theories of practice have already addressed several forms of variation, even if these have not always been articulated as characteristics of variation *per se*. In order to summarise briefly what this work has revealed, this section identifies three different forms: variation as a basic feature, variation as meaningfully constructed and variation in the constituent elements of a performance.

Variation as a basic feature

First, variation can be understood as a feature to consider in understanding and analysing all practices – that is, no matter their particularities, they are marked by continuous internal variations. The conceptual distinction between practices as entities and as performances (Shove and Pantzar, 2007: 154) helps to reveal and reinforce the centrality of variation within a world of practices. A practice-as-performance takes place at a particular space and time when understandings, materials, practitioners and activities come together in a particular way. For example, at 12.37 p.m. on 4 December 2015, I made a sandwich in my kitchen at home using a plate, knife, bread, toaster, ham, mustard and cheese. Many such performances, undertaken by multiple practitioners in diverse spaces and times, can be conceptually brought together in considering a practice-as-entity. In this case, the entity in question could be the practice of making lunch, or more specifically of making sandwiches, or even of making ham and cheese sandwiches, depending on how the analytic boundaries are drawn. What is important in making this summary move to practice-as-entity is that entities are inherently varied internally – they cannot help but encompass differences because of the unpredictable and diverse nature of performances. Even if I make ham and cheese sandwiches every day for lunch, this routine precludes exact repetition. Despite my best efforts, I will never get the same amount of mustard on the bread in exactly the same pattern. Some days the toaster might make the bread more or less crispy, in response to the latter's age and texture. There may be more significant irritations or disruptions – the store not stocking my normal brand of bread or receiving a text in the middle of the sandwich-making process – that alter the performance further. The patterning that makes practice-entities intelligible to practitioners and researchers alike is inseparable from and consistent with the variation that is an inevitable dimension of performances (and thus entities).

Variation as meaningfully constructed

A second aspect of variation within practices concerns the limits of their intelligibility. Variations not only emerge through performance, but are also made sense of through shared meanings, understandings and goals. As a result, practitioners (re)produce distinctions that articulate and evaluate variations within a practice. Going beyond tacit limits disrupts working or practical understandings of 'the' practice.

Within birdwatching, for example, practitioners distinguish types of involvement and levels of knowledge – with 'birdwatchers' being those with more casual commitment and limited knowledge, 'birders' being more involved and knowledgeable and 'twitchers' being not only obsessively engaged with the practice but also far more mobile – seeking rare or far-flung birds. These terms articulate different variants of meaningful participation in the practice and the communities that gather around them.

The enactment of variations within practices also involves the establishment of meaningful boundaries within which practices are conducted and understood. Hägerstrand discusses the 'tolerable flexibility' that exists for the successful performance of any project – 'to what extent projects can "survive" interruptions' (Hägerstrand, 1996: 669). Although he does not use this concept in relation to social practices, I suggest that it is important in relation to the meaningful construction of variation. While categories may seem simply to name variations within a practice, they may also mark what are understood to be the limits of tolerable variation – bounding the difference that is understood as still plausible or acceptable for participants. Where variations threaten to derail a practice, obstruct the achievement of a goal or transform a performance beyond acceptable bounds, practitioners acknowledge them as intolerable and therefore inappropriate. In this way, while all categories create boundaries and help articulate variations, within practices they can also become enrolled in normative assessments and processes whereby some variants are encouraged and others discouraged.

How tolerable variation is made meaningful is thus highly consequential for potential courses of action. Consider again practices involving food. Despite having the potential to cook and eat a wide range of food types at any meal, there is remarkably little overlap between the types of food consumed at breakfast, lunch and dinner in the UK (Yates and Warde, 2015). The variation between meals is marked by the different names given to them and is also shaped by understandings of socially appropriate and 'normal' foods for each. While it would be possible to make and eat a roast chicken for breakfast, socially such variation contravenes established sets of meanings and would therefore likely be deemed absurd. Variation within practices is therefore acknowledged and limited in important ways by the shared meanings that are constructed and reproduced by practitioners.

Variation in the constituent elements of a performance

The third aspect of variation within practices relates to the varied sets of elements that can be integrated into any one performance. As Reckwitz highlights, many different elements are brought together in a practice: 'forms of bodily activities, forms of mental activities, "things" and their use, a background knowledge in the form of understanding, know-how, states of emotion and motivational knowledge'

(2002b: 249). While multiple elements are needed for a performance, there are different possibilities that might suffice. That is, 'a practice involves different sets of objects that are used in different circumstances' (Hui, 2012: 206). Toast can be made using a toaster or a grill or a wood fire and mustard can be spread using a knife or, if none is available, the back of a spoon. In addition to the variation that occurs when the same set of elements is used in multiple performances, there is also variation that emerges from using different sets of acceptable elements. Discussions of how variants of practices emerge through global circulation often rest upon the recognition that changing the spaces and cultural contexts in which performances occur involves changes in elements that prompt new variations (Shove and Pantzar, 2005a; Maller and Strengers, 2013; Hui, 2015).

Another example of this can be found in the variation of funeral services. In modern Western countries, funeral services have evolved into three primary models: those that are institutionally commercial (led by a funeral director), institutionally municipal (led by municipal officials) or institutionally religious (led by religious officials) (Walter, 2005: 177). Within each institutional model, religion may or may not play a cultural role – as for instance in the USA, funeral home services that are structured as Christian services or the predominance of church services in culturally secular Sweden (Walter, 2005: 182). Each of these models involves different types of space with diverse collections of things, understandings, institutional rules and practitioners coordinating the service. Participants might have quite diverse suggestions and expectations of what elements a funeral service should include – based both on personal histories of participation in funeral or religious practices and their knowledge of and familiarity with the deceased. As a result, even within the same country, city or building, funerals can involve widely differing sets of elements, with services an eclectic mix of activities of varied provenance and with diverse relationships to the family, attendees and deceased. Humanist services can include the Lord's Prayer (Holloway, Adamson, Argyrou, Draper and Mariau, 2013: 41), Pink Floyd may be played at a church service (Szmigin and Canning, 2015: 755) or, as I experienced, the deceased's refusal to convert to Catholicism can be discussed during her Catholic wake. Depending on the institutions and practitioners involved, some variations may be deemed outside acceptable bounds while others are permitted because they contribute to the funeral's aims of meaningfully memorialising the departure of a loved one. The practitioners and institutions involved in any performance of a funeral negotiate and shape the set of elements that end up being incorporated, contributing to the combination of similarities and differences that distinguish it from other performances.

Attending to such variation in sets of elements is also important in relation to the potential flexibility of any one type of element. That is, there is more flexibility regarding exactly which elements are used in some practices than in others. Think for instance of the range of identification cards, such as drivers' licences, passports and birth certificates, that 'establish the identity of the bearer for purposes of state administration' (Torpey, 2000: 159). These documents are used for a range of activities: verifying one's identity when applying for a bank account or commencing new employment; one's age for alcohol purchases; or one's citizenship when accessing 'certain rights of democratic participation (e.g. voting), public services (e.g. medical care) and transfer payments ("welfare")' (Torpey, 2000: 165; Wang, 2004). In most cases, any one of a number of reputable forms of identification would be acceptable for each of these checks. Yet in the case of migrants, passports may become the *only* acceptable form of identification due to the inconsistent language and format of international drivers' licences and birth certificates. Moreover, when one is engaging in a border check at an airport or roadside border station, only passports are appropriate, as other forms of identification do not have the same international status or capacity to be stamped and thus do not fulfil the requirements of this practice.

Elements such as materials can thus vary in terms of their importance to particular practices. On one hand, they can be obligatory when there are no other elements that can be substituted and their presence is a necessary condition for continuing essential processes – as in passports at border checks. On the other hand, they may be substitutable – as in the case of different types of identity documents – or negotiable – if different processes can be conducted in their absence – or entirely optional. There are differing degrees of potential flexibility for particular elements within any practice, as well as for the variations associated with the different combinations of elements that characterise any one performance.

Variation in relation to the nexus of practices

Although multiple forms of variation can be identified within practices, focusing exclusively upon these provides a restricted account of how variation matters for theories of practice. Many important questions about relations between multiple practices relate to variations in the links and connections between practices and the consequences of these variations for the trajectories both of the practices involved and the complexes they form. Therefore, while variations within practices are not necessarily independent of those between practices – changes in one could affect the other – it is useful to distinguish between them in order to highlight different methods and approaches needed to study and analyse them.

The question therefore becomes: how do intersections of practices reveal and relate to variations between practices? This section addresses three types of intersection – spatio-temporal, practitioner/material, and conceptual – using these to identify features of variation and suggest future lines of investigation.

Variation in terms of spatio-temporal intersections

As many authors have discussed, the particularities of practices emerge alongside their spatial and temporal dynamics. Bourdieu, for instance, suggested that 'practice is inseparable from temporality, not only because it is played out in time, but also because it plays strategically with time and especially with tempo' (1990: 81) and practices are similarly inseparable from their mobilities (Hui, 2013: 892). Schatzki elaborates upon these points by noting that the doings and sayings of practices are anchored at a range of paths and places (2010b: 59) that enrol past, present and future through 'acting toward an end from what motivates' (2010b: 37). Limited work has been done thus far to explore the implications of these insights for not only individual practices but also for the project of conceptualising interconnections between practices.

Such an exercise depends on identifying and working with methods that reveal connectivity. Understandings of clock or calendar time and geographical space as dimensions that exist independent of human activity have long been used as bench-marks against which to reveal and assess variation. Take for example cross-national time use studies based on diaries that record activities undertaken at particular times of day by participants residing in specific countries. When analysis is undertaken, comparing data from two different years or from two different countries in the same year, it is the temporal structure of clock hours in a day and the spatial container of a country's political-geographical boundaries that are taken to be common reference points in terms of which notable variations are identified. Warde, Cheng, Olsen and Southerton (2007) for example, use time use data to reveal 'considerable national variation in patterns of food preparation, eating at home and eating out', which they relate to how consumption is institutionalised in each country (2007: 363). Varying links between food preparation and eating, food provision and regulation, as well as comparisons of the time spent engaged in different patterns of eating, are used to dispute the idea that there has been global convergence in food cultures and related practices (Warde *et al.*, 2007: 380).

In such cases, temporal or spatial characteristics are treated as relevant common-alities in the field of practices in relation to which varying links and dynamics of practice might be revealed. While providing useful insights, this approach falls foul of Bourdieu's warning about eliding the differences between analysts' and practi-tioners' logics and spatio-temporal foci:

> like the map which substitutes the homogeneous, continuous space of geom-etry for the discontinuous, patchy space of practical pathways, the calendar substitutes a linear, homogeneous, continuous time for practical time, which is made up of islands of incommensurable duration, each with its own rhythm, a time that races or drags, depending on what one is doing.
>
> *(1990: 84)*

Nonetheless, focusing upon temporal or spatial intersections can reveal important variations in how practices are interlinked and interrelated, including variations in the meanings and understandings that guide their spatio-temporal dynamics.

A study by Markham Schulz (2015), for example, uses comparative research (between France, the United States of America and Norway) to reveal variations in how people negotiate the transition from work to non-work practices. Focusing on the 5–9 p.m. period when professional workers are most likely to be finishing work and moving on to personal activities in non-work spaces, Markham Schulz uncovers different understandings shaping these transitions in space and between practices. In France, managerial cohorts gain social prestige by working late (and thus delay leaving work), while in Norway those who do not leave work when expected are stigmatised for the apparent lack of a fulfilling personal life. In the USA, he found more internal differentiation and discovered that individual companies interpret acceptable boundaries and shifts between work and personal time in different ways. Treating the temporal zone of early evening hours as an intersection between practices in different countries allows Markham Schulz to investigate how relationships between work and non-work practices are negotiated – and to reveal the specific understandings, institutional contexts and sequencing of activities that constitute 'variations' between countries.

Variations in the nexus of practices can thus be identified through reference to shared spatio-temporal characteristics. Although objective features – such as clock time – are often used in this role, there is room for exploring how other aspects of spatio-temporality (shared rhythms, paths, sites, etc.) could be mobilised in analysing variation.

Variation in terms of practitioners or materials at the intersection of practices

In addition to intersecting spatially and temporally, practices intersect through practitioners and materials that are shared between them. People, Reckwitz argues, are crossing points: 'As there are diverse social practices, and as every agent carries out a multitude of different social practices, the individual is the unique crossing point of practices' (2002b: 256). They thus embody intersections of numerous practices – working, cooking, eating, washing, banking, fundraising, exercising, gardening, training and more. This positioning can bring benefits – such as the development of skills or understandings that can be incorporated into a different practice – and challenges – involving seemingly incompatible meanings or the competition between skills that degrade or obstruct each other (e.g. muscular strength and flexibility). Some aspects of this positioning have been investigated within literature on multiple careers – for example, in relation to women's careers as mothers and professionals (Crompton and Sanderson, 1986; Evetts, 1994; Eaton and Bailyn, 2000). Much more remains to be understood, however, including how embodied skills or competences develop through involvement in more than one practice and how these differences underpin variations both in the performance of specific practices and in how multiple practices hang together.

The material components of practices can be similarly understood as intersections between multiple practices. Elements of practices are 'a point of *connection* between them' – albeit not fixed and static points but ones more akin to 'zones of overlap and intersection' (Shove *et al.*, 2012: 113) or 'a form of connective tissue that holds complex social arrangements in place, and potentially pulls them apart' (Shove *et al.*, 2012: 36). While not using the concept of material 'elements', Schatzki highlights the ability of practices to 'overlap': 'a particular doing, for instance, might belong to two or more practices by virtue of expressing components of these different practices' organizations' (2002: 87). Since practices are seen by Schatzki to be 'intrinsically connected to and interwoven with objects' (2002: 106), it follows that objects might similarly be points of overlap and intersection between multiple practices.

Having acknowledged that practitioners and material components can be positioned at the intersection of practices, there are several implications for analysing these features as vectors of variation. First, one might extend a consideration of multiple elements of practice to investigate not variation within practices (as discussed above), but rather variation between them. The materials used to make a sandwich, for example, are also included within the larger set that is used at funerals (e.g. for serving snacks after a memorial service), even if other materials such as flower arrangements or printed orders of service are not included within both sets. The sets of materials used in multiple practices overlap to varying degrees and provide links and interdependencies of varying strength. Compared to the set of objects used in food preparation, funerals have a more complex and wider-ranging set extending beyond food preparation and also including religious rituals, public communication and memorialisation, bureaucratic procedures and burial. Examining sets might thus help to reveal variations in the density and patterning of material links between practices.

Second, questions about how variations between practices affect practitioners could be pursued through a consideration of what multiple practices require of the same person. This line of investigation could extend work on multiple careers, for instance, to consider relationships between practices other than work and family life. It could also usefully extend understandings of the intertwining of careers in different practices. Some relationships between practices are marked by commensalism wherein performances of one benefit from, and also presuppose, careers in another. When dual careers are not present, as in this example of religious and funeral practices, it becomes problematic for practitioners:

> Ian['s funeral] was in a church because he was buried in the churchyard, but I'm not religious at all so there's no religious aspect for me. We had some hymns, two or three hymns that his mother chose, and nobody knew them. I thought that was hideous, because nobody was singing, everyone was just looking around a bit, embarrassed, they were just hymns no one had ever heard of.
>
> (*Szmigin and Canning, 2015: 756*)

Such moments of discomfort demonstrate that while participation in funeral practices is not dependent upon participation in religious practices, the symbiotic relationship between these practices – with activities and knowledge used in one having been developed in the other – places demands upon practitioners that cannot always be fulfilled. Practices vary in terms of the extent to which they cultivate the skills, understandings and knowledge that are demanded of practitioners performing them. While funerals regularly draw upon elements from religious practices, identity-checking procedures do not similarly do so. Where practices involve many elements that practitioners would need to develop through other practices, this can be an indicator of the closer intertwining of practices.

Third, the temporalities of materials' or practitioners' links to different practices could shape processes of transformation and thus constitute forms of variation. Elements and practitioners do not exist out of time – like practices they have histories and temporal characteristics. A skill cannot be demonstrated before it has been learned, or a material used before it has been created. The situation of materials and practitioners at the intersection of practices is therefore indicative of chains of interaction between practices – processes whereby inputs to one practice are transformed into outputs that may become inputs of another practice.

Take passports for example. Before passports can be checked during identity procedures, they must be created, and this involves what have grown to become elaborate practices including filling out forms, taking carefully specified photos, collecting professional attestation of likeness or personal acquaintance, providing supporting identity documents and submitting biometric measures such as fingerprints. These activities and their traces now feed into administrative procedures wherein forms, photos, attestations and documents are reviewed, assessed and processed before the production of the object itself – a document that often remains the property of the state and is connected to a myriad of databases through computer-readable codes. These passports, themselves traces of administrative and identification practices, have from their moment of creation a defined lifespan noted by their expiry date, as well as spatialities of expected relevance – the border checkpoints and immigration halls where they become a part of different bureaucratic processes.

Practices thus relate to passports in different ways. For the person completing a passport application, the passport is something only imagined – a goal towards which activities are oriented. For those working in passport offices, it is an output and trace of activity – something generated and circulated if valid inputs have been provided and appropriate documentation processes are completed. For border agents, the passport is a prerequisite input that is then scanned, examined, considered, recorded and potentially stamped. Through these linked practices, a necessary temporal sequence is established for any one practitioner, wherein border checks are not possible without having previously applied for and received a passport. In addition to being 'a necessary but not sufficient condition to be admitted into a country' (Wang, 2004: 357), passports act as a necessary but not sufficient condition for the performance of certain practices. The sequences of which they are a part include the orchestration of practices involving multiple sets of practitioners – applicants, government administrators and border security agents – often situated in different locations.

As this example highlights, materials (and similarly practitioners) are wrapped up in chains of actions, inputs and outputs. Practices transform materials and people's bodies into different forms. Series of inputs and outputs thus help to determine possible sequences through which practices are linked. Birth certificates are needed to obtain passports, which for migrants are needed to obtain health cards or numbers, which are needed to give birth to a child in a hospital, which will then prompt a further application for a birth certificate. Rawolle (2010) has used the term 'chains of production and consumption' to discuss such sequences in relation to Bourdieu's work, emphasising that attempts to circulate specific traces or accounts between practices can be more or less successful. This is an important point, as even seemingly established sequences and chains can transform or be interrupted. Yet I have resisted the terms 'production' and 'consumption', because Rawolle's account foregrounds the intended orientation of chains: 'the production of specific practices is oriented towards… likely consumption patterns' (2010: 127). Although identity documents are produced through practices thus oriented, they are also more ambiguously situated – with passports being used for example to check in to hotels even when other forms of identification would be sufficient. Chains of actions, inputs and outputs can thus be at times unintended or unanticipated by participants engaged in one or more of the interlinked practices.

Such sequences where one material is required for the production of another, or one set of experiences and skills are required for participation in another practice, represent dimensions of variations. For example, practices may vary in terms of how many inputs or outputs they have – and the extent to which these are consequential for other practices. In addition, variation between practices may be identified in relation to the materials or practitioners involved: not all materials will appear equally frequently as inputs or outputs, and some embodied skills or knowledge may be developed only by carefully selected practitioners in specific practices – think for instance of companies whose food production relies upon a 'secret sauce' or 'special technique'. Practices also vary in terms of their position within temporal sequences – the extent to which they draw upon particular inputs and outputs and thus need to occur before or after other practices. Investigating these temporal sequences can additionally pinpoint variation in the accessibility of practices to particular practitioners – the inability to obtain materials or develop competences may constrain continued participation in interconnected practices.

Variation in terms of groups and categories

While the bodies of practitioners and materiality of objects function as tangible points of intersection between practices, there is also a range of more ambiguously tangible things that can be similarly positioned. For Shove, Pantzar and Watson, meanings exist alongside materials as elements of practices that are shared and therefore 'zones of overlap and intersection' (2012: 113). Likewise, Schatzki discusses how components such as rules can apply to multiple practices (2002: 87). The diverse traces left by meanings, rules, concepts or categories can be difficult to follow as they weave through the nexus of practices. In order to focus this final subsection,

I therefore take up a very specific set of meanings and categories related to groups – in particular those through which groups of practitioners are defined.

This focus is useful in a number of ways. First, it builds upon practitioners' roles as crossing points within the nexus of practices. For each practice a person participates in, there is a group of other practitioners – some with whom performances are shared spatially or temporally, and others with whom direct contact might be established occasionally, or never. Being at the intersection of many practices is therefore also being at the intersection of many groups of practitioners. Second, the importance of groups that gather together by virtue of shared practices has already been established within literature on communities of practice. Dissatisfied with predominant understandings of learning as formal knowledge transfer from teachers to pupils, Lave and Wenger (1991) proposed that learning instead be situated within and as an outcome of a range of shared practices. In addition to foregrounding practices, they argued that learning is relational and therefore needs to be studied by attending to collectives or groups rather than individuals (Fuller, 2007: 19). There is scope for both extending this interest in groups beyond the topic of learning and for further questioning how groups are themselves conceptualised. Nicolini, for instance, suggests that by reifying the notion of 'community', Wenger draws too strongly upon positive framings of the term (2012: 90–1). More commonly, concepts that indicate particular groups of people – girls/boys, Christians/Muslims, professionals/manual workers – are regularly evoked in representing specific practices, even though they differ from groups of *practitioners*, and yet the implications of such categories for *multiple practices* have not been discussed at length by practice theorists.

Before considering how such categories might help to constitute or reveal variation within the plane of practices, I outline three means whereby groups – multiple things or people that are understood to be related – are formed. Communities of practice literature focuses upon the formation of groups through co-present interaction and shared performances. Families, for instance, eat and cook together, at more regular temporalities for immediate family members or less regular ones for extended family. Yet this is only one way that family groups are made. The family as an intelligible and meaningful group is also enacted by those not belonging to it: clerical staff in governmental agencies enact the family through procedures such as the registration of marriages and births and the production of identity documents or dependent visas that give families rights in relation to other practices legislated by governments. Groups are thus (re)produced through practices that label, codify and create traces of their existence. Such traces can then lead families to be treated as a group in other practices – for instance being allowed to approach border agents together rather than individually. Third, general understandings of what family is and what family means are also produced through practices that refer to non/fictional families. Novels, television programmes and housekeeping magazines as well as blogs, portraits and songs all contribute to how the category of 'family' is made meaningful. Children begin learning such meanings through picture books and early schooling and continue encountering them as adults in the anthropomorphised descriptions of animals in documentaries and the deriding of problematic families in news stories. 'Family' groups are thus made through the circulation of cultural products enacting diverse meanings, the creation of material traces with implications for other practices and the performance of shared practices. Other groups are constituted in similar ways, although with different emphasis upon the various forms of enactment involved. Groups of 'birders' or 'birdwatchers', for instance, are made meaningful through blogs, websites and birding books and are performed by groups of co-present enthusiasts, but are rarely defined or recognised in these terms by non-birdwatchers or by formal institutions.

What are the implications of a category such as 'family' for conceptualising variation in the nexus of practices? For one, looking at how 'family' is invoked or reproduced across different practices demonstrates that people can have quite different roles depending on how they are positioned in relation to different practices. Practices vary not only in how they incorporate and enact groups, but also in terms of the extent to which these groups generate variation within the practice. When the O'Brien family goes through border-crossing procedures at an airport, there is no expectation that the border agent's questions and passport-stamping procedures will differ from those adopted only moments earlier for the Rossi family and no expectation that the families will respond differently. However, these two families would be likely to generate and reproduce significantly different variants of funeral practices should one of their members pass away. Moreover, they will each reproduce different nexuses of practice – not all families ski or play board games.

In addition, reference to different groups and categories could be useful in identifying patterns of accessibility within the plane of practices. In some instances, the ability to participate in a practice depends upon one's membership in a particular group. While such dynamics have been well-considered in sociological literature on socio-demographic distinctions such as gender, class and religion, this could be extended to encompass the implications of other groupings – such as alumni of a particular school who might be given special rates on insurance packages or musicians who belong to a union and therefore have access to jobs that are not available to others. In some instances, groups may be determined within the practice in question, but in others the definition or membership of a group is imported from one or more other practices – thus enacting links and relationships between multiple practices. Categories of appropriate and inappropriate participants may thus be meaningful only in relation to a nexus of practices and variations in accessibility only intelligible through a consideration of how group categories are enacted and drawn upon across multiple practices.

Considering the groups and categories that are enacted within practices can reveal other dimensions of variation, since not all practices reproduce group membership in the same ways. Identity checking practices enact families, national citizens, il/legal mobiles, migrants and asylum seekers through carefully orchestrated bureaucratic procedures. By contrast, performances of cooking and eating enact such groups as families, friends, foodies, chefs and amateurs, but the categories involved are often ambiguous, with unclear implications for other practices. Some practices enact more formalised groups, for example through the recording of members or explicit codes of conduct, while others reproduce informal associations (e.g. a group of 'regulars' at the pub). Variations in the types of groups enacted provide one means of differentiating types of interdependence between practices. For example, those which involve and reproduce formalised categories with accompanying material traces – such as official records – may engender more intelligible chains of action and more precisely defined sequences of inputs and outputs than those through which more diffuse meanings (e.g. cultural representations) are carried. Moreover, any such differences and observed chains will be variable over time even where group categories remain present. For example, looking at how 'family' has been enacted historically will reveal changing links between practices – illustrating further variations in how 'family' functions as an intersection between practices. For many years the importance of religious practices and organisations was central to the constitution of families – both through marriage ceremonies and teachings about the impropriety of conceiving children out of wedlock. Yet today even families that are not recognised by certain religious groups (e.g. homosexual partners with adopted children) are formally recognised through civil ceremonies and adoption documents. Transformations in the nature and prevalence of family businesses and multi-generational homes similarly indicate that the meanings and practices of families have changed over time, transforming patterns of linkages in the nexuses of practices.

Conclusion

As this chapter has made clear, dimensions of variation are themselves varied. Identifying variation depends upon a point of reference in terms of which judgements of similarity and difference are made. There are endless possibilities for specifying terms and instances of variation. My aim in this chapter was not to characterise all possible variations within a world of practices – such a task is impossible. Instead, I have articulated different analytic strategies that can be used to name and discuss select types of variation and I have considered some of the implications these distinctions raise for understanding a world of overlapping and interconnected practices.

Variation is a feature of all practices and of relations between them. Analysing variations therefore generates further questions about how practices interconnect and about change within a field or nexus of practices. Discussions of variation prompt further thought about how varied temporalities and spatialities are constitutive of not only practices but also nexuses of practices. Articulating dimensions of variation is also crucial for addressing questions about power and norms within a field of practices: how do variations between practices inform understandings of accessibility, power and interdependence? On what basis might normative assessments of acceptable or intolerable variations in practices be made? Extending analyses of variation along these lines could also inform more empirically focused questions such as: on what basis should practices be selected for empirical study? While this question must be answered in relation to the concerns and questions at hand, being able to articulate dimensions of variation within a nexus of practices is important for justifying why some practices might be more suitable for investigating particular issues than others. While these questions have not been taken up in detail here, this chapter has helped develop a language and set of analytic tools for articulating variations within and between practices that will support their exploration in the future.

Acknowledgements

Many thanks are given to the participants and discussants at the Windermere (2014) and Lancaster (2015) workshops, who provided very helpful comments and suggestions on previous versions of this chapter.

5

EPIGENETICS, THEORIES OF SOCIAL PRACTICE AND LIFESTYLE DISEASE

Cecily Maller

Introduction

In the spirit of investigating new frontiers and territories, this chapter is situated between two different types of theory: social practices and epigenetics, a sub-discipline of genetics. Its purpose is to examine the effects of practices on practitioners' bodies[1] and in so doing, advance theories of social practice towards new frontiers in health. So-called 'lifestyle diseases' are a persistent and growing global issue and the leading cause of death and disability despite decades of intervention (Daar *et al.*, 2007). In regard to the many varieties of practice theories and practice composition, this chapter draws on the work of Shove *et al.* (2012) as it incorporates central tenets of theoretical and applied work to date. Explorations of the possible benefits and tensions of joining ideas from social and natural theories, or the 'soft' and 'hard' sciences, are not new. In fact, they are consistent with the materialist tradition of which theories of social practice are a part (Nicolini, 2012; Schatzki, 2001a).

Aside from sub-disciplines such as evolutionary psychology and human sociobiology, other more metaphorical explorations venture between the social and natural sciences (e.g. Shove and Pantzar, 2005b). Although these explorations have potential, they also have their challenges, some of which are highlighted by Schatzki (2001b).

For example, recent work on theories of social practice has benefited from numerous concepts sourced from the natural sciences of population biology and ecology, including terms like 'recruitment', 'reproduction', 'convergence' (Shove *et al.*, 2012), 'competition', 'cooperation' and 'predation' (Pantzar and Shove, 2010a). Similarly, ideas about muscle memory from sports medicine and exercise science are useful in understanding how practices are remembered in bodies through 'practice memory' (Maller and Strengers, 2014). Practice memory, like muscle memory (Shusterman, 2011; Staron *et al.*, 1991), 'relies on the notion that through performance, imprints of practice elements are codified and can remain linked in the mental and bodily patterns of the performer' (Maller and Strengers, 2014: 150). These theoretical moves, although not free from the problem of incommensurability (Kuhn, 1970), have the potential to break new ground by offering transformative ideas about social change and how it might be (re)directed in more sustainable, equitable or healthier directions.

There is a need for positive change in regard to health and wellbeing and the rise of chronic non-communicable diseases (NCDs), characterised as typically not passing from person to person and being largely preventable (Daar *et al.*, 2007). NCDs are attributed to 'unhealthy lifestyles' associated with post-industrialisation (WHO, 2015a). However, evidence suggests that the distribution of NCDs is uneven, since aside from socioeconomic differences, 'social habits, routines and conventions provide a source of general resistance' (Warde *et al.*, 2007: 381). NCDs include cardiovascular diseases, respiratory illnesses, some cancers and type 2 diabetes – responsible for killing 38 million people each year (WHO, 2015a), or 60 per cent of all deaths globally (Daar *et al.*, 2007). Obesity and being overweight – 'a highly predominant nutritional problem and one of the world's greatest health issues' (Patel, Choksi and Chattopadhyay, 2015: 430) – are associated with NCDs, in particular cardiovascular disease and type 2 diabetes. According to the WHO (2015b), in 2014, an estimated 1.9 billion adults were considered overweight and 600 million were obese. Public health programmes have had only marginal success so far and despite decades of apparently productive research into methods of intervention, 'no country to date has reversed its obesity epidemic' (Roberto *et al.*, 2015: 2400). NCDs and obesity are particularly interesting health challenges as they are defined by the complex interplay of people, their bodies and environments (Roberto *et al.*, 2015).

The chapter has two aims. First, to work through possible points of intersection between theories of social practice and epigenetics to explore the effects of practices on performers' bodies. Second, to see if ideas from epigenetics can extend the reach of theories of social practice to encompass intergenerational and environmentally related health problems attributed to 'lifestyle'. As there are a number of possible diseases attributed to lifestyle, the chapter focuses on obesity. The challenges that arise when aligning two very different theories and when reconciling the objects of study, the sites where action occurs and conceptualisations of bodies are presented.

The chapter begins by providing an overview of the main ideas in epigenetics relevant to a discussion about social practices and practitioners' bodies. The next section explores possible points of intersection between theories of social practice and epigenetics, highlighting tensions and potential incompatibilities. Using obesity as an example, the chapter takes familiar ideas about performance and recruitment and explores them at a detailed level. This exercise raises a series of questions about the inner workings of practice, the intricacies of action and doing and effects on practitioners' bodies. The subsequent section uses ideas outlined previously to consider how a social practice-epigenetics perspective might further encourage the application of theories of social practice to the problems of understanding and intervening in lifestyle disease.

Epigenetics: what is it?

Epigenetics is a relatively new and somewhat 'controversial' (Bird, 2007) field of study in genetics that seeks to understand and explain the effects of gene–environment interactions on bodies, in other words, 'the interface between genetics and the environment' (Milagro, Mansego, De Miguel and Martínez, 2013: 784). Its focus is at the cellular and molecular level: how environmental exposures change the way genes are expressed, thereby changing the physical appearance – or phenotypes – of bodies without changing the underlying genetic makeup, or genotype (Skinner, 2014; Tammen, Friso and Choi, 2013); in other words, epigenetics studies changes to the physical form of individuals that occur in response to *environmental* instead of *genetic* factors (Handel and Ramagopalan, 2010).

Various environmental exposures change the way genes are expressed (switched on or off). They include weather, drought, chemicals and environmental toxins, high or low calorie diets, stress, exercise, drugs, including tobacco and alcohol, as well as pathogens (Skinner, 2014; Tammen *et al.*, 2013). Exposures can result in changes to the phenotype, affecting conditions such as physical shape, disease susceptibility, stress response, behaviour and longevity (Tammen *et al.*, 2013). These conditions are associated with a range of pathologies, from obesity, diabetes, cardiovascular disease and cancer (Milagro *et al.*, 2013), to changes in social behaviour (Keverne and Curley, 2008; Skinner, 2014) and mental states (Karlic and Baurek, 2011), although the evidence for social and mental change is inconclusive (Januar, Saffery and Ryan, 2015). This means:

> Epigenetic marks are therefore a reflection of an individual's environmental exposures and as such change during the lifetime of a cell/tissue. Thus, we are 'acquiring' changes to our epigenome all the time.
>
> (*Handel and Ramagopalan, 2010: 2*)

Epigenetics is proposed as an explanation for why monozygotic twins with identical genes often diverge in their physical appearance and disease susceptibility over time (Fraga *et al.*, 2005).

One of the most exciting prospects of epigenetics is that it represents a form of 'soft' inheritance (Handel and Ramagopalan, 2010: 2) or 'epigenetic memory' (Karlic and Baurek, 2011: 279). Accordingly, past environmental exposures and their effects on bodies pass to future generations, despite the fact that the genes themselves are unchanged and that future generations do not necessarily experience the same exposure as parents and grandparents (Skinner, 2014; Tracey, Manikkam, Guerrero-Bosagna and Skinner, 2013). Epigenetic inheritance arises from a number of mechanisms. In *multigenerational inheritance*, more than one generation is exposed to the same stressor at the same time (e.g. via pregnant females). *Transgenerational inheritance* occurs when transmission of epigenetic changes passes through the eggs and sperm to future generations not directly exposed to the same environment (Skinner, 2014).

Theories of epigenetic inheritance have been developed in both the social and natural sciences, variously focusing on the prospect of inheriting artistic talent or a propensity for genius (Karlic and Baurek, 2011; Shenk, 2011) or for disease and obesity (Patel et al., 2015; Rhee, Phelan and McCaffery, 2012). Not surprisingly, epigenetics is considered to represent 'some of the most exciting contemporary biology' (Bird, 2007: 396).

How could these ideas link to theories of social practice? To begin, environmental exposures may occur during the performance of practices – where genes and environment interact. Following this, the logic of epigenetic changes and how human–environment interactions leave imprints on bodies parallels theories of practice where 'a social practice is the product of training bodies in a certain way' and 'can be understood as the regular, skilful "performance" of (human) bodies' (Reckwitz, 2002b: 251). This is a principal point of intersection between these theories.

Linking epigenetics and theories of social practice: points of intersection, tension and the role of bodies

Theories of social practice have long recognised the importance of doing and performance (e.g. Bourdieu, 1990; Giddens, 1984), more recently distinguishing moments of enactment from the 'pattern' or 'block' of the recognisable practice entity that persists over time (Reckwitz, 2002b; Schatzki, 1996; Shove et al., 2012). In the moment of doing or performing a practice, all the elements are integrated. In this state of action, two things occur: (1) bodies interact materially with the world and its artefacts; and (2) in carrying out action, bodies experience certain material conditions, receiving a range of environmental exposures. Both affects can result in material changes in and to bodies. Performance is where genes, bodies and material environments interact – and consequently where epigenetics and theories of social practice interface.

Theories of social practice are concerned with the 'enduring' practice entity (Shove et al., 2012: 8), whereas epigenetic theories are concerned with the gene, or more precisely, its expression (Patel et al., 2015; Tammen et al., 2013). These differences in the objects of study are where the theories potentially diverge. However, despite having different foci, both involve human bodies and change over time. This possible point of tension serves to highlight the point that action and its effects are taking place at multiple levels or bodily scales and have varying impacts over time and space. This multiplicity generates further questions of timing and sequence. In epigenetics, there are likely to be multiple instances of exposure that trigger a series of cellular events or molecular processes culminating in a change of gene expression and phenotype at a later date – or even in another generation (Milagro et al., 2013). Similarly, a practice does not arise from a single performance; instead, it requires multiple performances by many performers across time and space (Reckwitz, 2002b; Shove et al., 2012). Recognition of these temporal patterns leads to further speculation about how these theories describe different types of action that fit together, or link, in a causal or dependent fashion such that epigenetic changes to bodies are reliant on, and the result of, the performance of practices. As performances are repeated over time, bodies are continually shaped by and through practice in different ways in order to generate 'skilful performances' (Reckwitz, 2002b: 251). These include mental patterns and corresponding bodily development of muscles, tissue and bones consistent with theories of social practice on one hand, and biochemical or metabolic processes leading to epigenetic changes on the other.

Given that material changes to performers' bodies are central to both theories, this observation raises questions about how bodies are conceptualised in each and whether correspondence, commensurability or compatibility should be expected (Kuhn, 1982).

In contrast to epigenetics, in theories of social practice, bodies have a 'present-absent' status. They are clearly present in that bodies are the carriers of practice, essential for the continuing performance and persistence of practice entities and in that practices are 'embodied' by their performers. Bodies are also 'absent' in the way that their physical and sensory qualities are largely unrecognised or *dematerialised*. It could be argued that in theories of social practice, human bodies are recognised as carriers: as contributing to the elements of meanings and skills or competence (Reckwitz, 2002b; Shove *et al.*, 2012) and as 'sites of embodied understanding' (Reckwitz, 2002a: 212). However, it is not clear how they might be conceptualised beyond this. In particular, there is no specificity or delineation as to what parts of bodies might be implicated in certain practice performances. This is despite the trend to '[put] the body back into sociology' (Shilling, 2003: 17). Reckwitz briefly acknowledges the materialities of bodies in this way:

> One can say that both the human bodies/minds and the artefacts provide 'requirements' or components necessary to a practice. Certain things act, so to speak, as 'resources' which enable and constrain the specificity of a practice.
> *(2002a: 212)*

However, in this instance, Reckwitz again refers to bodies in general. There is clearly a bodily presence in Bourdieu's concept of 'habitus' (1984) as 'a system of dispositions' (Bourdieu, 2005: 43) where habitus is considered both 'a medium and outcome of social practice' (Wainwright and Turner, 2006: 240). More recent work pays scant attention to the materiality of bodies, perhaps because there has been greater interest in the material roles of non-humans in the conduct of practice, or because there has been less practice theoretically inspired research in the area of health. For some of these reasons, the materiality of bodies has been underplayed; exceptions include Pink (2012; Pink and Leder Mackley, 2014) and Wallenborn (2013; Wallenborn and Wilhite, 2014).

Concerning the health outcomes of practices, the central role of bodies is paramount. Most practices have health implications, whether for good or ill (Blue, Shove, Carmona and Kelly, 2016; Maller, 2015). Furthermore, as NCDs and obesity arise from people–environment interactions (Patel *et al.*, 2015; Roberto *et al.*, 2015), there is an opportunity for theories of social practice to contribute to understanding and intervention in these issues (Andrews, Chen and Myers, 2014; Blue *et al.*, 2016; Maller, 2015).

Before proceeding, it will help to provide a brief review of some of the ways bodies could be further conceptualised in theories of social practice to foster links with epigenetics. As an obvious first step, bodies and their constituent parts could be considered material elements, depending on the practices at hand, and; second, bodies could be considered as an 'assemblage'. In what follows, I discuss these conceptualisations and in particular, consider bodies as material elements.

That bodies rarely count in a physical sense as contributing to the material elements of practices is somewhat surprising as bodies – literally – can provide a number of possible material aspects of practice/s. These include energy in the form of physical strength, cellular and molecular processes and substances of various kinds necessary for basic and higher order functioning. Furthermore, they are a substrate or repository for practices (Bourdieu, 1984; Maller and Strengers, 2014; Shove and Pantzar, 2005b; Wallenborn and Wilhite, 2014). Bodies also offer a range of sensory capacities that enable or participate in practices (Pink, 2009; Pink and Leder Mackley, 2014).

Some practices require more active bodily involvement, movement and skill than others, for example, dancing or playing a sport compared to working at a desk or commuting to work. To do professional ballet, or indeed any sport or artistic performance, performers' bodies must be 'fast, strong, supple and have impressive stamina' (Koutedakis and Sharp, 1999, as cited in Wainwright and Turner, 2006: 242). In these performances, bodies move in deliberate and precise ways, often formed through years of training in which movements are tightly coupled with the other practice elements (competences and meanings) (Shove *et al.*, 2012; Wallenborn and Wilhite, 2014). Another way bodies materially contribute to physically demanding practices is aesthetically, meaning that they must be shaped, sculpted, presented and tightly maintained through rigid routines of training and body care to meet visual requirements and expectations (Wainwright and Turner, 2006). The bodily requirements of these practices contrast with others that are arguably less demanding in terms of corporeal precision, aesthetics and discipline. In other practices, bodies have a more biological role. For example, in relation to pregnancy and childbirth, bodies contribute a large range of materials to the developing foetus, including genetic information, proteins and blood. Whether bodily components of genes, fat or muscles will be relevant to a particular study depends on the line of inquiry, but these examples serve to highlight the fundamental *material* role bodies play in practices.

In underplaying what bodies offer materially, theories of social practice and their proponents have rarely considered the bodily impacts of practices in relation to health. Some practices shape bodies and have more profound health outcomes than others. As I discuss in more detail below, recent evidence shows that due to epigenetic changes and nutritional exposure in utero, obesity is now considered a heritable condition (Rhee *et al.*, 2012; Skinner, 2014). In relation to the aims of this chapter, there are also different time scales to consider, as practices have different bodily impacts in the moment of performance compared to the accumulated effects on bodies from performing over a lifetime. One example is smoking tobacco (or the practices that involve smoking tobacco). In the moment of performance and of inhaling cigarette smoke, nicotine immediately causes the release of dopamine, meanwhile over the lifetime of the performer, this can result in damaging bodily changes, including lung cancer (Hatsukami, Stead and Gupta, 2008). These examples show that bodies do not only provide vital materials to practices without which they could not be performed (Wallenborn and Wilhite, 2014); they are also systematically affected and made by them, sometimes in profoundly detrimental ways.

Another way to conceptualise bodies relevant to theories of social practice and epigenetics is as 'human–non-human assemblages' (Bennett, 2010; Greenhough, 2011) or 'extended bodies' (Wallenborn, 2013). Thinking of human bodies as assemblages is not a new idea (see Deleuze and Guattari, 1987: 4; Greenhough, 2011; and Fox, 2011), but it is worth briefly reflecting on this notion in the current context. Assemblages can take many and multiple forms, as summarised by Marcus and Saka (2006):

> [An assemblage] can refer to a subjective state of cognition and experience of society and culture in movement from a recent past toward a near future (the temporal span of emergence); or it can refer to objective relations, a material, structure-like formation, a describable product of emergent social conditions, a configuration of relationships among diverse sites and things… And of course, if not explicitly delineated, *it can refer to all of these at once.*
>
> *(2006: 102, emphasis added)*

The above definition reveals the multiplicity inherent in the nature of assemblages, which assists in considering how to link theories of social practice with epigenetics. For example, the body as an assemblage might include muscles, genes, tissues and bones, together with the practice elements of meanings, materials and competences. Furthermore, there are vast numbers of microorganisms which bodies host (bacteria, viruses and parasites), as well as the things, objects, technologies or other materials required for the performance of a practice.

There is also recognition that objects and other organisms permeating bodies as part of human–non-human assemblages have agency; in Bennett's (2010: vii, xvi) terms they have 'vital materiality' or 'thing power'. In the case of any practices related to the ingestion of materials like food or drugs, these actors have a material presence in practices in interacting with bodies and create certain effects leading to varying health outcomes. As Bennett (2007: 137) argues in relation to fat:

> It is more likely that an emergent causality is at work: particular fats, acting in different ways in different bodies and with different intensities, even within the same body at different times, may produce patterns of effects but not in ways that are fully predictable – for a small change in the assemblage may issue

in a significant disruption of the pattern. The agentic assemblage in which persons and fats are participants ought to be figured as a nonlinear system.

The same point applies to the vast number of microorganisms that enter or are already part of bodies, as Turnbaugh *et al.* (2007: 804) observe, 'the microorganisms that live inside and on humans (known as the microbiota) are estimated to outnumber human somatic and germ cells by a factor of ten'. In concluding this brief summary, one of the most useful aspects of thinking in terms of assemblages is that boundaries are immediately called into question; not only boundaries between organisms, but between bodily parts and their components. This type of conceptualisation allows for thinking about permeability and unsettles the illusion that human bodies – and practices – have fixed or discrete edges in the world, unconnected to life, matter and action around them (Bennett, 2010).

This section has reviewed two possible ways bodies could be thought of that are commensurate with theories of social practice and epigenetics – as materials or as assemblages. In epigenetics, bodies and their materiality play a central role. In fact, bodies are scrutinised and quantified from their phenotypic states right down to their molecular processes and genetic material. In theories of social practice, the role of bodies is less clear, leaving room for more detailed investigation and definition as this chapter initiates. Interestingly while body–environment interactions can be the central focus, in neither case are bodies themselves the key units or sites of study. When thinking about health, the strategy that makes sense to both epigenetics and theories of social practice is that of taking bodies to be the medium or pathway through which change happens. To explain this idea in more detail, it is useful to work through an example.

Obesity seen through the combined lens of epigenetics and social practices

Obesity is a complex, contested and moralised condition that is a classic outcome of human–environment interactions. It cannot be explained by environment or genes alone, but is instead the product of interactions between the two (Rhee *et al.*, 2012). In obese[2] people, fat deposits are said to be the result of 'an imbalance between energy intake and expenditure', attributable to the availability of high calorific foods and a lack of physical activity (Milagro *et al.*, 2013: 783). Multiple genes have been associated with obesity such that there is a 'human obesity gene map'. However, the main contributors are environmental, including lifestyle, food consumption, levels of physical activity and sleeping patterns (Patel *et al.*, 2015: 430). Hence, the causes of obesity are not as simple as an energy-in/energy-out equation. As Patel *et al.* (2015: 451) explain:

> Research suggests that inherited genetic factors under the influence of environmental signals determine susceptibility of individuals to developing obesity and associated complications.

What is clear is that from an epigenetic perspective, obesity arises from a range of environmental conditions or exposures (Milagro *et al.*, 2013; Patel *et al.*, 2015; Rhee *et al.*, 2012). As mentioned earlier, environmental exposures associated with epigenetic changes to bodies are often material (Skinner, 2014; Tammen *et al.*, 2013). Of relevance to obesity, these materials are likely to include food, alcohol and other drinks or substances consumed by bodies.

From a practice perspective, having a body labelled as obese could be described as the outcome of recruitment to certain practices and not others. Evidently, like genes, a single practice cannot explain obesity. Shove, Pantzar and Watson, referencing Evans' (2006: 261) critique of obesity policy and research, state that 'the concept of obesity brings *multiple practices* together in its moralising fold' (Shove *et al.*, 2012: 111, emphasis added). Hence, taking a practice-centred approach, obesity is the outcome of recruitment to a set of practices, bundles or complexes (Shove *et al.*, 2012). These might include formulations or arrangements of shopping, cooking, eating, food provision, exercise, socialising or commuting to work, or in other words, the 'disparate practices' of everyday life (Shove *et al.*, 2012: 110).

Recent work in epigenetics has discovered that some epigenetic changes pass from one generation to another. This means past human–environment interactions – or the effects of practices performed on bodies – can persist over time, affecting not only the lives of people in one generation, but as inherited by successive generations under certain conditions (Skinner, 2014). Epigenetic inheritance of obesity has been associated with the practices of pregnant mothers that result in epigenetic changes affecting their descendants in adult life (Rhee *et al.*, 2012; Skinner, 2014). For example, epigenetic mechanisms affecting genes regulating glucose, insulin responsiveness and appetite can result in changes to the mother's phenotype as well as her adult children (Patel *et al.*, 2015). It seems early developmental periods 'during which the epigenetic code is partially removed or reset, are vital' (Patel *et al.*, 2015: 446). These epigenetic changes and how human–environment actions might imprint bodies is interesting from a social practice perspective, especially when contemplating interventions to improve, or at least understand better, diseases such as those relating to obesity that are blamed on lifestyle. The following section explores this idea.

Intervening in lifestyle diseases: a social practice-epigenetic perspective

It is clear that global trends in deaths and illnesses said to arise from lifestyle are escalating and are unlikely to shift in the short term. In order to modify this trajectory, there is a need to reconceptualise how such health conditions arise, focusing on new understandings of wellbeing and disease from the latest thinking in both the natural and social sciences.

In the natural sciences, epigenetics is emerging at the forefront of innovation, in particular in regard to obesity. In the social sciences, theories of social practice are beginning to make a similar impact in analysing a range of health and wellbeing outcomes. In bringing these two fields together, this chapter explores new ways to intervene. The timing is ideal as there is growing recognition in public health, and health promotion in particular, that existing approaches have not delivered desired outcomes. For example, Roberto *et al.* (2015: 2401) examine the 'false dichotomy that obesity is driven by either personal choice or the environment' and instead suggest 'these two competing perspectives be merged to show the reciprocal relationship'.

The first contribution from a combined practice-epigenetics perspective is the problematisation of lifestyle diseases. The main point is that while individuals perform practices, they are not the unit of study or of intervention. Instead, the proposition is that health problems arise from *practice–gene–environment* interactions realised through the performance of specific practices. In carrying out or performing practices, practitioners (individuals) are exposed to (and ostensibly create) a number of environmental conditions that make and remake bodies, resulting in varying states of health or disease. Therefore, interventions must target the practice, not the performer (Blue *et al.*, 2016; Maller, 2015; Shove *et al.*, 2012; Spurling, McMeekin, Shove, Southerton and Welch, 2013; Strengers and Maller, 2014).

There are four other aspects of how problems of obesity would be framed from this perspective, all of which are consistent with other work based on theories of social practice. These are: (1) practices are intricately linked to other practices to form bundles and complexes: no practice exists in a vacuum; (2) bodies and their parts count as material elements that are made and remade through performance and bodily processes and mechanisms, including epigenetic means; (3) there is more than just the agency of human bodies involved in practices, such that other various materials, objects, technologies and organisms also have agency; and (4) the marks of practices on bodies can be heritable such that the effects of practices performed in one generation can pass to the next, during pregnancy – all changing ideas about disease aetiology. These contributions involve thinking beyond individuals and their 'lifestyle choices' said to result in health or ill health (Blue *et al.*, 2016; Maller, 2015). As Fox (2011: 360) writes, 'ill-health is too quickly accepted as an attribute of an individual body, rather than a wider, ecological phenomenon of body organisation and deployment within social and natural fields'.

Although bodies are not the entity of study or the only target of intervention, they are taken to be the medium or pathway through which change happens and health outcomes are realised. Blue *et al.* (2016) and Maller (2015) have usefully considered types of health interventions that would follow from and be consistent with a social practice framework. I expand on these types of intervention below, but with a practice-epigenetic twist. The approach resembles Wallenborn's (2013: 149) argument for a 'practice perspective combined with a body-centred analysis'. However, it is noted that:

> Whilst a turn to practice makes great strides in overcoming critical, problematic dichotomies between individuals and social structures, rational actions and habits, it does not generate simple guidelines for intervention.
>
> (*Blue et al., 2016: 11*)

This difficultly is in part explained by the emergent nature of practice phenomena (Shove *et al.*, 2012). Their 'ceaseless movement and incessant rearrangement' (Schatzki, 2002: 189) presents a challenge to any attempts at control. Another point is that as practices interconnect, effective interventions can sometimes come from other quarters or be unintended outcomes of seemingly unrelated policies (Blue *et al.*, 2016).

There are, nonetheless, methods of directing interventions at the practices of which everyday life is made. From this perspective, relevant targets include seemingly innocuous ways of going about everyday doings, so habituated they almost become invisible, or, at the very least, unremarkable. Epigenetics is demonstrating the profound impact of the everyday practices of parents and grandparents on the health of future generations 'pervad[ing] all aspects of development' (Keverne and Curley, 2008: 398).

By implication, forward-looking interventions seeking to influence the health of future populations should focus on the practices of current (and possibly previous) generation/s. At the same time, this link suggests that practice-based interventions also need to take a long-term view, as already recognised (e.g. Schatzki, 2015a; Spurling and McMeekin, 2014).

Aside from this, the key strategy to change health outcomes from a practice-epigenetic perspective is to (a) intervene in relevant practices and their elements of meanings, materials and competence and (b) orchestrate the making and breaking of links that sustain practices, as well as those between practice bundles and complexes (Blue *et al.*, 2016; Shove *et al.*, 2012; Spurling and McMeekin, 2014). For example, controlling fat as a material element in multiple practices causing multigenerational obesity could include: changes to practices of shopping and food consumption by developing competencies in preparing and consuming low-fat meals or developing new practices of meal preparation; changes to the meanings and materials of meals in relation to frequency, size and content; new or changed practices of policymaking to reduce the availability of fatty, sugary and highly processed foods and drinks and medical or surgical practices, such as bariatric (lap band or gastric) surgery. The latter has been shown to be effective in circumventing epigenetic changes that result in the birth of overweight children (Rhee *et al.*, 2012). Of course, these are not new ideas. However, from a practice-epigenetic perspective, the difference is to recognise and capitalise on where and how these attempts intervene in *practices*, *bundles* and their *elements* and therefore better to coordinate and systematise what are usually treated as one-off, separate or unrelated interventions, directed at individuals and their behaviour at single points in time. In Spurling and McMeekin's (2014: 79) words: 'intervention should not be viewed as "external" or "one-off" but as continuous and reflexive, historical and cumulative'. From a practice-epigenetic viewpoint, intervening may also involve targeting new, or to date unrecognised material elements, such as genes, cells and molecules implicated in epigenetic modifications.

Other options would be to focus on the recruitment and defection of practitioners from practices contributing to ill health. A practice-epigenetic take on this would involve a multigenerational perspective, as suggested elsewhere (Maller and

Strengers, 2014). In public health, childhood is already recognised as a key part of the life course in creating future health outcomes, as established by the social determinants of health literature (see Wilkinson and Marmot, 2003). The importance of maternal health and early childhood development is already embedded in a range of public health interventions, particularly those aimed at reducing multigenerational health inequities (Klawetter, 2014). Similarly, from a practice-epigenetic point of view, the importance of childhood and interventions in practices associated with (or occurring during) pregnancy and child rearing should be recognised.

There is further scope to consider the recruitment and training of children as new practitioners and of the effects of such processes in creating lasting imprints and practice memories (Maller and Strengers, 2014) that matter for health. Work inspired by theories of social practice has not yet ventured into childhood or child rearing, both being areas in which the potential of practice theoretical research remains to be realised.

Finally, attempts to intervene to reduce lifestyle diseases from a practice-epigenetic outlook would be directed towards monitoring and responding to shifts in practices (Blue *et al.*, 2016). As Schatzki (2015a: 17) observes, 'changes of all kinds constantly befall practices, arrangements and bundles, which undergo halting, irregular, not necessarily infrequent, and sometimes rapid development'. Examples might include interventions aimed at redirecting practice trajectories as well as other emergent changes arising from the inherently dynamic nature of social practices and practice–gene–environment interactions. In particular, it would make sense to undertake long-term monitoring of practices and epigenetic variations across generations as programmes and policies are introduced or modified. Finally, it is important to recognise that all policies and interventions regardless of intentions will affect the emergence, persistence and disappearance of practices (Shove, 2014), implying that interventions are an ongoing phenomenon in addition to being practices in themselves.

Conclusion

This chapter had two aims: to explore the territory between theories of social practice and epigenetics, focusing in particular on the relation between practices and performers' bodies; and to consider what such a focus might offer in terms of health interventions. In undertaking this theoretical exploration, I have discussed differences in the units of study and in conceptualisations of bodies, and have also identified points of connection between the two theories. A main point of intersection is that neither social practice nor epigenetics takes human bodies as the unit of study or as the site of change. Instead, in epigenetics, it is the gene (or the processes that change its expression) that is of interest, and in theories of social practice, it is practices in moments of performance and as entities. However, both strategies recognise bodies as media or substrates of change.

This discussion draws attention to the effects of practices on practitioners' bodies at a very detailed level, both in the moments of performances and over one (or more) lifetimes. These processes are important for understanding complex health issues involving human–environment interactions such as obesity. Linking theories of social practice to epigenetics generates further related questions about the terms in which lifestyles, practices and related diseases are passed from one person to another. The mechanisms at stake may vary but such ideas question the heritability of diseases and forms of ill health currently in the NCD category.

Finally, such approaches have the potential to open up new frontiers in health promotion, health education and medicine. In particular, there is an opportunity to work with theories of social practice, drawing on a practice-epigenetic stance in conceptualising and analysing practices of childhood and child rearing. There is a strong case for this move considering the importance of early childhood development in most aspects of health and wellbeing. Furthermore, interventions based on ideas of recruitment, training and heritability generated through practice-epigenetics thinking have the potential to shift the current burden of disease and to promote greater and more equitable forms of wellbeing, although the timeframes will necessarily be long term and over several generations.

Empirical research informed by theories of social practice and epigenetics is challenging but also critical in the face of the scale and global impact of diseases now attributed to lifestyles.

Although there is new research developing in epigenetics that will have profound implications for future work on lifestyles – and more intriguingly, social practices – more needs to be done, in particular in understanding the underlying molecular mechanisms of transfer. These concerns aside, according to Bird (2007: 396), epigenetics has 'caught the general imagination' and there are no signs the enthusiasm it has generated will slow down any time soon. Dawkins classic text *The selfish gene* (Dawkins, 1978) proposed a new gene-centred view of evolution. Looking ahead, could we and should we anticipate a gene-centred view of social practices? Only time will tell.

Notes

1   The term 'bodies' refers to 'body-minds' or 'doings and sayings' as Schatzki (2002) and Reckwitz (2002a) among other more recent practice theorists have noted (e.g. Nicolini, 2012).

2   'According to medical convention, overweight and obesity are defined on the basis of body mass index (BMI), which is calculated by dividing weight (in kilograms) by height squared (in meters). The BMI of healthy, overweight and obese individuals is defined as 18.5 to <25; 25–29.9; and ≥30kg/m², respectively' (Patel *et al.*, 2015: 430).

6

TECHNOLOGIES WITHIN AND BEYOND PRACTICES

Janine Morley

Introduction

The incorporation of material entities as integral elements of social practices, or as inextricably bundled with them, is a significant development in theories of social practice (Reckwitz, 2002a; 2002b; Schatzki, 2002; 2010a; Shove *et al.*, 2012). As Reckwitz notes, '"artefacts" or "things"… necessarily participate in social practices just as human beings do' (2002a: 208). Reflecting a similar idea, Shove *et al.* (2012) describe materials as one of three broad categories of element that are actively integrated when a practice is enacted. Yet materiality is diverse and additional material roles in the life of practices beyond their status as direct constituents of performance have received less attention. This chapter aims to characterise some of these more indirect material–practice relationships by exploring two examples of automated 'machines': central heating and fully automated factories.

My intention is twofold. First, I hope to extend the conceptual tools for positioning technologies of different kinds within accounts of practice. In so far as practice theories focus on what human bodies do, they may be limited when it comes to a wider consideration of what humans do collectively *beyond* their bodies; that is, through technological systems that carry out processes at varying degrees of distance, in time, space and awareness from the activity of people. Typically, these extended relationships are not recognised if technologies are only or mostly conceptualised as tool-like elements implicated in the 'practical' doings and sayings that define practices. Such interpretations become increasingly problematic as new forms of digitally automated and autonomous technologies come into use. A broader view is also required if we are to represent and analyse changing patterns of resource use, especially energy, which enables various forms of automation.

Second, I argue that other ways of conceptualising technologies and their dynamic relations to and within practices are important in analysing social change more generally. In principle, materials and technologies are highly significant for how practices develop and change over time, not only as 'elements' of practice, but in other ways as well. In broad terms, technologies have dramatically altered the nature, range and qualities of the contemporary 'population' of practices by reducing and reconfiguring the contributions and qualities of human participation, how such practices are reproduced and whether and how they persist, evolve or dissolve. The concept of automation, for instance, indicates the potential for machines to 'take over' work that was previously carried out by people. In other words, some technologies appear to be important for how practices persist and change without directly 'participating', as elements, within their performance. How can these relationships be represented? And what is their significance for analysing the dynamics of practices?

To explore these questions, I start by examining how technologies have been positioned within theories of practice. The idea that practices are comprised by elements and that they change as these elements and their interrelationships change has been central to developing understandings of social change in terms of practices (Shove *et al.*, 2012). Although valuable, I argue that such conceptualisation of materials and of their role in change is limited. In the second section, I provide an example: I consider how automated machines are powerfully implicated in modulating another mechanism by which practices change as 'populations' of practitioners change. In the third section, I extend the example of automated production to the contemporary phenomenon of fully automated factories and also draw on a contrasting example of automated central heating to conceptualise a variety of relationships between automated technologies and practices that form interconnecting constellations of practices and materials. In the fourth section, I reflect on what might be distinctive about the dynamics of such machine–practice relationships.

Materials as elements of practice and beyond

The idea that '"artefacts" or "things" … necessarily participate in social practices just as human beings do' (Reckwitz, 2002a: 208) is largely derived from the ideas of Latour and others within science and technology studies, who argue that action is 'distributed' between people and objects (or 'non-humans') such that 'implements … are actors, or more precisely, *participants* in the course of action waiting to be given a figuration' (Latour, 2005: 71, original emphasis). In incorporating this line of thinking, Reckwitz (2002a: 221) remarks that 'the things handled in a social practice must be treated as necessary components for a practice to be "practiced"'. Yet, they are not the only components, as indicated in Reckwitz's much cited definition of a practice as:

> [A] routinized type of behaviour which consists of several elements, interconnected to one other: forms of bodily activities, forms of mental activities, "things" and their use, a background knowledge in the form of understanding, know-how, states of emotion and motivational knowledge.
>
> (*2002b: 249*)

Drawing on this general idea, Shove, Pantzar and Watson identify three broad kinds of elements (material, competence and meaning), which constitute practices when actively integrated by practitioners (Shove and Pantzar, 2005a; Watson and Shove, 2008; Pantzar and Shove, 2010b; culminating in Shove et al., 2012). These elements define the practice as an entity distinct from other activities, act as a set of 'resources' that organise the practice and are themselves constituted through instances of engagement in the practice (performances). Through this recursive interplay, practices come into being as links between elements are established through performances, evolve as new elements and/or new interlinkages are (per)formed and disappear as links are broken. That is, practices change as the elements of which they are composed change or as relations between these elements are reconfigured.

However, when viewed as 'things and their uses' or as 'things handled', material elements are conceptualised as tools or implements. Indeed, the concept of the *active* integration of elements, as performed by the practitioner, tends to focus on materials that are directly mobilised, attended to or manipulated in practical activities. But as Rinkinen, Jalas and Shove (2015: 1) remark, objects are encountered and engaged in multiple relations beyond 'enactment of social practices'. It seems other kinds of materials and relationships figure in the lives of practices, too.

Arguably, the category of materials, or material elements, in the plural is also problematic by its apparent reference to discrete and bounded physical entities, 'encompassing objects, infrastructures, tools, hardware and the body itself' (Shove et al., 2012: 23). Yet also referred to by Shove et al. (2012) as materiality, this category is reasonably interpreted more broadly: to represent the inherent materiality of doing and saying including structures in and on which this takes place, aspects of the environment like air and water, as well as less tangible phenomena such as sound and heat. As a dimension or aspect of practice, materiality involves, but is not necessarily synonymous with, the material entities that are present or necessary.[1] Specifically, the *relationships* and interactions between entities, such as bodies and technologies, might also be considered as part of the materiality of practices.

Yet the conceptualisation of materiality *within* practices is not my departure point. Instead, I focus on relationships that appear to matter *beyond* performance, at least, of single practices. This is the case with automated machines that carry on forms of 'activity' that are distanced, in different ways, from the flows of human activity, and as such would normally be absent from an account of materiality *in* practice. Accordingly, the potential roles of such materials in giving form and shape to practices and to the mechanisms by which they change is also not fully captured by a discussion of 'material elements'.

In this respect, Schatzki's (2002; 2010a) framing of materiality as material arrangements that are linked to, but conceptually distinct from, practices is of interest. Here, practices and material arrangements each provide a context for the other and are accordingly bundled together, persisting over time in interlinked patterns. While 'practice-arrangement nexuses' (Schatzki, 2010a: 130) or 'bundles' (Schatzki, 2012) are not dissimilar from Shove et al.'s (2012) notion of practices (Schatzki, forthcoming), the concept of material arrangements is not restricted to the materiality of practice performances. This allows Schatzki (2012: 4) to list a number of other ways in which 'practices effect, use, give meaning to and are inseparable from arrangements while… arrangements channel, prefigure, facilitate and are essential to practices' through relations of causality, prefiguration, intelligibility intentionality and constitution (Schatzki, 2010a; 2012).

From this perspective, artefacts like machines have a certain default independence from practices, even though they are necessarily linked to them in a variety of ways. The challenge therefore comes not in thinking about *whether* the automated processing undertaken by machines is related to practices, but *how*. Specifically, are other interrelations, beyond co-constitution, salient in positioning and understanding such machines in practice theoretical accounts, especially those concerned with processes of change and stability? And how are these relations performed through bodily interactions? This is implied since, to Schatzki, as to Shove and colleagues, the actions involved in practices are 'bodily doings and sayings… that people directly perform' (Schatzki, 2002: 72).

It is worth noting before proceeding that for purposes of clarity, and despite my comments above, I continue to refer to machines as examples of 'materials' following the established understanding of this category as one of physical entities, including artefacts. More specifically, I understand machines to be examples of technologies, again understood as artefacts (Mitcham, 1994) and, in particular, ones that in any given historical period 'materialise' relatively new adaptations in design, techniques or tasks.

Modulating human participation: when machines 'take over'

The account developed by Shove et al. (2012) has more to say about what is involved in the conduct, reproduction and dynamics of practices than is captured in the language of elements alone. Specifically, in addition to changes in the elements of practice and their interconnections, they note that practices also change as the populations of practitioners who sustain them change and as the connections between practices change (Shove et al., 2012; Watson, 2012).

For instance, Shove, Pantzar and Watson note that 'the contours of *any one* practice – where it is reproduced, how consistently, how long and on what scale – depend on changing populations of more and less faithful carriers or practitioners' (2012: 63, original emphasis). In other words, who undertakes a practice, and how, has implications for how that practice changes from within, through the creation and circulation of variety (thus the configurations of elements). In addition, if practices can be seen to colonise 'peoples' time and energy' (Shove et al., 2012: 65) these are important 'resources' by which practices connect to each other, for example, through forms of competition and collaboration. In simple terms, time spent 'energising' one practice cannot be spent on others, with the exception of multi-tasking and blending of multiple practices (Shove *et al.*, 2012).

It is therefore important to reflect on the ways in which forms of participation are modulated and mediated through material relations and therefore how they might figure as a source (and also an outcome) of change. For example, Shove, Watson, Hand and Ingram (2007) describe how the redesign of materials as inert as radiator fittings or varnish enables people with less-specialist skills and experience to use an apply these products. This is important for who can get involved in home improvement and hence how DIY and professional practices are reproduced. Equally, ready meals and pizzas are forms of technology that modulate and in a sense delegate the competencies involved in making dinner thus influencing who cooks at home and what it means to do so. Moreover, with the development of digital technologies, there is increasing debate, and also concern, about the redistribution of knowledge and service work to programmable machines in post-industrial economies (e.g. Ford, 2015).

Indeed, there is no shortage of narratives that explain or foretell dramatic social changes as a result of new or different technologies. Machines, as contrasted against tools, have been the focus of much of this debate (e.g. Hegel, Marx, as discussed by Heilbroner, 1967; Mumford, 1934; Illich, 1973; Schumacher, 1989). The following account is provided by Leder in an endnote to his book *The Absent Body* (Leder, 1990: 179–81), drawing on Tondl's (1974) categories of technology. It is characteristic of a widespread understanding of the significance of machines, but is also notable for its focus on the body.

Tondl (1974) outlined three broadly chronological stages of technological development in which the 'body-implement relationship' differs (Leder, 1990: 179). The first phase is an era of 'tools proper' that are wielded and powered by the body. Through skilled use, such tools become habitually incorporated into experience in an 'embodiment' relation, defined by a diminishing awareness of the tool itself, as a focal object. Tondl's second phase of technology is characterised by machines, which are devices powered by non-human energy sources, originally 'natural' ones such as water and animal power, and later mechanical power. People are still involved in working with machines, but in a very different way: they guide and control machines but do not provide the motive force. This places the body into a mode of 'background disappearance' (Leder, 1990: 180), having a supporting relationship to the machines whose 'needs and rhythms' provide the 'pattern for the work' instead of those of the human body. The third phase is one in which 'automated machines' carry out many of the control functions for themselves, through monitoring and regulation. Leder suggests: 'direct bodily involvement is even further reduced… primarily because it has been put out of play' (1990: 180).

In this account, three categories of technology are defined by their interplay with humans and specifically by whether the body 'powers' them and/or 'controls' them. It echoes Mumford's (1934: 10) typology of technology in which the 'essential distinction between a machine and tool lies in the degree of independence in the operation from the skill and motive power of the operator'. As Mitcham (1994: 168) notes, this is a key shift since: 'as the machine becomes increasingly independent of direct human energy input, it becomes not just a static object but the bearer and initiator of operations or of special physical, chemical or electrical processes'. In other words, while tools are 'handled', or otherwise controlled directly and thereby 'participate' in the activities that comprise social practices, machines denote a degree of autonomy from direct bodily power/energy and intervention. As machines are developed and deployed, there are exchanges between human and technological 'participation' in work. In essence, Leder's account is of the progressive 'taking over' or 'delegation' (Latour, 2005) of previously human roles by or to technologies resulting in the effective reformulation (or even dissolution) of former production practices.

Before turning to consider this outcome in more detail in the next section, it is worth noting that such general narratives should be treated with caution and this is no exception. First, the idea that the transfer or delegation of work from people to machine (or vice versa) are ever directly or successfully achieved must be tempered. As Latour (2005: 70) warns, the term delegation should not be taken to imply that people (as *Homo faber*) are fully in control of what technologies do or that they deliberately hand over certain aspects of work and responsibility to them (machine or tool). Instead, and as Ruth Schwartz Cowan (1989) argues in her analysis of the changing nature of female domestic work over the twentieth century, technologies designed to automate and ease (house) work, have had unintended consequences, often introducing new forms or standards of work of their own. Moreover, not everything that technologies do is a replacement or substitute for human effort. Technologies are often useful in practice because of the way they *extend* the capabilities of human bodies and the possibility for human action (Kline, 2003; McGinn, 1991; Wallenborn, 2013).

Second, the distinction between machines and tools is not an essential feature of the artefacts themselves, but rather an outcome of their (changing) relationships within practices. For instance, Idhe (1993: 34, quoted in Verbeek, 2005: 117) argues that 'once taken into praxis one cannot speak of technologies "in themselves", but as the active relational pair, human-technology'. Since practices involving an artefact or its 'contexts of use' vary, technologies have more than one definition, a concept Ihde (1993: 20) describes as 'multistability'. Yet, 'contexts of use' also imply relations between technology and other materials, such as those that are stored, provide power or are powered and other mutual transformations. Thus, in addition to tool and machine, Mumford (1934) distinguishes further types of technology: utensils (pots, baskets) and apparatus (dye vat, kiln), both of which affect chemical transformations, and utilities (roads) including those that are powered (railway, electricity), to which Mitcham (1994) adds structures (buildings).

Nevertheless, it seems that through the progressive transformation of work practices, automated machines have powerfully modulated who participates and how and thereby whether certain practices persist or disappear. So let us return to the question of what happens to the relationship between machines and practices when the machines 'take over'.

Machine relations: conceptualising dark factories and central heating

In this section, I consider how to conceptualise programmable, automated machines in relation to practices, with the help of two examples. First, I extend the example of automated production to the contemporary prospect of *fully* automated factories. Known as 'lights-out' or 'dark' factories, they require no routine on-site involvement from human workers, thus such facilities can be unlit and unheated and offer an extreme example of how humans are 'put out of play' in work that continues by other means. Although reputed to exist in 2016 (for example, a Phillips factory in the Netherlands that produces electric razors and a FANUC factory in Japan that builds robots for automated production lines) and although, more commonly, it is only certain aspects of production processes that are fully automated rather than whole sites, I use this as an emblematic example of situations in which practice (involving human participation) has ostensibly been 'replaced' by machines. This implies that such machines are no longer elements, at least not in the same practices of production, since these particular practices have themselves expired.

My second example is of another technology designed to operate independently of ongoing input on the part of active practitioners: central heating. The operation of central heating systems is not necessarily accompanied by or contingent upon the heating-directed activities of people, nor is central heating a necessary component of the many other possible practices that are, at times, performed in heated spaces. In other words, there is a sense of decoupling or divergence between the heating 'work' carried out by central heating systems and the flows of human activity that transpire within the same automatically heated sites.

The question, then, is how are these machines,[2] both of which independently carry out transformations on other materials (fuels, water, air, components and other 'raw' materials), to be analysed in a system of thought organised around practices defined as distinctly bodily doings and sayings? If these operations fall outside the scope of practice-based analyses, then a lot of what constitutes the social world through the progressive accumulation of ever-more complex and 'intelligent machines' (Schatzki, 2002: 179) may be lost from view. For understandings of consumption, particularly of energy as used to power all sorts of social-material processes and practices, along with the many other resources that are transformed as a result, this would be deeply problematic.

Below, I consider several ways in which such technologies may be figured in relation to practices. First, they can be positioned as part of interconnected agglomerations of practices, in which, second, people and technologies are mutually 'engaged' in various ways and which are, third, organised by reference to cross-cutting end-oriented processes.

Extending practices: systems and constellations

If bodily doings and sayings in dark factory production and central heating are reduced, and routinely removed, do (former) production and heating practices dissolve and disappear? Or are they still carried on by the machines? There is a distinction to be drawn here: it is fully consistent with Shove *et al.*'s (2012) framework and with Schatzki's theory of practices (2002; 2010a) to claim that the processing machines undertake is not *in itself* a practice, if there is no bodily activity that is a part of this process. This suggests that, indeed, *some* production practices may disappear as production tasks are automated. But this is not to say that such automated processing is not still *part* of a practice or sets of practices or, in Schatzki's approach, adjoined or bundled to them.

The concept of practices might be 'extended' to include the operation of machines that share or take over the same tasks as human practitioners, but which occur at some temporal or spatial distance from a range of human–enacted activities. For instance, Schatzki (2010a: 137) refers to 'the practice of warming houses'. This is a collective and dispersed definition of practice in which no single performance or practitioner carries out *the* practice of heating houses at any one time. Rather, it is achieved across the distributed activities of builders, engineers, planners, plumbers, safety regulators, window and insulation fitters, energy companies, as well as the efforts of inhabitants to understand and configure systems as they 'set things up' (Schatzki, 2010a: 129).

From this point of view, there might not be much difference between thinking about automated machines as part of a wider set of practices as opposed to being part of *a* single (but broader) practice. However, the former is preferable if we choose to work with a 'tighter' definition of practices and if we reserve this term to describe activities that are meaningful and identifiable to their practitioners. This strategy gives us more opportunity to think through what these less-than-direct relationships between practices and technologies mean for analysing change.

To conceptualise larger sets of practices and the forms of interconnection that characterise them, a number of concepts have been suggested. For instance, Shove *et al.* (2012) differentiate between bundles and complexes of practices, depending upon how interdependent and necessary are the interconnections between them. Kemmis, Edwards-Groves, Wilkinson and Hardy (2012) formulate inter-practice relationships in terms of ecologies of practices, while Watson (2012) refers to a 'systems of practice' approach. In contrast, Schatzki (2002; 2010a; 2015a) provides a multiply interconnected account in which practices are linked to other practices, arrangements to other arrangements and practices to arrangements, the latter forming bundles. Bundles connect to other bundles forming constellations, which together form a plenum, 'an immense maze of interconnected practices and arrangements' (Schatkzi, 2015: 16).

Positioned as elements that circulate and play roles in multiple practices, materials (just as with other elements) are important in conceptualising how practices relate to one another. For instance, they might be shared or competed for. In addition, the products of one practice often serve as inputs to others, forming the basis for sequences and other temporal connections (Shove *et al.*, 2012; Nicolini, 2012). In such ways, 'material systems' like infrastructures coordinate and configure connections between practices in 'a trellis-like framework through and around which the combining and loosening of practice complexes occurs' (Shove *et al.*, 2015: 10; see also Shove, 2016). In fact, reconfigurations in the ways that practices connect, bundle together or compete, is one of the key mechanisms identified by Shove *et al.* (2012) through which social change occurs. Conceptualising materials as elements helps to recognise and follow these dynamics. So can automated machines be positioned as elements within systems of practice? Or might such materials also play other roles in these systems?

In the case of dark factories, just as with central heating, we can identify a range of related practices in which the factories, their component machines and the inputs and outputs of their processing (raw components and products) might represent elements: in the activities of managers, engineers, mechanics, designers, marketeers, delivery drivers and so on. So while the practice of directly operating the production machines on a day-to-day basis may have disappeared, there is a whole system of other practices that remain firmly interconnected with the now fully automated machines. Below, I consider how these connections might be analysed by reference to an extended notion of the production process.

At the same time, it seems that the dark factory and its machines do not feature in associated practices in the same ways: in some, such as management practices, the machines might not have any direct or immediate material role in enacting such practices. Similarly, in the case of central heating, despite the range of practices that enable the operation of such machines, their primary significance resides in their ongoing detachment from practice. Thus, to situate automated machines *as elements* of potentially multiple practices is only a partial answer to the question of how to conceptualise them. Questions about the nature of these relations remain and if anything, are deepened by bringing into view the variety of practices to which central heating systems and dark factories connect. This observation is not unique to automated machines, but these examples are useful for exploring some of the varied roles that technologies may play. So before returning to the question of how to conceptualise systems (or constellations) in which central heating and dark factories are embedded, it is important to consider further what these roles may be.

Human-technology relations

To do so, I turn to Ihde's (1990) phenomenological analysis of the relations between humans and technologies as implied in praxis or action. He outlines three major kinds of relationship: (1) mediation, in which humans relate to the world via technologies, as tools or perceptual extensions of the body (embodiment relations) or through which the world is represented (hermeneutic relations); (2) alterity relations, in which technologies are acted upon and interacted with; and (3) background relations, in which technologies shape experience by remaining in the background. In fact, Ihde uses the very example of central heating to illustrate the latter:

> … there is some necessity for an instant deistic intrusion to program or set the machinery into motion or to its task. I set the thermostat; then if the machinery is high-tech, the heating/cooling system will operate independently of ongoing action.
>
> *(1990: 108)*

Central heating systems imply a close interaction between bodies and the technology, but one that is not necessarily dependent upon ongoing practices. The purpose of automated central heating is to promote the experience of physical, bodily comfort, but to do so automatically, that is, to minimise the time and timing of any attention required. Thus, 'in operation, the technology does not call for focal attention' but as an 'absent presence, it nevertheless becomes part of the experienced field of the inhabitant, a piece of the immediate environment' (Ihde, 1990: 109).

Ihde (1990) argues that such relations are relative to practices and as noted earlier, artefacts can exist in more than one kind of relation. Thus, when the central heating system breaks down or when it is programmed or installed, it is the focus of attention, it is worked upon directly and the technology and its processes are in full view (in a focal, alterity relation). Incidentally, when engaged with heating in this manner, a plumber might act on the heating system with a spanner, and if very skilled, the spanner withdraws from his/her attention, becoming an extension of his/her body in practice (an embodiment relation).

Dark factories are similarly figured in sets of practices that define them differentially as machines to be acted upon, tools to be acted with, or part of the background field of other practices. Yet, the relationship between operator-bodies and fully automated factories is one of more thorough decoupling, not just backgrounding. Other practices do necessitate bodily co-presence at the factory and direct manipulation, as in the case of engineers maintaining the machinery. But it might be argued that the absence of operators *per se* from the core process of production implies that this process is somehow 'bracketed off' from practice and 'black-boxed' as if it were a single technology or artefact in its own right. Thus, although a dark factory is more than one machine, it may be figured as a singular entity in certain human-technology relationships.

Intriguingly, relationships between dark factories and practices like management, design or marketing, become rapidly complex: they are multiply mediated by other technologies and practices and may be thought to exist between groups of people (organisations or 'corporate bodies') rather than single human beings. In addition, some of these relationships with materials are not themselves necessarily material: or rather, in this case, they don't involve the material substance of the factory directly. In Schatzki's (2012: 4) terms, 'thoughts and imaginings' about dark factories must be an aspect of design and management practices and they (intentionally) link together these practices and material arrangements. But do thoughts and imaginings qualify as *material* elements of the performance of these practices?

Whilst this is an intriguing question, I wish simply to note some of the additional less-than-direct 'modes' in which technologies might be 'engaged' in practices: as acted on practically or in thought, as acted with or through and as acting in the background. I also wish to underline the point that these are relational roles that for any one technology may be more or less apparent from moment to moment, within and across the different practices that 'surround' them.

Extended processes: patterns of temporal relations and material flows

In thinking about the systems of practice in which central heating and dark factories are situated, a discussion of the extended range of potential human-technology relationships suggests that such systems are materially interconnected through more than the circulation of the material elements of performance. Following Schatzki, I will refer to these agglomerations as constellations, that is, as interconnected nets of materials and practices. In taking this approach, I still consider practices to be constituted through elements of materiality, yet I also wish to show how materials are interconnected to one another in flows and complex interactions, which may be decoupled from performances, the very fact of which conditions the sequences and other connections that form between practices. Let me elaborate.

Even apparently passive objects *do* things when they are not being actively mobilised in practice at a particular time. For instance, roofs are useful precisely because, once set up, they do not need to be attended to in order to keep out the rain. Such 'passive' material interactions include storing, channelling or providing surfaces, and may apply to clothes, teacups, buildings, and so on. The fact that things tend to remain 'set up' in absence of human interaction is also significant: that furniture, equipment, roads and so on remain where they are put thereby holds space open in which practices can readily take place, at another time. Practices are therefore connected to such material arrangements and interactions temporally, that is, in various intermittent sequences that might involve setting up, monitoring, maintaining and putting away.

The same is true of relationships between materials that involve active, energy-demanding processes such as the sculpting, welding and mixing that might take place in dark factories, and the burning and pumping that central heating systems perform. In this regard, heating systems are much like automated production factories in that 'they carry on, overtaking the formal roles that, at one time or another, have been assigned to them' (Rinkinen *et al.*, 2015: 12). For example, as Rinkinen *et al.* (2015) explain, there are significant differences in ways that small-scale wood-fired heating processes organise human inputs compared to those associated with automated central heating systems (Jalas and Rinkinen, 2013). Both require attention but in very different ways and both follow and reproduce quite distinctive rhythms. In other words, there needs to be a way of accounting for the temporal ordering associated with automated heating or production systems that extend beyond the machines involved and that include various forms of remote or indirect involvement in multiple practices.

In some ways, this is a question of how practices and material arrangements mutually impose order on each other. This is evident in Schatzki's conceptualisation of mutual patterns of causation between machines and practices:

> Whenever humans build machines that something other than human effort powers or use living organisms and things for their purposes, the causal contribution to and significance of these entities (and arrangements thereof) for human coexistence is either set up by or otherwise relative to human practices (actions, ends, projects).
>
> *(2002: 117–18)*

Just as practices articulate ends, the achievement of which is likely to require at least some temporal and material ordering; certain materials, in their dynamic relations with others, also impose order on the timing and duration of related practices. This might include 'natural' biological processes such as thermoregulation, sleep and eating/digestion and fermentation. Also, according to Leder (1990), automated machines generate temporal demands in relation to the practices required to set up, maintain and control them. Where such mutually shaping patterns emerge in relation to shared ends, it may be helpful to refer to an '*extended process*' that is organised across the constellation of practices and materials and that is itself formed by virtue of these interrelations. Thus defined, extended processes are characterised by sequences of activity and material interactions that are temporally and teleologically ordered, referring not just to the operations of automated machines, but to what they help achieve *as part* of constellations. Central heating and automated production (of particular products) are good examples.

In sum, a concept of extended processes (or something similar) may be useful for thinking about how some constellations are organised, how they are reconfigured, and even, potentially, reproduced on an ongoing basis. For example, if taken as a unit of analysis, we can analyse how production or heating processes change over time, or how they vary, with the inclusion of different kinds of technologies or practices and as certain practices disappear and as others emerge. When analysing change, the qualities of these extended processes are important for understanding changes in the temporal and material relations that connect constellations, how such relations and constellations are stabilised, maintained and adapted, and the modes of engagement between humans and technology they call for.

Shifting constellations: the distinctive dynamics of automated machines?

In positioning central heating systems and dark factories within larger sets of practices, I have considered a number of relations through which these automated machines relate to practices (and other materials), in addition to their role as direct material elements. This includes temporal-material patterns and intentional and background relations. In this section, I turn to consider some of the implications of these, now extended, relations for analysing processes of change, again drawing on the examples of central heating and dark factories. In this, I am particularly interested in what might be distinctive about how automated technologies and related practices co-evolve.

I briefly consider six speculative ideas: (1) that these dynamics might resemble those associated with the elements of single practices; (2) that patterns of human and machinic involvement change across constellations in ways that reflect the processes that connect them; (3) that processes in which automated machines are embedded might be more stable than those achieved only through practices; and (4) that they might also be more readily standardised; (5) change more rapidly; and (6) that such constellations might become an irreversible yet background-like condition of society.

Elements of systems

Just as technologies might be situated as constitutive elements of practices, they might also be considered as necessary aspects of the existence and continued reproduction of sets of practices. In arguing that socio-technical systems of mobility can be reframed as systems of practice, Watson (2012: 493) refers to 'systemic elements – including infrastructures, technologies, rules, norms and meanings – which those practices constitute and maintain'. Thus, the idea that single practices change as their elements change can be extended to systems of practices. Importantly, this may apply in the case of elements that are not directly constitutive of, or shared by, all the practices within a system. For example, relationships between practices within a system may be reconfigured by the technological development or redesign of elements of one central, or highly interconnected, practice. Equally, elements may change as the system changes: not only in physical form as objects are redesigned to reflect the ways they are used, but also in the sense that meanings and functions develop as practices and the relationships between them change. In effect, this positions automated machines as interpretively flexible and co-evolving technologies-in-use (e.g. Hand and Shove, 2007) in relation to a system of practices, rather than as a distinctive part of any single practice.

Elements of constellations: reconfiguring temporal–material patterns

In a similar way, it makes sense to think of automated machines as elements of processes that are organised across constellations. With the introduction of automated machines, cross-cutting interconnections are reconfigured in ways that matter for types of human and machinic participation and for the temporal and material organisation of the whole constellation (here bounded by the processes of production or heating). For instance, automation might involve the re-allocation of person-hours from one practice to another within the constellation, for instance, shifting 'work' from tasks of machine-operation to those of programming and monitoring remotely sensed feedback. This may require quite different skills, with the result that populations of suitably qualified practitioners may also change. In addition, more extensive automation may have further consequences, perhaps entailing changes to delivery schedules or the types of materials used as inputs.

Beyond the 'immediate' constellation – i.e. the production process itself – other adaptations may follow across wider sets of practices. For example, automation may render some populations of previous or would-be practitioners redundant, thus 'freeing up' time for practices in other constellations. Economic and political changes associated with mass-automation are at least partially associated with the re-allocation of time between different sets of practices. And in the case of heating, for example, time not spent collecting fuel and preparing fires may be used for other pursuits, perhaps resulting in less seasonally distinct schedules of activity.

Persistence and stability

In principle, a largely machinic 'extended' process is likely to evolve differently to one that is largely performed by human practitioners. We might expect such a process to be more stable compared with situations in which practices are continually reproduced through human performance and are consequently subject to ongoing, if minor, variation. Human performances occur across different spaces, times and settings and this is widely understood as a means by which practices change from within, albeit slowly (Warde, 2005; Røpke, 2009; Shove et al., 2012).

In contrast, certain material arrangements and technologies sustain the stability and durability of practices over time in part because of their physical durability (Latour, 1991b; Gieryn, 2002). Thus much like buildings, which do not have to be continually re-performed in practices, even if they often are re-interpreted and re-configured (Gieryn, 2002), it could be argued that fully automated technologies provide something of a stabilising and structuring context to the practices that connect to them and within the constellations in which they are embedded. For instance, and at a minimum, a process that requires no human intervention presents a different set of challenges for managers caught up in the wider flux of economic, political and industrial changes as compared to situations which involve large numbers of workers with particular skills.

Standardisation

Processes that are largely undertaken by machines can be engineered in ways that seem infeasible for processes that are enacted by people, no matter how 'rationalised', well regulated or 'mechanical' they are. This suggests that automated systems may be amenable to higher degrees of standardisation. As others have observed, heating and air conditioning technologies are inextricably implicated in global circulations of standardised expectations and actual conditions within buildings (Shove, 2003; Healy, 2008). In part, it was the development of machines that could automatically maintain a set point temperature that first raised the question of what indoor temperatures should be like. The scientific process of specifying comfort parameters has subsequently provided a rationale for the promulgation of air conditioning systems that can reliably deliver these fixed conditions, whatever the weather.

Rate of change

In contrast to the prospect of stability, it is also plausible that a largely machinic or automated process is more amenable to intentional re-engineering or reconfiguration and rapid change than a process that largely depends on human performance. As Schatzki (2013) notes, it is not just technologies that lend durability to social life, but also slowly changing competences and understandings. From this point of view, software updates and new robotics might well outstrip the speed of change in bodily competence. Moreover, by reducing or removing the temporal and material challenges of coordinating and organising human work, such as operating conditions (light, heat, safety), shift patterns and working hours, it may be possible to re-imagine and re-organise extended processes in different ways.

Irreversibility and transformation

As indicated above, production processes, in particular, appear to be transformed through processes of automation. One consequence is that it becomes increasingly difficult, if not impossible, to 'reverse engineer' these processes of production and return to forms of work powered only by the human body. This may not be the result of any one moment of automation, but rather an outcome of successive sequences of automation and transformation such as those which enable the range of products, infrastructures and even foodstuffs that are common today.

The irreversibility of what were once apparently negotiable distinctions and delegations between bodily and machine-centred work is deepened as competences change: just as new skills, for instance, in controlling and making automated machines emerge, others are lost. More broadly, the economics of work adapts and shifts as 'work' time is reallocated and re-evaluated, as competences change and as the 'working' population is redefined. This adds to a sense of deepening interdependence between fully and partly automated production processes and the wider net of constellations in which they are positioned, as both co-evolve. Economic and social organisations predicated on advanced automated production processes emerge as these processes and systems become part of the more materially durable fabric of society, much like buildings or roundabouts.

Discussion

It seems obvious that practices, technologies, bodies and other material and immaterial flows are intimately and variously related in ways that shape and are shaped by each other. It is hardly contentious to claim that they co-evolve. However, it is more difficult to differentiate and conceptualise the kinds of relationship and modes of change involved in this co-evolution. To date, much of the discussion about how practices emerge, transform and disappear has focused on objects that are manipulated and used. Thus conceptualised, technologies are seen as one of several interlinked elements of practices between which a number of recursive dynamics can be traced, including connections to other practices. As others have noted, this is not the only way in which material relations figure in the dynamics of practice, meaning that it is important to 'unpack' and differentiate between the distinctive roles that different materials and arrangements play in practices and their dynamics (Shove, this volume; Shove *et al.*, 2015; Rinkinen *et al.*, 2015).

In this chapter, I have furthered this discussion by focusing on relationships between practices and automated machines. Such relations are marked by the relative absence and decoupling of human practitioners, rather than being defined by forms of interlinkage and co-participation. At the same time, I have shown that such machines are indeed embedded in wider sets of practice and that when viewed in these terms, entire factories might be considered as technologies-in-use at a more aggregate scale. Even so, modes of 'engaging' with or relating to fully automated technologies differ significantly from direct interactions with tools that are handled. This suggests that different dynamics may operate in constituting and transforming the constellations in which automated machines are embedded, as compared to processes that are reproduced through active human participation. The implications are ambiguous: it seems that machinic arrangements are at once seemingly more stable and at the same time more open to intentional redesign than processes that are reproduced by multiple, variously skilled bodies.

At a more general and equally speculative level, a distinction between tool and machine-based relations points to two primary modes of social reproduction: one of practices and one of 'extended processes', as sets of procedures organised around a particular project or end. In many cases, practices and processes overlap. Where projects involve machinic and other material processes, the roles of things are heavily interconnected and coordinated with and by doings and sayings. However, through more sophisticated forms of control, learning and interconnections with other machines, some machinic operations become increasingly independent, only requiring setting up, adjustment and maintenance: activities which are typically concentrated among a smaller group of practitioners.

The practical, political implications of such generic shifts are uncertain. However, the bracketing off, or decoupling, of an increasing array of processes from the realm of human-centred practice suggests that the dynamics of at least some areas of practice depend upon the operation of ever-more complex material structures and infrastructures. Moreover, as sophisticated, digital control technologies are integrated with complicated mechanical procedures, as in the case of fully automated factories, the boundaries of technological artefacts may be reconstituted. As they get 'bigger', such technologies cannot be 'used' by single bodies, nor can they be interacted with directly – although they are clearly worked on and 'used', but in a different, more distanced sense. In addition, through their routine operation, they stand in something like a background-relation to larger systems of practice, simultaneously constituting and reconfiguring them in subtle and indirect ways.

Attending to these kinds of practice-material relationship is challenging. It calls for a willingness simultaneously to think beyond the body and to consider a range of relationships less familiar than those of direct manipulation and perception, while, at the same time, being able to account for the ways in which these less-than-direct relationships remain anchored in the bodily doings and sayings of which practices are composed.

Notes

1   One might also argue that such artefacts or physical entities are themselves not *only* material, but also constituted through meanings, capabilities, and processes. I explore a related 'relativistic' notion (Ihde, 1990) that artefacts can only be defined in relations, rather than as things in themselves, later in the chapter.
2   The boundaries of these 'machines' as artefacts is not straightforward, yet if defined as complex collections of artefacts of different kinds that share certain tasks or roles, reference to central heating systems and factories as single machines makes more sense.

7

IS SMALL THE ONLY BEAUTIFUL?

Making sense of 'large phenomena' from a practice-based perspective

Davide Nicolini

In this chapter I will discuss how a practice-based sensitivity can be used to address big issues and 'large-scale phenomena'. Examples of big issues include the nature and functioning of the financial market, large institutional arrangements, the education system, bureaucracy and the future of the planet. The topic is central to the advancement of practice-oriented studies. Practice-based sensitivities are often pigeonholed as part of microsociology and thus deemed unsuitable to deal with some of the big issues of our time and are of scarce importance outside academic circles. How we address 'large-scale phenomena' is therefore closely related to the issue of the relevance of practice-based studies and the practical uses of practice theories.

In the chapter, I will use the terms 'practice-based studies', 'practice approach' or 'practice lens' to denote a family of orientations that take practices as central for the understanding of organisational and social phenomena. Authors who embrace this orientation suggest that matters such as social order, knowledge, institutions, identity, power, inequalities and social change result from and transpire through social practices. While they all agree that the study of the social needs to start and end with social practices, they use different sensitising theoretical categories, research methods and discursive genres. As I argued elsewhere (Nicolini, 2012), I see no merit in trying to reduce this multiplicity in search of a unitary or unified theory of practice and this equally applies to a discussion of how practice-based scholars approach large-scale phenomena. Accordingly, my aim here is not to build a practice-based theory of big social phenomena or to theorise large-scale social phenomena by building upon a specific type of theory. Rather, more modestly, I am interested in the different methodological and theoretical strategies that authors in the practice-based camp have used to address large-scale social phenomena. While I do have my own view of what practices consist of,[1] I will here simply examine the question from different practice-based vantage points and discuss how 'large phenomena' transpire amid and emerge through different theories of practice.

I will start my discussion by contrasting the position of practice-based approaches to 'large-scale phenomena' vis-à-vis the idea of macro-phenomena, levels of reality and localism. I will then critically survey some of the ways in which practice-oriented scholars have addressed 'large phenomena' and comment on their affordances and limitations.

On 'large-scale phenomena' and praxeology

Practice approaches and the 'macro': flat ontologies and layered reality

One of the common characteristics of practice approaches is the belief that concrete human activities – with blood, sweat, tears, and all – are critical for the study of the production, reproduction and change of social phenomena. Pierre Bourdieu, for example, indicated that to understand crucial aspects of French society, we need look into ordinary settings such as kitchens and dining rooms rather than focussing on abstract domains populated with structures, functions, and the like (Bourdieu, 1984; Bourdieu and Wacquant, 1992). Similarly, one of the greatest recent social changes in North American history was triggered in the back of an old bus by a small number of courageous women and men who refused to leave their seats and in so doing interrupted the reproduction of segregation – in practice (Parks and Reed, 2000). This theoretical orientation has critical methodological implications. It suggests that in our investigation of social matters, we need to engage with real-time activity in its historical situatedness – although how this should be done constitutes one of the dimensions along which different practice approaches diverge.

More broadly, practice theorists disagree on how to deal with the issue of scale and the traditional distinction between micro and macro social phenomena (Knorr Cetina and Cicourel, 1981). A first distinction exists between practice theorists who embrace a flat ontology and others who uphold a more traditional layered view of the social.

Some, albeit not all, practice theorists adopt a flat ontology and join forces with other relational sociologies that suggest that all social phenomena, small-scale and large-scale, are constituted through and experienced in terms of 'micro' situations (Emirbayer, 1997). For these authors, so-called 'large-scale phenomena' are constituted by and emerge through the aggregation of interrelated practices and their regimes of reproduction. The task of social scientists is to account for such processes of constitution and reproduction; they also have to display these processes in their texts, that is, reassemble the social in front of the eyes of the reader, viewer or listener (Latour, 2005). Authors who embrace a flat ontology caution that although practitioners customarily use abstractions to refer to 'summaries of the distribution of different microbehaviors [sic] in time and space' (Collins, 1981: 989), these abstractions and summaries do not have causal power and should not be turned into entities with autonomous existence. Social reality has no 'levels': when it comes to the social, it is practices all the way down.

Not all practice theorists embrace a flat ontology. Two examples are Bourdieu and Giddens. Both authors believe that such things as structure, power and fields exist in their own right, although they need to be reproduced in and through practices. A similar stance has been adopted by authors such as Fairclough (2005; 2013), who combines an attention for (discursive) practices with a critical realist position and Glynos and Horwarth (2007) who, building on a Lacanian sensitivity, suggest that practices are governed by a dialectic of social, political and fantasmatic logics – the latter providing an affective explanation of why specific practices and regimes grip subjects. Concepts such as structure, field and logics indicate that for these authors, practices alone are not sufficient to explain social phenomena and the constitution of society.

This ontological position is reflected in conceptions of what counts as large phenomena. Authors like Bourdieu, Giddens, Fairclough and others who admit the existence of phenomena outside of the realm of practice, conceive 'macro' social phenomena in terms of long-term, complex and far reaching social processes. These processes, which are beyond the discretion of any individual, constitute 'external forces' which structure people's daily conduct. As such they should be treated as self-subsistent entities: social classes, discourses, the market, the state, etc. For these authors, such entities need to be explained in terms that are different from those used to explain mundane social intercourse: in common parlance they constitute a different level of social reality. Micro and macro large-scale social phenomena are made of different ontological stuff, so to speak.

Authors who embrace a more relational standpoint, on the contrary, reject this view and denounce it as a theoretical sleight of hand. Complexity and size have nothing to do with the existence of so-called 'macro' phenomena, or at least they do not warrant granting such phenomena a different ontological status. For one thing, plenty of evidence exists that even the most ordinary 'micro' situations and discursive interactions are extremely complex and intricate. For example, the extensive work of conversation analysis has unearthed a Pandora's box of mechanisms, effort and skilled performance in even the most mundane of discursive interactions. At the same time, social conduct that according to the accepted views are considered 'small-scale' – for example, the practice of greeting other people at the beginning of a social encounter – are in fact ubiquitous, pervasive and critical to sustain the fabric of social relationships and its orderliness. Indeed, one can hardly think of a phenomenon that is more 'macro' and 'large-scale' than greetings.

For authors who subscribe to flat ontology, then, the idea of large phenomena points at issues that are highly ramified in time and space and for this reason difficult to grasp *and* represent. From this point of view, the ascription of a special ontological status to 'large-scale phenomena' is a combination of lack of knowledge and frustration with the fact that we are unable to get our heads around them. In short, 'macrosociology' is a sociology for impatient people.

Not all flat ontologies are equal: individualism, situationalism and relationalism

Fundamental distinctions also exist among authors who subscribe to a flat ontology. These distinctions are closely related to the praxeological orientations they adopt.

First, there is a tendency – or maybe a risk – for practice-oriented authors to fall back on the idea that large-scale social phenomena can be explained because people perform or follow something that pre-exists them (a logic of action, a praxis, a template for action, a routine). In this view, social phenomena arise from the fact that people perform practices – the emphasis being on *people* as in 'well-formed individuals'. This position is conducive to an overdetermined and over-theorised outlook, which explains social affairs in terms of rational individual choices or (more or less successful) efforts to realise pre-existing rules, plans of action or mental schemes (see Schatzki, 1996; 2002 for a discussion).

Second, a group of authors usually associated with ethnomethodology and its later development and diaspora endorse what Knorr Cetina (1981) describes as 'methodological situationalism'. The notion of methodological situationalism adds a critical restrictive condition to the flat ontology principle that 'concrete social interactions' should be considered the building blocks for macrosociological conceptions' (Knorr Cetina, 1981: 8). The supplementary condition is that nothing can be said of what happens beyond in situ social interactions. From this perspective, the only empirically acceptable objects of conceptualisation in social investigation are orderly scenes of action taken one at a time; nothing can be said outside these restrictive boundaries (Schegloff, 1997; Sarangi and Roberts, 1999). In this extreme version, large-scale phenomena are not accepted as legitimate objects of inquiry *per se*. Phenomena can be considered large only by virtue of the number of their repetitions and their relevance in sustaining the texture of the social (as in the example of greeting, which is ubiquitous and critical for society to function).

In this very narrow interpretation, methodological situationalism risks becoming an instance of what Levinson (2005) calls 'interactional reductionism'. The term foregrounds the risks of reducing all social phenomena to self-organising local interactions. According to Levinson, this approach turns the potentially fruitful suggestion that social phenomena are assembled amid and through situated practices into an empirical straightjacket. This in turn restricts the range of empirical options and practical uses of practice approaches.

A third group of scholars, to which I belong and that will constitute the focus of the rest of the chapter, maintains a form of relational or *connected situationalism*. The basic intuition that distinguishes this group of scholars from the previous one is that the basic unit of analysis is not a single scene of action or a specific situation or instance of the accomplishment of a practice, but rather a chain, sequence or combination of performances *plus* their relationships – what keeps them connected in space and time. From this perspective, which practice theorists share with other traditions such as multi-sited ethnography (Marcus, 1995; Falzon, 2012), social phenomena are effects of and transpire through associations in time and space of situated performances. Performances therefore can be understood only if we take into account the nexus in which they come into being. What happens here and now and why (the conditions of possibility of any scene of action) is inextricably linked to what is happening in another 'here and now' or what has happened in another 'here and now' in the past (and sometimes in the future). The study of large-scale phenomena from a methodological connected situationalism position is predisposed towards a rhizomatic sensitivity. A rhizomatic sensitivity sees associations of practices as a living connection of performances; it offers an image of how practices grow, expand and conquer new territory; it suggests that to study how large phenomena emerge from and transpire through connections between practices, we should always start from a 'here and now' and follow connections (Nicolini, 2009); and finally it offers a model for representing the gamut of connections in action. As we will see below, depending on the sensitivity of the researcher, this can take the form of an overview – so that large phenomena appear as textures, nexuses, meshes or assemblages of practices – although this is not inevitable and other options to praxeologise large phenomena are also available.

In summary, from a connected situationalism position, the study of large phenomena amounts to (1) the investigation of what large rhizomatic assemblages of situated activities look like, how they come into being, are reproduced and change; and (2) how these evolving assemblages are made available and become relevant and consequential in other situated activities and their assemblages by virtue of being turned into summaries and/or representations. How this can be done in practice is the subject of the rest of the chapter.

Three theory method packages through which to study large-scale phenomena from a practice-based perspective

In this section, I will examine three ways to respond to the question 'how can we understand large-scale phenomena using a practice-based sensitivity'? The first builds upon what I call textile metaphors (texture, net, fabric, weaving), the second focuses on how the global manifests in the local, the third concentrates on the practices through which large-scale phenomena are assembled. As we shall see, these broad approaches constitute what elsewhere I called 'theory method packages' (Nicolini, 2012). Although they are related in more than one way, these packages embrace slightly different ontological assumptions and propose different practical approaches to making sense, studying and representing large-scale phenomena from a practice-based perspective.

Large-scale phenomena as a fabric of interconnected practices: from metaphor to method

The first approach, which as we shall see includes some variants, builds on the work of authors who propose that large-scale phenomena emerge from and transpire through the living and pulsating connections among practices. Schatzki (2015b: 4), for example, suggests that large phenomena are 'constellations of practice-arrangement bundles or of slices or features thereof'. The difference between small and large phenomena is essentially one of extension and number of the practices involved:

> A bundle is a set of linked practices and arrangements. A constellation is a set of linked bundles … the kinds of link that exist among bundles are the kinds of link that connect practices and arrangements. A constellation, consequently, is just a larger and possibly more complex bundle, a larger and possibly more complex linkage of practices and arrangements.
>
> (*Schatzki, 2011: 8*)

Gherardi (2012a) mobilises the image of texture (and sometimes web) to capture the interconnected nature of practices. According to her, fields of practices 'arise in the interwoven texture that interconnects practices' (2012a: 131) and extend all the way to society. The concept of texture is used in an evocative way 'to convey the image of shifting the analysis between studying practices from the inside and the outside' (Gherardi, 2012a: 2) and 'to follow the connections in action and investigating how action connects and disconnects' (Gherardi, 2012a: 156). Czarniawska (2004) similarly uses the image of the action net to achieve the same result. Large social phenomena such as institutions, business organisations and regional waste prevention programmes are conceived as the result of weaving actions together and stabilising the resulting arrangement, inscribing it in text, bodies and artefacts (Lindberg and Czarniawska; 2006; Corvellec and Czarniawska, 2014). The concepts of texture and action net are thus meant to capture both the connectivity and the work that goes into establishing and maintaining these ties. As with Schatzki, the view is that large phenomena are made of a complex web of living connections between practices.

Concepts such as net, network, web, bundle, texture, confederation, congregation, assemblage, mesh and ecology are often used by practice-oriented authors (and other relational social scientists) to describe how practices work together. All these metaphors conjure and promote the idea that large social phenomena emerge from the interconnection of social and material practices and evoke the image of a pulsating, yet seemingly chaotic, anthill-like world. However, these concepts are often used figuratively rather than analytically. While authors nurture the *imaginaire* of a world made of practices, they offer relatively few pragmatic indications of how we could make sense of it or approach the study of such a world empirically. In short, the issue is how to operationalise this *imaginaire* in ways of seeing and writing.

Uncovering the interconnection between practices through systematic analysis

Among the few authors who have offered a practical way to study and represent interconnections among practices and their effects are Stephen Kemmis and his colleagues (Kemmis, 2005; 2010; Kemmis and Mutton, 2012; Kemmis *et al.*, 2014). In a number of works spanning a decade, these authors have developed a sophisticated grammar and set of methodological principles to understand and represent practices and their ecologies. Kemmis and colleagues conceive of practices as socially established cooperative human activities composed of the hanging together of saying, doings and social relatings. These activities are organised around projects and by virtue of being reproduced in time, they assume the character of practice traditions. When participants engage in activities in the pursuit of projects, they do the things and they speak the language that are characteristic of the practice and enter relationships building on the 'memory' provided by the practice tradition. Critically, however, doings, saying and relating only become intelligible within the pre-existing set of cultural-discursive, material-economic and social-political conditions. Such conditions both enable the unfolding of a practice (the practice memory, for example, is sedimented in the physical arrangements, language spoken, discourse used, etc.) and constrain them (they establish what can be said and done). Kemmis and colleagues call this intersubjective space, 'the architecture of practice' in effect, Kemmis' Habermasian reinterpretation of Schatzki's 'orders'. To paraphrase Marx, people bring practices into being, but not under conditions of their own choosing. However, in contrast to the traditional Marxian interpretation, the relationship between practices and architectures is two-way (Schatzki (2002) calls this a contextural relationship). When practices happen, they become part of the happening: they take up available doings, sayings and relatings; they modify them; and they leave behind traces that in turn become part of the practice architecture of future activities. Activities and the architectures within which they unfold are therefore shaped by other practices and their architectures, and in turn shape them. Practices thus 'feed upon each other' (Kemmis *et al.*, 2014: 47) and in so doing constitute ecologies understood as 'distinctive interconnected webs of human social activities that are mutually necessary to order and sustain a practice as a practice of a particular kind and complexity (for example, a progressive educational practice)' (Kemmis and Mutton, 2012: 15).

Kemmis and colleagues use this detailed theoretical construction to develop an empirical method to analyse practices and to study how they combine into large phenomena. They do so by providing an analytical tool (in the shape of an analysis checklist) for examining individual practices in terms of sayings, doings and relatings; their project; and the architecture amid which the practice unfolds. The same categories are then used to compare how different practices influence, enable or constrain each other and to examine how one practice 'feeds upon', 'is interconnected with' or shapes or is shaped by other practices and whether the relationship is one of hospitability, symbiosis or suffocation (all these terms are used in Kemmis *et al.*, 2014: chap. 3). The result of this second type of analysis is a two-ways table that allows investigators to examine, for example, how the practice of student learning is shaped by teaching, teacher learning, leadership processes, etc. It might be, for example, that exposing teachers to the practice of democratic and participative forms of school leadership creates a hospitable condition for specific active and participative teaching practices that in turn affect the practice of student learning. The table also helps show how student learning influences other practices. We thus find that the teacher's practices are reflexively shaped by her observations and interpretations of how students respond to her teaching and that positive changes in the practices of student reinforce the utilisation of democratic learning practices and initiatives at school district level.

The analytical 'table of invention' (a term underscoring its heuristic use) aims to support the empirical mapping, with some level of systematicity, of relationships between practices in specific parts of the ecology. Although in the existing practical examples, the approach and the 'sequential, systematic and repeated' empirical analysis are limited to a specific part of the ecology, Kemmis is adamant that the same principle applies everywhere:

> [T]he educational practices in the Education Complex are not vast 'social structures' that order the world uniformly throughout a classroom, school, School District or national jurisdiction. On the contrary, they are realised in everyday interactions between people, and between people and other objects, in millions of diverse sites around the world.
>
> *(2014: 52)*

While ecological relationships may turn out to be more complex and less linear than this combinatorial approach suggests (Kemmis and Mutton (2012) begin to explore how principles from biological system theory can be brought into the discussion), the basic approach remains valid: if the world is flat, large-scale social phenomena can be examined in terms of mutual relationship among practices.

Studying large-scale phenomena by rhizomatically following connections between trans-situated practices

The work by Kemmis and colleagues has the advantage of enabling empirical analysis by making concrete the idea that large social phenomena are the result of nets, large confederations and vast ecologies of practices tied together. It also offers a practical way of investigating them. One may not agree with Kemmis' approach, which can be accused of being a bit mechanical and simplistic, recycling several elements of old style systems theory (via the action research tradition from which Kemmis derives). However, Kemmis' work sheds light on what is at stake when using metaphors like web and net to study large phenomena from a praxeological perspective. For example, one of the things that becomes clear is that such metaphors are especially suitable for situations where there is *direct* interaction and contact among practices and their human and non-human carriers. However, this approach is not well suited to studying the increasing number of social phenomena that are global in scope and do not embrace direct interaction (or even prohibit it, as in the terrorist movement studies by Knorr Cetina (2005)). The challenge is to find ways of studying such phenomena that hold fast to the idea that practices are always social and materially situated and involve real-time empirically observable scenes of action. This can be done if we reconceptualise the notion of interdependence – expanding the variety of ways in which practices can influence each other – and replace a textile view (based on metaphors of web and net) with a rhizomatic approach. Progress in this sense has been made by a group of scholars who substitute the idea of web, net and network with the idea of nested relationality (Jarzabkowski et al., 2015), trans-situatedness (Nicolini, Mørk, Masovic and Hanseth, 2017), and complex global micro structures (Knorr Cetina, 2005; 2009). These authors offer a further way to translate in practice the assumption that large-scale phenomena emerge from and transpire through connections among practices, which differs from that proposed by Kemmis and associates. The idea in this case is that a number of large-scale social phenomena emerge from active relationships between highly localised forms of activities that take place in dispersed places and time zones. What keeps these distant local practices in a nexus of connections is not some superordinate form of coordination, such as that exerted by NATO. Rather, the connectivity stems from the nature and fabric of the practice itself. A concrete example will help to explain what is at stake here.

Jarzabkowski et al. (2015) have utilised this approach to study the global market of reinsurance – that is, the place where insurance companies buy insurance policies for themselves. Using a zooming in and out research strategy (Nicolini, 2009; 2012), they patiently followed the practice of reinsurance, studying it in (extreme) depth in the five main global hubs where it unfolds through highly situated activities (meetings, conversation, calculations in offices, restaurants, parties). In each hub, they identified the practices through which consensus prices emerge, risk is modelled and trades are finalised. Among other things, they discovered that what makes this vast nexus of diverse elements and competing trades function as a recognisable market is that each of these practices constitutes the context for each other – first locally and later trans-locally. The complex web of relationality that they patiently unravel is sustained through practitioners' membership of the same community of practice and utilisation of specific scoping technologies (i.e. technologies that summarise the instant state of the market on a screen and allow at the same time to intervene in it, see Knorr Cetina, 2005). Most important, maintenance of the web also depends on the organising effect afforded by (1) collective sharing by traders of the same set of *practical understandings*, that is, the know-hows that govern ordinary activities such as arriving at a quote in the absence of a centralised market or dealing with large adverse events; (2) the circulation of the same *general understanding* of how the network of relationships works, why and what is legitimate and acceptable within this particular regime of practice; and (3) the specific temporalities inscribed in and reproduced by the collective practice – e.g. periodical renewal dates punctuating the process which provide specific time horizons for the different activities and constitute an object towards which the gamut of activities converge and precipitate. Unlike other markets where participants are connected through embodied presence (e.g. a traditional trading room full of screaming brokers) or response presence (e.g.

modern trading floors where the market is transformed into moving indexes on a computer screen to which human traders or non-human trading algorithms react), here we have a global market which is built on a form of relational presence. In short, the market is brought into existence because the practices of underwriters are relational to one another and collective activities are coordinated by virtue of being part of a same practice, despite the lack of spatial co-presence.

The approach is very promising in that it makes such relations tangible and further develops the idea that understanding and representing large-scale phenomena requires a reiteration of two basic movements: zooming in on the situated accomplishments of practice and zooming out to their relationships in space and time (Nicolini, 2009; 2012). This approach can be extended to phenomena that have a broad, even global, breadth. The approach also invites us to expand the palette of methods through which we interrogate how these relationships are established, maintained and consumed beyond the transactional 'quid pro quo' principle that is built, for example, in Latour's (2005) notion of interessement. General understandings, for example, connect practices mainly through discursive mediation and operate at a level that is both rational and affective. As authors like Laclau and Mouffe (1985) convincingly argue, discourse can govern and bring together practice at a distance through structuring the field of intelligibility and the related demands that this makes on social identities, relationships and systems of knowledge and belief – a case in point being the construction of national identity and other imagined communities (Anderson, 1991). Much of this takes place at a level that is affective rather than rational and builds on the power of preconscious drives and impulses, such as the sense of lack and incompleteness built into the fabric of individualisation (Laclau and Mouffe, 1985).

The point has been highlighted by Karin Knorr Cetina (2005), who studied complex global microstructures – structures which, similar to the reinsurance market above, are driven by micro-interactions, but are global in reach. Asking how the fragmentary kaleidoscope of often unconnected cells of Al Qaeda make for a global movement, she draws attention to the transcendent sense of temporality shared by affiliates (a temporality that transcends individual life and survival and that implies waiting, patience and preparedness); the use of media to communicate to the rest of the diaspora (terrorist attacks are also messages with a strong sensory, affective and motivating intent); and the strategic use of the narrative of an ongoing and persistent confrontation between a religiously defined Arabic diaspora and various Western empires (Knorr Cetina, 2005: 23). Al Qaeda as a global large-scale phenomenon thrives on the principle of nested relationality and can only be studied by zooming in on its practices and following connections, provided we are prepared to think of such connections in much broader terms than in some current practice-based approaches.

In summary, the concepts of practice architecture, nested relationality and the related methodological principles of examining mutual influences between practices in situ and of tracking distant connections among local practices following human, material and discursive intermediaries, constitute a first practical answer to the question of how we can represent large-scale phenomena from a practice-based perspective. The two strategies are complementary in that they operationalise the textile metaphors often used to conceptualise large phenomena from a practice perspective. They do so by holding fast to the ideas that practices are always manifest in empirically accessible social sites of activity (as this is how they perpetuate themselves) and that explaining how practices form constellations and wider configurations does not require presupposing the existence of mysterious superordinate entities. Trans-situated practices are connected through other practices such as those of visiting, writing and circulating artefacts; writing blogs to proselytise on the internet, etc. We can thus understand the global, using the same approach we use to examine the local.

Examining the global in the local

A second practical answer to the question of how we can represent large-scale phenomena from a practice-based perspective is by focussing on how the global manifests itself in the local. In effect, the methodological movement in this case is complementary to the one used by the approaches above: rather than building on an inside-out strategy whereby researchers move from one locale to another until a 'global' overview emerges, here the focus is on how the global itself manifests in ordinary practices. As I discussed above, this view extends the intuition of ethnomethodology and conversational analysis by following sequences of action and talk in interaction beyond the boundaries of the specific scene of action (or text) under examination. The goal is to understand how the practical understandings, discursive resources and member categorisations used to accomplish practices in a specific locale are reproduced in time – rather than limiting exploration to their rules of application.

This approach has been developed into an explicit investigation strategy by Scollon and Scollon (2001; 2004; 2005), who call it 'nexus analysis'. These authors, who build on the insights of discourse analysis, think of large-scale phenomena in analogy to large-scale discursive formations or 'big D Discourses' (Gee, 1999). Discourses here are understood as the conditions that bestow a certain order and meaning on the statements which belong to them. Discursive formations, such as medicine, ethnicity, modern science or being a rock musician (or fan), were obtained by assembling existing discursive and non-discursive elements in a novel way through the institutions of new social and discursive practices. These large discursive formations are socially constitutive in that they enact social identities, relationships between people and bodies of knowledge. While most discourse analysts limit their focus on statements, text and how they are assembled and produced, for the Scollons, semiosis necessarily spills over beyond texts and into the world. Discursive formations provide the conditions for the accomplishment of all activities, not only discourse. In turn, discursive formations are socially and materially reproduced through the very conditions that they institute. Nexus analysis is the investigation of the forms of discursivity that circulate through specific sites of practice and which lead to the emergence of specific mediated actions and regimes of activity, for example, doing a class or appearing in court.

In detail, the analysis starts by examining a specific site of engagement (a time/space station where some practice is customarily reproduced) with special attention given to the social arrangements (interactional orders), the historical bodies of the participants (their lived experiences) and the discourses that are active in that particular scene (the discourses toward which participants' attention appears to be directed). Analysis of the site of engagement and of mediated actions there enables the crucial discourses that operate in the scene to be identified. This is, however, only part of the task. The next step of the analysis consists of navigating between these discourses 'as a way of seeing how those moments are constituted out of past practices and how in turn they lead to new forms of action…' (Scollon and Scollon, 2004: 29). This is achieved by 'circumferencing' the existing cycles of discourse (and practices), examining their historical origin and showing how they constitute local action through anticipating consequences and providing motives. Key to this task is the idea that discourse mutates in time through 'resemiotisation' (Iedema, 2001; 2003); and the deliberate use of different time scales by the researcher.

The idea of resemiotisation captures the process through which discourses are progressively materialised from situated and quite 'local' talk, towards increasingly durable – because they are written, multiplied and filed – forms of language use (Iedema, 2003: 42). When introduced into a different scene of action, these durable manifestations of discourse are re-performed locally. For example, it may be decided (talk) to organise a focus group on certain social policies and to invite a number of heads of household. The decision is then resemiotised in an invitation letter (text) that is sent to male addressees or householders (who are very often male). These people accept the invitation and participate in the focus group (talk). The site of engagement actively reproduces a gender bias that is brought to bear by a cycle of discourse. The gender-based discourse is both manifested in and perpetuated through the nexus of practices: the focus group. The situation is compounded by the fact that male participants are likely to carry into the scene historical bodies/ideas that predispose them to perceive themselves as the family spokesperson (even if they are not necessarily the actual breadwinner). The two cycles of discourse render participants doubly blind to the gendered nature of the practice. They do not see this gendering and they do not see the discourse that makes them not see. Retracing the multiple socio-historical chains of resemiotisation, it is critical to uncover 'how and why what we confront as "real" has come about through networks of transmission and assemblage of semiotic resources' (Iedema, 2003: 48). Nexus analysis therefore provides an understanding of which discourses circulate in any form of practice and accounts for how such large-scale discursive formations are reproduced.

Critical to this endeavour is also the deliberate deployment and manipulation of different time scales, the assumption being that when we change the temporality taken into account in our investigation, different types of phenomena become noticeable. For example, Scollon (2005) lists a number of cycles within which different aspects of human existence are entrained: respiratory cycles; metabolic and digestive cycles; circadian cycles of waking and sleeping; lunar cycles; solar cycles and the seasons; entropic cycles; and the formation and decay of material substances. The list, which is not meant to be exhaustive (for example, it does not include socially produced temporalities and cycles), is only a reminder that what counts as relevant and consequential changes depending upon which temporal horizon we employ. Large-scale phenomena need to be made – they are not given – and what counts as large is very much an effect of our interests and practical concerns.

Studying scalography and playing with it

A further way to answer the question of how we can represent large-scale phenomena from a practice-based perspective is to address them directly through the idea of scalography (Hinchliffe, 2009). This third way is rather different from the two strategies examined above.

Scalography refers in fact to the ethnographic study of scalar objects and practices, that is, the study of practices through which large-scale phenomena are constructed. Scalography can be used in a literal or in a reflexive way.

Used literally, scalography is the study of the scoping technologies (Knorr Cetina, 2005) and representation activities through which specific classes of practitioners construct and circulate large-scale phenomena. Practitioners in several scientific domains use all manner of 'summaries of the distribution of different microbehaviors in time and space' (Collins, 1981: 989). These abstractions are expertly created for specific practical uses: guiding an army, controlling a city, producing a news bulletin, making policy or investment decisions. They are manufactured through ordinary practices and mobilised in centres of calculation, such as control rooms, military command centres, news rooms, boardrooms of large corporations, etc. (Latour, 2005). From this point of view, large-scale phenomena exist only as the object of work in specific occupations. To understand large-scale phenomena, defined in these terms, it makes sense to investigate the ordinary work of those who produce overviews, vistas and summaries of distributions. This can be done, for example, by attending to the creation of mobile intermediaries, following their circulation and examining the assembling powers of skilled humans and scopic technologies (Callon and Latour, 1981; Knorr Cetina, 2005).

Because such work is concrete and localised, we can apply one of the two strategies discussed above to investigate in which buildings, bureaus or departments large phenomena were and are manufactured and how this works. While the study of the practices through which macro-phenomena are brought into being and differences of scale are produced is not specific to practice theory (the topic has been examined extensively by both science and technology studies and actor network theory, see Latour, 2005; Hinchliffe, 2009), how these themselves are examined is new.

Scalography, however, can also be used in an intentional yet reflexive way. As I suggested above, for practice-based studies and cognate approaches, the problem is not that large phenomena are manufactured and used, but rather that this process is hidden from view, ignored or forgotten, so that the map is confused with the territory. Social scientists are perfectly entitled to create partial, thumbnail abstracted representations of large phenomena for practical use, as long as they do this in plain view and do not sever the link between representational practice and practice represented. In this sense, we can study large-scale phenomena by taking the regular performances of a large number of similar activities across time and space as the object of interest. We can attribute a collective name to a number of individual instances and treat the resulting epistemic object as quasi-entity: for example, the 'macro-practice' or 'practical regime' of showering, shopping in supermarkets, washing, teaching, cycling and trading in the market (all cases discussed in Shove *et al.*, 2012). Such representational and processual quasi-entities can then be used to construct narratives of growth, survival and disappearance at a large spatial and temporal scale. The critical reflexive step is to refrain from granting such quasi-entities direct causal power. Growth, competition and disappearance must also be explained by reference to specific events, local conditions and ordinary practices. This manoeuvre, which has been successfully adopted by a number of practice-oriented scholars (see, e.g. Warde, 2005; Shove *et al.*, 2012; Shove and Spurling, 2013), lends itself to studying the relative success of practices in terms of competition for practitioners (their time and attention) and other resources 'consumed' by the practice. We can thus explain why showering seems to have won the competition with bathing, at least in most Western countries, by focussing on how an incremental change of techniques, know-how and ways of understanding bodily cleanliness came together to create 'a space for showering to challenge the previously dominant way of doing bodily cleansing (that is bathing)' (Southerton, Warde and Hand, 2004: 42). By focussing on the particular connections between the 'infrastructural, technological, rhetorical, and moral positioning of showering vis-à-vis bathing' (Hand, Shove and Southerton, 2005: 15), the approach provides an alternative, practice-based explanation of the process of 'diffusion' and how local innovations turn into large-scale phenomena. It also leaves plenty of room for, and in fact invites us to take into account, individual calculation (costs), social mechanism (imitation and fashions) and affective as well as preconscious elements (for example, the subsconscious interpellation of cleanliness associated with late modernity, see Leader, 2002). By the same token, the approach also allows us to reason in terms of alliances, mutual support between practices and their components and even competitive appropriation.

For example, the rapid success of car mobility can be explained by the fact that cars first shared and then appropriated (or 'stole') skills, material forms and even spaces that belonged to competing systems of mobility: horse carts, cycles and in certain case buses and train (Urry, 2004; Shove *et al.*, 2012). Finally, and most important, the approach can be offered to practitioners who can use it to question regimes, ask how they were established, what different arrangements are possible and what it would take to transition to them. All this is at a level of detail that is compatible with practitioners' daily experience and that they can therefore grasp.

In summary, by partially 'entifying' practices themselves and becoming reflexive scalographers, practice-oriented scholars open the possibility of studying practices in ways that are precluded by the other two approaches. We can thus learn interesting things by counting the frequency and variation of practices in time and across locales and studying them historically – something that other approaches struggle to do. This approach has the benefit of making room for contradictions, conflicts and tensions in the study of practices, all elements that tend to disappear when large phenomena are built from the bottom up as in the strategies described in the two previous sections (see Kwa, 2002, for a discussion). It, however, is not without its own risks. One of the main challenges facing this third strategy is to maintain a consistently reflexive attitude towards what is only ever temporary 'entification'. It is easy to slip between the step of constructing practices as analytical objects to reifying them as a 'thing with boundaries'. Questions about 'what is practice?' and 'what are its limits?' soon emerge, mostly because we are so bad at dealing with performances. The solution is to move quickly into Mrs and Mr Bourdieu's dining room and ask: 'in which building did it happen?' and 'who did it?' In short, it is important not to get lost in this complex game of foregrounding and backgrounding and to remember that it is a game of our own making.

Concluding remarks

Let's return to the initial issue of how a practice-based sensitivity can be used to address big issues and 'large-scale phenomena'. The above discussion suggests that the question admits multiple related answers, even among practice-oriented scholars who subscribe to a relational and flat ontology (Emirbayer, 1997). Taken together, these answers, which very often can be used in combination, suggest that adopting a practice-based orientation offers some specific affordances vis-à-vis competing or cognate orientations.

First, practice-based approaches join forces with other relational sociologies and invite us to rethink certain entrenched distinctions starting with the idea that micro and macro-phenomena can be cleanly distinguished. Big issues exist, of course, but big issues do not necessarily concern large-scale phenomena and not all large-scale phenomena are big issues. Large-scale phenomena do not necessarily happen in places that are different from where 'small' ones occur. Presence and distance are not opposed and are only occasionally concerned with space and time. Large-scale and global phenomena are not always things that can be seen from space.

Second, practice-based approaches suggest that large phenomena are made and that differences in scale are produced in practice and through practices. They also invite us to manipulate, play and experiment with different methods of scale-making. The advantage of practice approaches vis-à-vis other theoretical sensitivities stems from their capacity to use more than one scale at the same time and to move skilfully between them. The challenge is how to conceive, talk and investigate large phenomena without letting old views return by the backdoor. The actors we encounter in our explorations also use abstract/vague entities such as 'culture' or 'the spirit of the times' to account for concrete activities. We therefore need to be vigilant and to refrain from colluding with them in believing that these abstractions are anything other than convenient summaries. This does not mean that 'these abstractions and summaries do not *do* anything', as suggested by Collins (1981: 989). Abstractions such as 'energy consumption' and 'leadership' in fact do a lot of work, for example, in parliament, in the stock market and in workplaces all over. Moreover, their capacity to produce effects is related to their assumed correspondence to what they summarise. Our job is not to denounce them as false idols, but rather to ask through what practices and technologies of representation were they produced, in which observable scenes of actions were these summaries created and, most important, what effects do they produce when deployed in practice?

Finally, practice-based approaches allow us to abandon the idea that producing big abstract theories is the only way to study large-scale phenomena. On the contrary, much is to be gained from resisting the temptation to study types of large phenomena as such.[2] Accordingly, the objects of inquiry for practice-based approaches are not the financial market or schooling in the abstract, but rather the market of reinsurance at the turn of the millennium or the school system in Alaska or in Australia. As soon as we set out to study 'the market' or 'institutions' or 'the state' in abstract theoretical terms (even if we use the word practice a thousand times), we abandon a practice-oriented project and start doing something else. In the words of Collins: 'sociological concepts can be made fully empirical only by grounding them in a sample of the typical micro-events that make them up' (1981: 988).

There are many good reasons for following this advice, but at least two in particular are worth mentioning here. First, there is increasing evidence that the idea that good social science is a science of abstract entities and systems is simply a symptom of what in jest we could call 'economics envy' or 'Parson's disease'. As Heuts and Mol nicely put it, 'crafting a rich theoretical repertoire… does not work by laying out solid abstracting generalisations, but rather by adding together ever shifting cases and learning from their specificities' (Heuts and Mol, 2013: 127).

Second, the type of representations produced by practice-based approaches are what practitioners often ask for. While practitioners at times make use of abstract concepts in making sense of problematic situations and charting new and unknown territories, they are always thirsty for descriptions of their daily practical concerns. This is because practitioners learn from others through hints, tips and examples; practitioners are always on the lookout for ideas and nuggets of wisdom that they can steal. Practice theory thus allows us to produce representations that practitioners can then use to talk about their own practice – and thereby to do something about it.

Notes

1 I think of social practices in terms of orderly regimes of mediated material and discursive activities that are aimed at identifiable objects and have a history, a constituency and a normative and affective dimension. For reasons of space, I will not discuss or defend this stipulation in the present text. Readers are referred to other texts where I do so (Nicolini, 2012; Nicolini and Monteiro, 2016).

2 I am in debt to Pedro Monteiro for this observation.

8

PRACTICES AND THEIR AFFECTS

Andreas Reckwitz
(Translated by Steven Black)

Theories of practice claim to be able to find new ways of seeing society and human behaviour. The intense international interest in practice theoretical approaches in sociology in the last ten years (see, among others, Schatzki *et al.*, 2001; Schmidt, 2012; Nicolini, 2012) comes out of a widespread dissatisfaction with the traditional sociological vocabulary, which has proved insufficiently inspirational to current empirical research. This dissatisfaction applies above all to the dualistic distinction between individualist approaches of economic rational choice theory on the one hand, and the holistic approaches on the other, which take their point of departure from norm systems or intersubjective communication processes. But it applies also to the dualistic distinction between a culturalism that studies discourses and sign systems on the one hand, and a materialism of biological processes on the other (see Reckwitz, 2002b).

The family of practice theories – irrespective of their internal differences – offers an alternative to these dualisms. Its main tenet is to seek the social in practices, in embodied routine activities subtended by implicit, collective knowledge. It is for this reason that practices belong to the realm of the genuinely social, at the same time as they are anchored in the bodies of individuals and act through them. Further, because the *social* practices depend on implicit schemes of knowledge, they are always *cultural* practices. And because they are anchored in bodies and in artefacts connected with bodies in specific ways, they are also always *material* practices. The social world consists then of more or less repetitive performances of doings and the widespread complexes which theses practices form.

This is of course a very general definition. In recent years, a good deal of conceptual and terminological work has been done on the development of a more systematic theoretical framework. In particular, the work of Theodore Schatzki (1996; 2002; 2010b) is of note here. However, there is still an amount of untapped heuristic potential in practice theories. It should, however, be pointed out that the purpose of this work is not to develop a new theoretical system called 'practice theory' simply for its own sake, as a rival to the systems of Parsons or Luhmann for instance. Instead, the aim is to obtain a heuristic aid and stimulus to empirical research capable of rendering visible phenomena and contexts that were previously off the radar. At this point, I want to address a special question of fundamental importance in current social theory. It concerns the status of emotions, feelings and affects in social theory and in sociological analysis. The new millennium has seen a special interest in the emotions and affects among social and cultural theorists. This has moved some to speak of an emotional or affective 'turn' (see, among others, Greco and Stenner, 2008; Harding and Pribram, 2009). I see this interest in the context of a broader movement within the theory of the last 15 years toward the inclusion of previously neglected categories as important ingredients of the social world. An analogous case is the social significance of space and spatiality (see Löw, 2001), of artefacts and things (see Latour, 1991a), of bodies and the corporeal (Shilling, 2003) and, finally, the rediscovery of the senses and sense perception (Böhme, 2001), all of which have been announced from different quarters.[1]

These calls for a general shift of perspective may seem at first glance unrelated to one another. However, they share a common tendency to refocus elements of the social in such a way as to align the cultural *and* the material, the symbolic *and* the objective (or the living) on the same level of sight. It is no wonder that all these attempts to bring about a turn (see also Bachmann-Medick, 2006) have come *after* the heyday of radical culturalism in the social sciences and the humanities, in structuralism and semiotics and to a certain extent in radical constructivism. Radical culturalism insisted rightly that the meanings of spaces, things, bodies, perceptions and affects are culturally determined, it regarded them consequently as cultural representations, and subjected them to corresponding sociological, anthropological, historical and literary analysis. But for the proponents of the new turns this does not go far enough. Instead of a one-sided emphasis on the cultural character of these elements of social life, they are concerned with them as both cultural *and* material entities.

Social space, for example, consists of the organisation of interrelated bodies and artefacts, interpreted by both participants and observers (see, e.g. Löw, 2001, and earlier, Lefebvre, 1991): it is both material *and* cultural. The same can be argued for sense perceptions, for things and for the corporeal. The new tendencies seem at first concerned to reinsert the material into the social, but on second sight, they turn out to be breaking down the whole cultural/material dualism. The demand for an affective turn must be taken this way. After all, affects are both cultural *and* material. As states of bodily excitation, they are persistent realities of their own right and yet their origins, effects and social intelligibility depend on cultural and historical schemata. This double character of affects is decisive for their place in the social and is therefore central to their analysis by the social sciences.

It is therefore evident that practice theory and affect analysis not only can, but must, be set in relation to each other. If the affective turn is about overcoming the culture/material dualism in the understanding of feelings and if practice theory seeks to overcome this dualism in general, then a specifically practice theoretical approach to affects seems promising. With few exceptions (see Burkitt, 1999, and also Harding and Pribram, 2009: 1–23), however, this has not yet been forthcoming. Classic theorists of practice such as Bourdieu, Giddens and de Certeau are largely silent on affects. The reason seems to be that the first generation of practice theorists in the 1970s and 1980s (who incidentally did not use this label) were chiefly occupied with following Wittgenstein in overcoming the individualism/holism dualism. The second dualism, the material/cultural binary, first emerged into the foreground as a candidate for overcoming around the year 2000, partly as a result of the Latour effect, but also due to the various turns mentioned above (this tendency is evident in the thematic shift between Theodore Schatzki's main works *Social practices* (1996) and *The site of the social* (2002)). Attacking this dualism first becomes relevant for the second generation of practice theorists. This does not constitute another turn in social theory, but rather the assimilation of a large part of the other turns propagated in the last years (spatial turn, pictorial turn, body or corporeal turn) into the kind of broader reconfiguration of social theory beyond the confines of the material/cultural dualism, a dualism which is ripe for overcoming.

What would a genuine praxeological account of affects look like? My basic claim is that it is not enough just to take affects 'into account' in social theory; the crucial insight is rather that *every* social order as a set of practices *is* a specific order of affects. If we want to understand how practices work, we have to understand their specific affects, the affects which are built into the practices. There can consequently be no social order without affects, but there can be vastly different types and intensities of affects within practices. What does this mean exactly? In order to answer this question, I will first briefly address the reasons why classical social theory has tended to overlook the constitutive social significance of emotions and affects. After that, I will outline the relationship between affects and practices and finally I will focus on the issue of how artefacts can act as 'affect generators' within practices.

The affects as blind spot

What prevented social theory so long from recognising the fundamental social importance of emotional and affective phenomena?[2] Since the 1980s, the exponents of the so-called affective or emotional turn (Clough and Halley, 2007) in the social sciences and humanities have been convinced of the need to alter fundamentally our understanding of the social. Of course, all this talk of turns is a means of dramatising and simplifying the situation. There does not exist some coherent block of traditional social theory that needs to be overcome, but rather a heterogeneous conglomerate of texts dating from around 1900 that later became the object of a specific style of interpretation in mainstream sociology. It is obvious that the work of certain authors from that period, such as Gabriel Tarde with his sociology of imitation (Borch and Stäheli, 2009), or Sigmund Freud and psychoanalysis (Elliott, 1992), demonstrated recognition of the fundamental social importance of affects. The dominant reception of Weber and Durkheim through Parsons and the theory of modernisation and on through to such diverse authors as Niklas Luhmann, Jürgen Habermas, Michel Foucault and Pierre Bourdieu is, however, characterised by a systematic neglect of affectivity. Two interconnected causes can be assigned to this tendency. One reason is the widespread assumption in sociology of the identity of the social with normative orders or orders of knowledge, resulting in an understanding of affects as non-social, non-cultural phenomena occurring within individual's bodies or individual's psyche. A further reason is that modernity used to be equated to formal rationality overcoming affects.

The first reason for the anti-affective attitude of large segments of classical and contemporary social theory seems to be the identification of the social with the intersubjective force of normative rules. Since the late nineteenth century, social theory has been dominated by dualisms opposing the social to the individual and to the natural or biological (Lukes, 1973). This pair of dichotomies usually occurs in combination with a third, even more abstract dualism between the rational and the irrational. Admittedly, the social sciences have not entirely overlooked emotional, affective phenomena. But they have located them on the second, inferior pole of these pairs of opposites. Emotions were regarded as properties of the individual and thus excluded from sociological generalisation or seen as natural, biological dispositions and drives belonging to the pre-social body. In both cases they are placed beyond the rational, regular and predictable social order.

There have always existed opposing tendencies, of course, the late works of Émile Durkheim, rediscovered in the last few decades, being the prime example. In *The elementary forms of religious life* from 1912, Durkheim (1912) discovers that in religious communities, emotional ties do not subsist outside of the social but rather exercise a stabilising, integrating force within it. Durkheim is nevertheless doubtful that these emotional aspects of social relations can be reproduced in modern societies (Shilling, 2002).

Strangely enough, the comprehensive paradigmatic shift in the social sciences since the 1970s, the variously titled 'cultural', 'interpretive' or 'textual' turn, has not overturned the anti-affective attitude. Structuralism, poststructuralism and social constructivism have transformed our understanding of the social by substituting semiotic and discursive structures and regimes of knowledge in the place of prominence previously occupied by normative orders. The paradigm of the social is no longer religion or law, but rather language: society must be understood in analogy to language. Affects, as states of bodily excitation, then seem to stand outside of the linguistically constituted social. Emotions appear for this reason only on the margins of classical works of cultural theory like Foucault or Bourdieu. If emotions are noticed at all in such culturalist approaches, then as objects of specific discourses, as phenomena of lingual construction. This reduction of emotions to discourse, such as was promoted by social constructivism in the 1980s (Harré, 1986), made the social, cultural representation of emotions accessible to analysis by social science, but remains imprisoned in the cultural/material binary.

The second reason why social theories have so long marginalised affects and emotions is to be found in the dominant sociological understanding of modernity.

Such disparate authors as Marx, Weber, Adorno, Parsons, Foucault and Bourdieu share the common conviction, whether affirmatively or critically, that modern society is most fundamentally characterised by formal rationality. The rationalisation of action and the social spheres is seen as increasingly displacing all affective aspects of action. The affects seem more to belong to premodern or traditional societies, which are then classified as natural rather than social. In this way, the dualism between modern and traditional societies underlies a distinction between different stages of social evolution in terms of the absence or intensity of affects. Norbert Elias's (1976) major theory that the process of civilisation toward modern society is equivalent to the increase of affect control would seem paradigmatic of this type of interpretation.

The traditional social theory thus adopts the premise that modern society is characterised by what in Parson's theory of modernisation is termed 'affect neutrality', implying that in the differentiated spheres of action in modernity, emotions are largely neutralised. Many authors, from Weber to Habermas, view this alleged affect neutrality in modern society as essentially positive. The suppression of dangerous emotions looks progressive when seen from the perspective of the rationalist opposition of enlightened understanding to mere feeling (a binary that nineteenth century theories of gendered character index onto the two sexes). The reverse image of this suspicion of emotions is their latent or manifest celebration, such as held sway at the interwar Collège de Sociologie, which attacked modernity for its claim to suppress emotions, hoping in Rousseauian manner for a return of individual and collective feelings, whether sensuous, physical or what not.

In summary, the strict dualism between the social and the biological or individual, in conjunction with the theory that modernity is distinguished by affect neutrality, whether benign or problematic, is the reason for the exclusion of affects and emotions from social theory. The affective is confined to the individual, the biological or corporeal or banished to premodern societies. It has all the trappings of the outside, constituting the inside of affectively neutral society.

Practice theory of affects

A practice theory perspective on affects is concerned neither to denigrate nor to celebrate the affects. The presence of affects in a society cannot be simply ignored. Whether they are menacing or benign they are a constitutive part of the social life which incessantly produces them. The diagnosis of modernity as affect neutral is therefore false. The affects may be shaped *differently* in some modern institutions but they do not vanish altogether. Practice theory avoids the cultural/material binary by approaching every social order, conceived as an arrangement of practices, as its own affective order; every social practice is then affectively *tuned* in a particular way and has, as such, a built-in affective dimension (see also Seyfert, 2011).

What then is the particularity of a practice theory perspective on affects? I would suggest three underlying principles of such a perspective: (1) affects are not subjective, but social; (2) affects are not properties, but activities; (3) affects are states of physical arousal, of pleasure or displeasure, directed at some definite person, object or idea.

The practice theory approach brings about a fundamental change of perspective on affectivity. It approaches affects not – as the terms emotion or feeling have traditionally suggested – as interior properties of individuals only accessible to an introspection plumbing the depths of the psyche, but places them instead on the level of social practices themselves. Affects are then properties of the specific affective 'attunement' or mood of the respective practice.[3] As soon as a person is competent to perform a practice and is 'carried away' by it, she incorporates and actualises its mood. This state of affairs is ordinarily obscured by an individualist bias in ordinary language. When, for example, an early twenty-first century person falls in love, it only seems to be an individual feeling (or even a basic anthropological constant). In fact, the feeling is embedded and informed by the bundle of practices called love that developed around the late eighteenth century in Western culture. 'Love' is a set of routine behaviours dependent on specific cultural patterns (the uniqueness of the beloved, fascination for their otherwise mundane seeming qualities) and containing a peculiar set of affects: physical desire, longing in the absence of the beloved, the existential pain of love unrequited or lost. These routine behaviours are clearly closely tied to discursive practices and fields, such as romantic novels and films in which the codes and affects of love are publicly represented for imitation.

It is apparent here how the affective practice of falling in love is both cultural and material at once. It is cultural in that it depends on the specific cultural, historical and local knowledge schemata referred to above and with which participants in the practice think, feel and remember in a certain way. The affect *must* be cultural since it is oriented on specific entities in the world, which first become desirable or repellent within the framework of certain systems of interpretation. The practice is at the same time material to the extent that the affects inherent to it are real states of physical excitement, manifesting in measurable physical reactions or at least in the subjective fact of physical feelings which can only be ignored with the greatest effort. Falling in love involves such physical facts, the cultural origins of which are no longer visible to the lover. The affective structure of a practice thus explodes the inside/outside binary (see Burkitt, 1999), by being internal and external at the same time. It consists in external, public, intelligible signs of emotion and internal, subjective states of physical excitement.[4]

The bundle of practices called love is manifestly affective. However, on closer inspection, all social practices turn out to be affectively attuned in one way or another, including the allegedly neutral ones. Academic practices in the modern fields of the natural sciences or humanities turn out to involve attitudes of curiosity and attentiveness to the nature of things. Affects enter into economic practices in the modern market economy, associated with success or victory in competition or the joy of creative work. The question is *why* this affectivity not only occurs in special cases of social practices but is a general phenomenon. Two main structural properties of practices can be said to require the presence of affects: motivation for the practice and the focussing of attention.

Social practices 'interpellate' the subject in a certain way. But how *can* the subject be interpellated in this way and thus participate in the practice?[5] The answer is that the practice must entail a specific motivation to perform it. From this perspective, it is not the individual who comes to the practice with their own 'psychological' motivation, but rather the practice itself of which the motivation is already an integral part. Motivation is where affects come into play; there must be some affective incentive to participate in the practice. This can be a positive desire, a defensive incentive to avoid displeasure or a combination of the two. Intrinsically creative work in late modernity operates characteristically on the basis of a built-in motivation for creative enjoyment, whereas a serf's labours will tend to be motivated by the threat of corporal punishment for disobedience. Generally, I would state that motivation without a process of being affected by something is not thinkable. However, we must leave aside the problematic 'individualist' connotation of the term motivation in favour of the praxeological idea of motivations 'embedded into' social practices themselves. Of course, this does not exclude the possibility that under certain circumstances individuals do not fully participate in the practice as they lack being successfully 'interpellated' into the underlying motivation structure. The possible failure to participate in a practice thus is not only a question of lacking corresponding skills and interpretations, but also of lacking corresponding desires and fascinations.

Just as every practice must have its particular built-in motivation structure, so too must the directedness of sense perception be organised in a specific way. The fundamentally volatile human sensory attention is guided by a practice toward phenomena relevant to the practice and deflected from irrelevant ones, which then drop out of the radar altogether. Of course, bundles of practices have diverse possibilities of how to direct attention. Above all, material artefacts are such means of influencing attention. A specific architecture and interior design, for instance, subtly directs the attention structure of the subjects in certain ways. Media technology succeeds in doing this in different ways. There might also exist explicit norms of attention, for instance at work or in school classes. However, in our context it is crucial that perceptual attention is laden with affects (see Ciompi, 1997) so that the affectiveness built in practices succeeds in directing attention in a profound way. In academic practices, for instance, it can be the curiosity or interest for certain themes that guides attention; in body practices, it can be the sense of shame at one's own impurity. Any perception involving strong positive or negative affects will enter the focus of sensuous attention, while entities with weaker or neutral affective significance will remain beneath perceptual attention, like white noise.

Clearly then, a practice theory cannot conceive the affects as qualities or properties, but must regard them as dynamic *processes* and *relations*. Within a practice, people can be affected in specific ways by other people, by things and ideas. Affectivity is therefore always a relation between different entities. For this precise reason, I prefer the term affect to that of emotion. The term affect may have the disadvantageous connotations of some spontaneous pre-cultural force. Yet the term emotion seems more problematic still, suggestive as it is of something a person 'has'. The concept of the affect, with its verb form 'to affect', is more fully the description of processes, of *affecting* and being *affected* (see Ott, 2010, and in the background Deleuze and Guattari, 1987). As such, the question must always be: who is affected by whom or what? From the point of view of the human subject, it can be said that the affectivity of a practice comprises specific stimulations attached to other people, things or ideas. These latter are interpreted within the practice in some typical way and so can become triggers for feelings of pleasure or displeasure. An affect is therefore always directed at something of significance, always intentional in the phenomenological sense, in that it involves the interpretation of some entity as desirable, revolting, etc. In contrast, the same entities trigger entirely different states in people within other practices or leave them indifferent. A basic capacity for reactions of desire and aversion, pleasure and displeasure, would seem to enter the human body at the point of birth. But the direction this desire or aversion tends, the objects it is formed by, is a question of the social practices. Luc Ciompi (1997) suggests we should assume the existence of five basic feelings – joy, interest, fear, rage or sadness – which list I would take on board rather as a heuristic catalogue than as a fundamental anthropological constant.

In the new debate, especially authors working in a Deleuzian framework such as Brian Massumi (2002) have preferred the term affect over emotion, because it denotes a disruptive force that breaks through cultured routines. Where does this disruptive element fit into the analysis being proposed here? At this point, we must back up a bit. Practice theory indeed presupposes that practices constitute social orders and as such are undergirded by a structure of social reproduction and repetition. Yet at the same time, practices also always harbour the potential for novelty, surprise and experiment, which can modify or transform the practice from within. Therefore, on the account I am proposing here, affects are *not per se* anarchic and disruptive, but rather among the main ingredients in culturally standardised, routine bundles of practices. However, there is always the chance that new and different acts of affecting will emerge from within social practices and explode their normality. These non-routine affective events are indeed no rarity, although it is in every case questionable whether they will constitute their own regular practice or disappear again. Such a non-routine affective event can occur on the individual level – some idiosyncrasy, viewed in some cases as pathological, a unique phobia or fetish – or on the level of collective spontaneous excitement, be it a state of pleasure, panic or other.

A practice theory perspective on affects is thus able to assign the affect discourses their proper place. The 'thematisation' or 'problematisation' of feelings has been itself a theme of intense discussion in cultural theory since the 1970s, which tended to regard feelings as 'culturally constructed'. As elaborated above, this kind of culturalist theoretical reductionism inevitably falls short of the mark by tending to confuse feelings with the semantics of feeling and so neglecting the physical facts of affects. The practice theoretical perspective in no way excludes such a discourse analysis of emotions and affects, but rather preserves them within the more comprehensive framework of a concept of practice-discourse formations. If we want to trace the ramifications of affects as formed in specific discourses at specific times, then we cannot view them in isolation, but must analyse the connections between discursive and non-discursive practices. Especially in modernity, affects are often not implicitly and traditionally present in social practices, but rather amplified, weakened or even brought into existence by being treated as a theme or problem on the level of discourse. These discursive practices always already exist in interconnection with non-discursive practices, oscillating between the discursive and the non-discursive, becoming physically internalised and causing real effects in the body.

Any theory of social practices would end up in a cul-de-sac were it strictly to oppose practice and discourse, doings and sayings, as though they were two separate orders of things. If practices are grasped instead as a meshwork of doings and sayings, then discursive formations are just social practices, neither more nor less; they are practices of representation in which objects in the world are represented, imagined and evaluated, with the aid of media technologies. However, depending on the context, these practices of representation are linked to other practices, into which their contents are 'translated' (Latour). For example, the discourse of psychology is translated into a therapeutic practice. The exact form of translation between discursive and non-discursive practices is then a question of empirical research. One of the best examples for the relevance of affect discourses in the context of a practice-discourse formation is the previously mentioned modern discourse of love at work in higher literature and film, as well as in popular and academic, psychological literature, and coupled with practices of dating and mating, sexuality and partnership.

Now, the affective orientations instituted by social practices and practice-discourse formations can invest meaning in different 'affective objects' that can be roughly divided into three classes: persons, things and ideas. Where sociology has dealt empirically with emotions (see, e.g. the interactive sociology of Erving Goffman (1971) or Arlie Hochschild (1983)), it has concentrated on inter-subjective emotions, on emotions directed at other people, such as envy, affection or hate. Affects directed at other human beings, be they present or absent, are characteristic of many social practices. The affect can be directed at whole groups, be they, once again present or imagined, at a labour force, a crowd in a football stadium, an ethnic group. Beside humans, affective inclinations can also be attached to pure ideas, to transcendent entities, such as in religious practices or abstract entities, such as with an aversion toward 'the system' or trust in 'the market'.

Above all, however, the relations between people and inanimate things have an enormous and generally underestimated significance for social practice and its affects (see Knorr Cetina, 2001). The artefacts involved in a practice are often not at all affect-neutral but rather intensely charged with negative, or, in modernity more often, positive qualities. The care in engaging with tools, the glamorous fascination of a piece of clothing, the fear or enthusiasm at finding oneself in a metropolis, are all examples of this. An appropriate framework for analysing affects therefore needs to keep this interobjective dimension in view in order to compensate for the predominance of the intersubjective in sociology. Within the sphere of artefacts two special constellations can be highlighted which, particularly in modernity, operate as prominent generators of affect: atmospheres of place and reflexive, symbolic or imaginary artefacts.

Artefacts as generator of affect

In principle, every artefact can be used within a practice as the bearer of positive or negative affects. The earliest such practices involve the use of weapons by hunters and gatherers, the use of agricultural tools by farmers after the Neolithic revolution and artisanal tool use. In abstract terms, we can speak of a 'tool paradigm' in relation to artefacts, present even in Bruno Latour's actor network theory examples of door openers and safety belts, where things are being used to some practical, rational end and are at the same time bound up with affects.

In addition to this tool paradigm, a different affect-structure in dealing with things grows up in the course of the development of culture and especially in modernity. Within this structure, things become primary affect generators within heterogeneous, often aesthetic, practices (see Reckwitz, forthcoming). In this con-stellation, things are produced or used expressly for their function as affect generators. We can speak here of a 'cult paradigm' of things. As in an archaic cult, the priority is not so much the practical use of things, but rather their ability to fasci-nate or repel (see, in a similar vein, Böhme, 2006). In modernity, but also in early civilisations, two types of artefacts function as affect generators: spatial atmospheres and symbolic or imaginary artefacts.

In the case of spatial atmospheres, the individual things are less important as isolated entities, but their location in three-dimensional space, their interrelations, the way they constitute an environment. This space is then not so much 'used', but rather entered into by people and experienced. Naturally, spaces like apartments and offices are made for specific purposes, but their holistic, three-dimensional character endows them with a special capacity to produce what Gernot Böhme (2000) has referred to, following the phenomenologist Hermann Schmitz (1998), as 'atmospheres'. People are affected by atmospheres arising from the sets of rela-tions of artefacts, as well as from other people, groups or practices. The experience of atmosphere is of course itself a practice requiring training in cultural codes and their corresponding sensuous receptivity. Artefacts can only become generators of affects within the framework of practices.

One privileged place for making atmospheres and the production and reception of associated affects in social practices within modernity is architecture, understood as built space in the broadest sense, encompassing not only the exterior architecture of buildings, but also interior design, traffic infrastructure, modified natural environ-ments and open spaces (see Delitz, 2009). Architecture draws the function of arte-facts as affect generators into the foreground. Architecture produces atmospheres by inducing affects like awe, admiration, a feeling of rest or stimulation. This can be said of cathedrals and palaces, gardens, shopping arcades, creative offices, fun parks, private houses, museums, public squares and libraries. If modern society, especially late-modern society, turns out actually not to be the affect-neutral, rational society it thought it was, but rather on the contrary a place of massive affects (see also Thrift, 2007), then the work of designing and generating atmosphere, especially in built space, is of key importance to understanding what modernity is really like. This encompasses a class of practices that can be called 'reflexively affective', meaning a practice involving artefacts produced primarily for affective uses. These reception practices are therefore bound up with corresponding production practices in which artefacts, in this case spaces, are designed for the purpose of producing specific affects in people.

The second class of reflexively affective artefacts that appears to bear a large responsibility for the affective concentration of modern society are semiotic-imaginary artefacts. Of course, even a simple artefact under the tool-paradigm is evidently a bearer of signs and potentially of imaginings capable of producing affects. But the semiotic-imaginary artefacts in the narrower sense are things produced primarily with the intention of transporting signs and imaginations calculated to affect people. In modernity, this means primarily written texts, images, and series of acoustic signals, especially music or combinations of all three. In addition, body accessories such as fashion clothing can assume the character of semiotic-imaginary artefacts.

Naturally, what applies to architecture applies here also: texts, images and series of acoustic signals can perform a primarily instrumental function, for example as vehicles of information. But for the understanding of modernity it is of central importance that these artefacts have been and continue to be employed regularly as affect generators in large scale practice bundles. Texts, for example, are written to generate certain affects in readers. This applies equally to literature (see Koschorke, 2003), political texts, in part to philosophical and to scientific texts (whether serious or popular) that aim to arouse feelings of identification or to change peoples' lives. It is even more palpably the case for images – whether paintings, photographs or film (see Prinz, 2013; also Hall, 1997; Crary, 2002) – producing affects of fascination for certain forms of subjectivity or compassion for discriminated social groups or providing training in a practice of feeling, such as love. Finally, musical sound sequences are genuine affective artefacts, since here the information function is minimal and the main purpose is the production of moods in the listener. In the case also of semiotic, imaginary artefacts, reception and production practices are interrelated. The production practices are aimed at making texts, images and acoustic signals in such a way that they can affect people, while the purpose of the reception practices is to be affected.

At this juncture, an interesting distinction emerges between affective practice-discourse formations and symbolic-imaginary affect generators. As symbolic-imaginary affect generators, entities like images, texts, music or fashion are embedded in non-discursive practices in the context of which they generate affects. These affect generators in images or texts can at the same time be integrated in discursive contexts, in which affects are frequently represented in different ways according to specific formation rules. Put simply, an image functions as an artefact generator when it functions affectively within a practice. On the contrary, as part of an image discourse it primarily represents affects. The film *Gone with the wind* is a massive affect generator, while at the same time participating in a complex sentimental Hollywood image discourse.[6]

The special importance I am here attributing to both spatial atmospheres in architecture and semiotic-imaginary artefacts for the analysis of the affective character of practices is therefore backed up by both on the level of a theory of the social and a theory of modernity. From a sociological viewpoint, practices in general and their affective dimension in particular can only be usefully analysed if they are understood as *practices with things*. From a theory of modernity viewpoint, the affective structure of those bundles of practices which constitute modern society, and in particular late modern society, are only graspable when we recognise the special status of architectural atmospheres and semiotic-imaginary artefacts and take adequate care to analysis the practice of these artefacts' reception and production. A practice theoretical affect cartography of modernity will have to concern itself, not exclusively but extensively, with these two bundles. To do this, traditional sociology will have to leave behind the 'anti-aesthetic and anti-technical hang' that has been attributed to it by Wolfgang Essbach (2001).

Notes

1   On this state of affairs in current theory generally, see Reckwitz (2013).
2   This section is based on passages from Reckwitz (2012).
3   The use of these terms can be read in the context of Heidegger's *Being and time* (1986, division 1, chap. 5).
4   Love is therefore more than just a form of communication, as Niklas Luhmann (1994) would have it, although it is also this. In system theory terms, love is a coupling of social, psychic and organic systems. This makes manifest the significance affects have independently of affect discourses.
5   For a somewhat different articulation of this, see Butler (1997).
6   Discourses on practices need not be themselves affect generators. Psychological texts, for example, deal with affects in an extremely influential way without needing to affect the reader.

9

SAYINGS, TEXTS AND DISCURSIVE FORMATIONS

Theodore Schatzki

Practice theories have brought much attention to the organised action nexuses where social life plays out. They have said relatively little, however, about language as an element of these nexuses. Pierre Bourdieu (1991) connected language to symbolic power, Andreas Reckwitz (2006, 2008) conceptualises the social as a network of practice-discourse complexes and William Hanks (1996) incorporates close attention to unfolding practice into a general account of language in human life. This is insufficient attention, however, for a phenomenon that some theorists have treated as constituting or instituting an abstract structure that pervades human existence – and that on any account is central to social life. The current chapter aims to work toward rectifying this deficit. Its central question is: What might practice theory say about sayings, texts and discourses? How can these phenomena be brought into accounts of a practice theoretical persuasion and be made part of their social analyses?

An immense literature discusses language, sayings and discourses and it is not possible presently to examine any appreciable part of it. I will, instead, take up the work of three so-called 'discourse analysts': Norman Fairclough, James Gee and Ronald Scollon. Ideas of Bakhtin and Foucault will also be considered. I focus on the accounts of these three theorists because these accounts broach issues that practice theories address and generally converge with practice theoretical approaches. Davide Nicolini (2012: 189) writes that these theorists' insights 'are directly applicable, or at least highly relevant, to the understanding of social practice'. I would say, more specifically, that ideas of theirs are highly relevant to grasping the *discursive* component of social practices. The pertinence of their ideas partly reflects the fact that they treat discourses, not as abstract structures as many structuralists and poststructuralists have done, but as something to do with utterances (see Reckwitz, 2008: 192–3, on this contrast). This pertinence also results from the fact that each of them works with a conception of social practices and accords practices general ontological significance.

This chapter begins by exploring congruencies between discourse analytic ideas and practice theories. Following this, the second section analyses sayings and texts as elements of practices on the basis of my own account of the latter. A third section outlines how sayings and texts form a kind of infrastructure that links practice-arrangement bundles. And a fourth, concluding section takes up the issue of whether large discursive formations exist in the plenum of practices.

The basic ontologies of three discourse analyses

The three versions of discourse analysis considered in this chapter approach language from what surrounds it. Instead of focusing on the properties of language as such (e.g. grammar, syntax), they treat language as an element of sayings and texts, which are embedded in social life. They theorise language as a social phenomenon and examine grammar and syntax only in so far as the latter either engage with fundamentals of social existence (as in Halliday's 1994 systematic functional linguistics) or reflect or implicate social phenomena.

As indicated, moreover, these three versions of discourse analysis highlight activity and set aside construals of language and discourse as abstract structures. These features reflect the ideas of two philosophers, John Austin and Ludwig Wittgenstein. Consider what is perhaps the most prominent definition of discourse: language-in-use. Because 'use' refers to activities, this definition treats discourse as an element or feature of activity. This way of thinking reflects Austin's contention that speaking is acting. Another widely cited notion of discourse is Gee's concept of Discourse:

> I use the term 'Discourse' … for different ways in which we humans integrate language with nonlanguage [sic] 'stuff,' such as different ways of thinking, acting, interacting, valuing, feeling, believing, and using symbols, tools, and objects in the right places at the right times so as to enact and recognize different identities, give the material world certain meanings, distribute social goods in a certain way, make certain sorts of meaningful connections in experience …
>
> *(1999: 13)*

This definition reflects an intuition that lies behind Wittgenstein's coinage of the term 'language game'. Wittgenstein (2009: §23) wrote: 'The word "language-*game*" is used here to emphasise the fact that the *speaking* of language is part of an activity, or of a form of life'. This quote claims that speaking, which is an activity, is part of broader activities. As suggested by the expression 'form of life', these broader activities encompass both further acts of speaking and non-linguistic doings (doings that do not use words, phrases, or sentences). Wittgenstein's intuition, in other words, is that linguistic activity is interwoven with non-linguistic activity in human life. This is exactly the thought expressed in the quote from Gee.

Discourse theorists advance different conceptions of the interwovenness of linguistic activity with other activity. Since each of the three theorists considered here works with a notion of practices, these different conceptions can be described as alternative understandings of the relation of language or discourse to practices.

Scollon nearly submerges discourse in practices. His starting point is the idea of mediated action (e.g. Wertsch, 1998). According to this idea, human activity is always mediated by (meaningful) entities distinct from the actor. Material objects figure prominently among such mediators, as does language: when a person speaks or writes, language mediates her activity, that is, it is a means whereby her action is accomplished. For Scollon, moreover, a practice is a repeated action: the practice of x exists when actions of x-ing have been sufficiently repeated to be recognisable as x-ings. The crystallisation of repeated x-ings as the practice of x also coordinates with the development of knowing how to x in the bodies of those who x (Bourdieu's habitus). In addition, actions, in the locales in which they are performed, for instance classrooms, stores, kitchens and airport terminals, are usually performed as part of combinations or sequences of actions. When each of the (types of) actions involved is a practice, the resulting bundlings of practices in locales are called nexuses of practice.

Gee, meanwhile, holds that discourse is language-in-use or strings of spoken or written sentences. As indicated, he adds to these the idea of Discourse, which denotes ways of combining language with non-language stuff. The notion of Discourse is particularly important for the project of analysing language as a social phenomenon, for according to Gee, society is composed basically of Discourses (2014: 128). Identifying a Discourse, however, reveals little about the particular configuration of language and non-language stuff that it embraces. The notion of practice performs some of this work. A practice, or game (as Gee Wittgensteinianly prefers), is a 'socially recognized [sic] and institutionally or culturally supported endeavour that usually involves sequencing or combining actions in certain specific ways' (Gee, 2014: 32). Examples are mentoring a student, lecturing before a class and playing Yu-Gi-Oh. Like non-discursive actions, discourses as strings of sentences or as language-in-use are components of practices. Practices, in turn, are concrete forms of Discourse.

Fairclough propagates related views. He distinguishes discourse and practice in the singular from discourses and practices in the plural. His conception of these phenomena, however, shifts. Sometimes, for instance, 'practices' refers to types and tokens of action (e.g. Fairclough, 2015: 61). At other times the plural form is not used and 'practice' more or less means situated action. In this usage, the expressions 'discursive practice' and 'social practice' mean speaking and writing as situated, respectively, in processes of text production, distribution and consumption and in social institutions and organisations (Fairclough, 1992: 66–73). At still other times (e.g. Chouliaraki and Fairclough, 1999), practices are analysed as entities that combine (1) material activity (i.e. non-discursive doings), (2) discourse (i.e. semiotic entities such as language and images as used in activity), (3) social relations and processes and (4) mental phenomena. This third view offers a rich conception of practices that treats discourse as part of practices. As I discuss below, Chouliaraki and Fairclough annex this account of discourse to Bourdieu's theory of field and habitus and hold (1999, 104–5) that it provides the account of this phenomenon missing and needed in Bourdieu.

Like practice theorists, the three discourse analysts under discussion disagree about whether the distinction between discursive and non-discursive action is fundamental (cf. Giddens, 1984: xxii). Scollon joins Giddens, Gherardi and Shove, Pantzar and Watson in upholding what might be called a 'monolithic' theory that portrays all activity as of one basic sort (e.g. mediated action in Scollon). By contrast, Gee and Chouliaraki and Fairclough join Reckwitz, Taylor, Bourdieu and myself in treating the discursive/non-discursive distinction as fundamental and in construing practices as composed of actions of both sorts.[1] In my opinion, the difference between discursive and non-discursive actions is fundamental to conceptualising practices and social life. Acknowledging it upholds the importance of language and facilitates a more nuanced understanding of what action accomplishes, for example, the varied differences and contributions that doings and sayings make to social existence. Consider, for instance, Gee's idea that when people speak or write they at the same time 'build seven things or seven areas of "reality"' (2014: 32). These areas are significance, practices, identities, relationships, politics (the distribution of social goods), connections (between things/topics) and sign systems and knowledge. Non-linguistic doings contribute to these building tasks, too, although they do so in different ways and to different degrees than sayings do. Making the discursive/non-discursive difference fundamental facilitates explorations of convergences, divergences and entanglements in these contributions.

However, the conceptions of practices promulgated by practice-minded discourse theorists lack a key element: organisation. Practices are *organised* sets of doings and sayings. The only organisations that Scollon and Gee recognise are sequences, combinations, repetitions and co-occurring repetitions of action. These phenomena are patterns and, thus, organisations only of the weakest, empiricist sort. What Scollon and Gee neglect is the organisation of what *informs* action, in particular, the organisation of what informs the actions that compose practices.

What organises practices in this way informs *both* the saying and the doings that compose given practices. This insight is fundamental to a proper understanding of practices. I noted that Chouliaraki and Fairclough distinguish discursive from non-discursive activities. They hold, further, that discourses are organised by what, following Foucault (see section below), they call 'orders of discourse'. Orders of discourse are socially ordered images, types of language and non-verbal forms of communication that structure particular social practices or fields (in Bourdieu's sense of field; Chouliaraki and Fairclough, 1999: 106, see also 50–1, 56). Orders of discourse, however, structure only the discursive dimension of practices and fields. They do not also structure the 'material activities', which according to Chouliaraki and Fairclough also compose practices: 'an order of discourse is a socially structured articulation of discursive practices which constitutes the discursive facet of the social order of a social field' (1999: 114). Thus, although orders of discourse organise practices, they do not inform both the sayings and the doings that compose practices. Below I return to orders of discourse and to the idea that the discursive component of practices has a distinct organisation. At this point I want to focus on the organisation that is common to doings and saying.

Elements of a practice theory of discourse

Elsewhere (1996, 2002) I have argued that the organisations common to doings and sayings are made up of rules, teleological-affective structures and both practical and general understandings. Practice organisations are teleological, normative and affectual structures, in the context, and out of a knowledge, of which humans who are brought up to act for ends, to heed normativity and to be affected emotionally proceed in their lives. The organisation of a practice also determines which doings and sayings belong to it. To say that practice organisations pertain to sayings as much as to doings implies, among other things, that sayings are intentional, oriented to ends, parts of tasks and projects and variously emotional, that they are carried out in light of rules and that they, to varying degrees, articulate general understandings. People do not just do, but also say, things when carrying on a given practice by way of pursuing ends, carrying out tasks or sets thereof and being imbued by particular emotions and general understandings. As people proceed through different spheres of life – work, family, religion, recreation, provision, etc. – they carry out practices through both sayings and doings.

Reckwitz's account of practice-discourse complexes contains an alternative conception of the common organisation of doings and sayings. Reckwitz construes practices (2002b: 249–50) as routinised types of behaviour (persisting blocks of bodily activity, mentality, background knowledge, emotion, motivation and things and their use). He treats discourses (2006: 43), moreover, as practices of the production of regulated representations, or practices of representation for short. By 'representations', he means textual and visual presentations (*Darstellungen*) of objects, subjects and contexts (which constitute these as meaningful entities in the first place). Practices of representation include those of speaking, writing, science, painting, filmmaking, sculpture, and the like. Note that this list can be usefully expanded to include practices (in Reckwitz's sense) in which representations are consumed, thus such practices as those of listening, reading, looking at and watching. Reckwitz claims that what holds practices and discourses together in complexes are orders of knowledge. These orders are composed of forms of implicit knowledge such as 'know-how, interpretive knowledge of routinised attributions of sense, and complexes of culturally modelled affects and motivations' (Reckwitz, 2008: 202). Such orders imbue practices and discourses, giving them their form. Discourses, in turn, produce knowledge orders and make them explicit (Reckwitz, 2008: 205). Knowledge orders, finally, are organised by cultural codes. These codes are networks of meaning patterns (*Sinnmuster*), 'systems of central differences and classifications' (Reckwitz, 2006: 44), for use in describing the world and dealing with it. These differences and classifications inform know-how, interpretation and forms of motivation.

Practice theories connect what people say (and do) to the organisation of social practices. Practices, in turn, fill out the social context in which people proceed. Like, therefore, the three discourse analyses considered in the previous section, practice theories approach language as a social phenomenon. Their general account also bears some resemblance to M. M. Bakhtin's (1986: 60, 78) theses that people always speak in specific speech genres and that such genres are determined by the different functional spheres of activity and communication in society, for example, science, the technical, commentary, business and everyday life. Each of these spheres, Bakhtin claimed, develops its own types of utterance, which are constituted by typical speech situations, typical themes, typical expressivities and typical addressees. These typicalities reflect the conditions and goals of the spheres in which the genres they help compose develop. Relatedly, a speaker's choice of utterance type reflects not just thematic considerations and the concrete speech situation, but also the nature of the activity-communication sphere in which s/he speaks. Note that speech genres, like Fairclough's orders of discourse, concern discursive activity alone. Oriented primarily toward discourse, both theorists overlook the common organisation of sayings and doings.

To illustrate what it is to analyse sayings by reference to organisations that are common to doings and sayings, consider Hanks's notion of the participatory frameworks that belong to communication practices (practices such as conversations in which sayings take the lead). His notion is based on Erving Goffman's (1981) idea of a speaker's footing. A speaker's footing is her relationship to her own words. Direct, indirect and quoted speech exemplify different possibilities. Goffman proposed that the status of speaker be replaced by a triumvirate of roles: the animator (the person who makes the sounds), the author (the person who selects the words and phrasings) and the principal (the person who is responsible for the statements and opinions expressed). This proposal underlies Hanks's idea (1996: 207) that communicative practices carry participant frameworks that are composed of communication roles open to those who speak or are the addressees of speech. According to my account, these communication roles, like roles more generally (see Schatzki, 2002), are reference points for the apportionment of a practice's organisation: which tasks, projects and ends, for example, are acceptable for or enjoined of a participant in, say, educational practices depends on the role(s) she occupies in them. In, for instance, the linked practices carried on by the animator of a speech act (e.g. Mr Grey, a teacher), the author of that act (e.g. Ms Wiggins, a bureaucrat in the superintendent's office) and its principal (e.g. Dr Lee, the superintendent), the tasks, projects and ends that normatively fall to Mr Grey as animator differ from those that normatively fall to Ms Wiggins and Dr Lee as author and principal, respectively. Such role-based apportionment can also affect which non-linguistic doings people carry out: different non-linguistic doings are acceptable for or enjoined of the person (animator) who speaks at a parent teacher association meeting and the person (author) who earlier typed the text on a computer. Finally, the apportionment of acceptable and enjoined tasks, projects and ends among people who occupy particular communication roles can be inflected by the wider roles that these individuals assume in the practices involved. For example, the doings that are acceptable for or enjoined of animators will vary partly depending on whether the animator is a school child quoting a friend, a teacher announcing a central school office policy or a drama coach acting in a play.

Any position that grants equal footing to sayings and doings is obliged to examine sayings as such. I will not say much on this topic. Sayings are a kind of activity. They are activities in which something is said. The idea, however, of saying something is ambiguous. What a person says in saying something is, first, the words, sentences and strings of words and sentences she utters. These words and sentences, as vocables, are texts. They are texts, of course, that usually perish in the event. What a person says in saying something is, second, what she says. If someone says, 'the sky is blue' or 'bring me an apple', what she says in this second sense is that the sky is blue and to bring her an apple. Saying something in this sense is sometimes construed as assuming a relationship (e.g. asserting, wanting) to a propositional content. When what someone says in the second sense is so understood, sayings can be described as representings – as Reckwitz suggests in construing (linguistic) discourses as 'sign-using practices viewed from the point of view of their production of representations' (2008: 203). Talk of representations (or of propositions) as opposed to representings raises a host of issues debated by philosophers for decades. This is not the place to take them up.

Sayings as a general category of doing have been well analysed in speech act theory (Austin, 1975; Searle, 1969, 1985). As especially Searle's version demonstrates, to treat sayings as doings is to subsume one's account of speech into one's account of action. For instance, since practice theory ties actions to practices and practice organisations, in treating sayings as activities, it holds that they are elements of practices subject to practice organisations. In this context, it is crucial to emphasise Wittgenstein's insight (2009: §23), affirmed in speech act theory, that sayings can be actions of countless sorts, for example, asserting, denying, explaining, asking, complaining, describing, insulting, bothering, ordering, remonstrating, begging, celebrating and so forth. Emphasising multiplicity makes clear that what people are typically about in speaking is, not speaking as such, but performing an action to which the use of language is useful or crucial.

Under 'sayings' I include acts of writing. Writing is a very different activity than speaking, but they share several key features. One is the use of language. A second is the saying of things. Reckwitz would add, controversially, that they both produce representations. What both incontrovertibly engender are texts, that is, collections of meaningful words and sentences, although these texts are usually evanescent in the one case and more durable in the other.

Sayings as activities qua token speech acts must be distinguished from what Bakhtin called 'utterances', types of which he called 'speech genres'. Utterances are not like particular acts of asserting, asking or ordering that a person can perform without ado by vocalising some words. For Bakhtin (1986: 71) held that the boundaries of an utterance are given by a change in speaking subjects, and this claim implies that an utterance can encompass a series of actions, all performed by the same person. From my point of view, Bakhtin's utterances can be conceptualised as tasks, which can be elements of teleoaffective structures and which people pursue by carrying out one or more actions, primarily sayings but also possibly non-discursive doings.

To conclude this sketch of elements of a practice theoretical account of sayings and texts, I point out that some phenomena that transpire within practices, or rather within bundles (see below), are best approached through bodies of investigation and theory that are different from practice theory but compatible with its ontology. A phenomenon transpires 'within' a bundle when it is essentially composed of or dependent on components of the linked practices and arrangements that compose a bundle. When either situation obtains, the bundle forms a constitutive context in which the phenomenon transpires, although what this more specifically involves can vary. Examples of phenomena that transpire within bundles in this sense are interactions; the dissemination of knowledge; power and domination; experience, including aesthetic experience; and the constant adjustments that actors make to the world. I mention all this because another example is understanding and interpreting texts and doings/sayings. Understanding is present within bundles both as action and as condition, and to theorise it, practice theory might be advised to draw on analyses of a philosophical sort. A further example is conversation, which is a type of interaction that transpires within practices. To theorise it, practice theorists might draw on the established body of work called 'conversational analysis' (see Nicolini, 2012). A final example is texts, which can circulate within and among practices. A sort of approach that practice theory might appropriate in analysing texts is text analysis: the analysis of their vocabulary, grammar, cohesion and structure (see Fairclough, 1992: 75ff).

Sayings and texts as connecting-and-threading-infrastructure

Practices – organised manifolds of doings and saying – connect to material arrangements – composed of bodies, artefacts, living creatures and things of nature – to form practice-arrangement bundles (e.g. Schatzki, 2002). Such bundles, in turn, connect to other bundles to form wider constellations of practices and arrangements. Social life transpires within these bundles and constellations; all social phenomena consist of sectors, slices or aspects of bundles and constellations. Bundles and constellations, moreover, assume diverse shapes and sizes. When, for example, bundles connect, the resulting constellations are typically larger (in the sense of spatial extension) than the original bundles; repeated connections that are not matched by significant decouplings result in very large constellations such as those in which governments or economic systems consist. Interconnected constellations, finally, blanket the globe and extend under the earth and into space. Taken together, bundles and constellations form one gigantic nexus of practices and arrangements, what I dub the 'plenum of practice' (Schatzki; 2016d).

I wrote in the first section that some discourse analysts neglect the organisation of practices. They also do not analyse this wider plenum. For instance, Gee, in addition to writing that society is composed of Discourses, claims that interactions among Discourses determine both the workings of society and much of history

(2014: 128). This is not, however, an idea he develops. Similarly, Scollon envisions practices forming nexuses (networks of repeatedly linked practices), imagines a form of analysis – nexus analysis – that would systematically and ethnographically study intersecting cycles of discourse (e.g. Scollon and Scollon 2004: 29; see Nicolini's chapter in the present volume), and analyses communities of practice as objectified nexuses, that is, as nexuses of practice that participants treat in discourse as bounded communities (2001: 155–6, 170). Like Gee, however, Scollon does not develop these ideas further, although some of his remarks suggest that he is not so much disinterested in social ontology as an advocate of a Garfinkelian view of the local occasionality of the social. Chouliaraki and Fairclough (1999), by contrast, are very concerned to connect discourses and practices to major issues in social theory. As suggested, moreover, they appropriate Bourdieu's notion of a field and, like him, construe fields as the principal container of practices. This is not, however, a matter they elucidate.

These observations are not criticisms. Discourse analysis is interested in discourse, not in social ontology, and it is not obliged to fill out the ontologies that it affirms or toward which its concepts point. At the same time, issues exist about the role of sayings, texts and discourses in the plenum of practices. One such issue is how sayings, texts and discourses contribute to the construction of the plenum, that is, to linkages among bundles and constellations.

Elsewhere I have written that practices and arrangements are linked by relations such as causality (e.g. activities effecting and responding to objects and arrangements), constitution (activities and objects/arrangements being essential for each other), intentionality (e.g. the directedness of activities and mental conditions toward objects and arrangements), intelligibility (practices making the entities that compose arrangements meaningful) and prefiguration (the bearing of arrangements on future courses of action). The resulting bundles, too, are related to one another in various ways, including via common actions, common organisational elements or common material entities; chains of action; common motivating events; participants in one bundle being intentionally directed to other bundles; overlapping, orchestrated or mutually referring places and paths; orchestrations of (i.e. mutual dependencies among) actions, material entities and organisational elements of different types in different practice-arrangement bundles; and physical connections and causality. It is out of relations such as these that practices link with arrangements and bundles form constellations.

Language, sayings and texts play a myriad of roles in these relations. Space considerations require that my discussion of these be schematic. Sayings can motivate people to intervene in or to respond to the world and also, as events, cause events that befall material arrangements; elements of practice organisation, like people's directedness toward entities, are articulated, that is, given (explicit) content in the terms of language; sayings and texts contribute to what makes sense to people to do and the intelligibility of things in the world; sayings and texts can indicate events and matters, to which people in different practices and bundles react; sayings and texts in one bundle can be about other bundles, the components of other bundles, or events occurring in them; and sayings can be links in chains of action as well as contribute to orchestration. Clearly, language, sayings and texts greatly contribute to the relations by virtue of which the plenum of practices is a mass of interconnected practices and arrangements. Collectively, they are a key component and means of connections among bundles.

Sayings and texts contribute to this interconnectedness in other ways. Texts, for instance, travel among bundles, among other things, disseminating ideas, topics, motivations, self-understandings and focuses of attention, establishing intentional directness among bundles and leading to individual or joint actions. An example is what Reckwitz (2006: 67) calls 'interdiscourses'. Interdiscourses are discourses, carrying descriptive-normative representations of subjects, that cross different social fields and diverse practices, thereby establishing representations of subjects as unified wholes. Closely related to the circulation of texts is what Fairclough calls 'intertextual chains', which are 'series of types of texts which are transformationally related to each other in the sense that each member of the series is transformed into one or more of the others in regular and predictable ways' (1992: 130). An example is a speech becoming a press release becoming both a webpage and an item on the evening news and in these forms peregrinating among bundles. Just like texts, sayings, too, both the activity and what is said, can give people ideas, shape their motivations, direct them to particular events and phenomena, lead them to respond and contribute to what actions they subsequently perform, individually, connectedly or collectively. In these ways, sayings contribute to the evolution of practices and bundles and, more broadly, to the course of history, in predominantly minuscule and occasionally large ways.

Sayings are also links, or parts of links, in what Bakhtin called 'chains of utterances'. Bakhtin (1986: 91) pointed out that utterances are full of echoes and reverberations of prior utterances. People quote others, appropriate words or phrases that they have heard or read, absorb ideas expressed in others' words and are motivated or oriented by what others have said. What's more, their utterances, explicitly or sotto voce, refute, affirm, supplement, rely on, presuppose and take what others say into account. Utterances also anticipate possible responses and, of course, become part of the stock of utterances to which subsequent utterances 'respond' in the ways just mentioned. By virtue of all this, utterances form chains, each link in which responds to previous links. These chains circle within bundles and constellations and pass through and between different bundles and constellations, thereby connecting them into larger bundles and constellations.

Finally, types of sayings such as explaining or describing peregrinate through the practice plenum, appearing in large numbers of practices and bundles and thereby forming a commonality among them. Reckwitz (2006: 66) develops this idea by noting complex dispersed practices that show up in various domains of modern life, that is, as parts of different constellations in the overall modern plenum. An example he mentions is the practice of experimentation, which marks postmodern culture in different domains of contemporary Western life.

Practices, bundles and constellations are replete with sayings and texts. These sayings and texts link up with other elements of bundles and constellations, connect bundles and constellations while also threading through them and make a considerable difference to the evolution of the latter. They are also thoroughly imbricated with the non-linguistic doings that are just as widely distributed through bundles and constellations. This distribution of sayings and texts gives concrete sense to the idea that discourse pervades the plenum of practice. Discourses as language-in-use and as strings of words and sentences are everywhere: connected, connecting, spreading, moving through and always making a difference.

An additional form of language-mediated connectivity in the practice plenum is captured in Kristeva's (1986) concept of intertextuality (foreshadowed by Bakhtin's notion of utterance chains). Intertextuality comprises the ways texts – written and spoken – are content-fully interconnected through links and explicit as well as implicit cross-references among their concepts, themes, topics, statements, stances, claims and orientations toward subject matters (see, e.g. Fairclough, 1992: chap. 3). As a significative net through which texts in different bundles connect, it links bundles and is an important dimension of the plenum of practices.

Large discursive phenomena

This section makes a start on investigating whether the practice plenum exhibits large discursive or linguistic phenomena. Given the variety of such phenomena that theorists have ascribed to social life, my discussion can only broach the topic. I just affirmed the existence of one sort of large discursive phenomenon: the intertextuality that pervades the practice plenum. The present section will consider two other putative sorts.

The first is Foucault's notion of discourse, which exemplifies the idea of constellations made up of sayings alone (see also Lyotard, 1988). Before turning to genealogy, Foucault (e.g. 1976) theorised discourses as discursive practices – arrays of statement-making sayings (Dreyfus and Rabinow, 1982: 44–8) – that are organised by multiple sets of rules pertaining to the objects, concepts, theories and discursive infrastructures (e.g. presuppositions) that characterise or are bound up with these arrays. The discourses that Foucault was particularly interested in were those of the human sciences (e.g. linguistics, natural history, demography, medicine, psychology). Discourses, accordingly, are different ways of structuring areas of knowledge (cf. Fairclough, 1992: 3).

Foucault's discourses illustrate what William James (1979) called 'vicious abstractionism'. Discourses are specious substantialising abstractions (extractions) from the plenum of practices. The statement-making sayings that compose Foucault's discourses always happen amid doings and material set-ups (offices, libraries, laboratories) that help compose bundles of which the sayings are likewise part. On a practice theoretical approach to sayings, it is crucial that the sayings involved be resolutely treated as components of these bundles and that these bundles be taken as the entities in which social phenomena consist. Foucault, by contrast, took these sayings, together with what is said in them, as composing distinct entities, which can be analysed and explained. He did not deny that sayings occur amid doings and material set-ups but failed to treat sayings essentially as parts of entities (practices) that also comprise the latter. Of course, it is true, as the notion of intertextuality indicates, that sayings are significatively connected to one another. They are significatively connected, however, *as* activities that are components of practices. It is not surprising that Foucault's analyses of discourses gave way to analyses of apparatuses (dispositifs; cf. 1980) in his subsequent genealogical studies. A discourse is composed of statement-making sayings alone, whereas an apparatus embraces sayings, non-discursive behaviours, and architectures.

A better way of construing discourses is exemplified in Hajer's (1995) notion of a discourse coalition, which is a group of individuals and organisations who work under the aegis of a particular set of ways of talking and thinking. The environmental discourse coalition, for example, coalesces around such concepts as sustainability, clean energy, saving the Earth, conservation and concern for the future, which it uses in particular ways in speech and writing. The discourse involved can thus be understood as a set of concepts together with their spoken and written (and thought) use in certain constellations of practices and arrangements.

This notion of discourse is unproblematic. It treats discourses such as environmental discourse as patterns in the use of particular concepts in certain interconnected bundles of practices and arrangements, for example, those of environmental activism, academic research, media reporting and politics. There is no attempt to isolate these concepts and uses from the acts and bundles concerned and to treat them as distinct discourse formations.

The second putative sort of large discursive phenomenon to be examined in this section is Fairclough's orders of discourse. Like intertextuality, discourse orders exemplify the idea of abstract discursivity.[2] As discussed, orders of discourse are composed of images, types of language and forms of non-verbal communication that are associated with particular social fields. (An earlier (1992: 124–30) version of the notion held that orders of discourse embrace genres, activity types, styles and discourses.) Such orders constitute potentials that acts of speaking and writing etc. can draw on. They are abstract structures because, as wholes, they are never encountered in experience, although elements of them are encountered when used in acts of communication. According to Chouliaraki and Fairclough, orders of discourse 'order' and 'regulate' communicative acts and interactions (principally, speaking and writing) in two ways: they structure, that is, enable and constrain these acts and interactions (1999: e.g. 63) and use of their elements is a means through which relations of power as forms of control are realised (1999: e.g. 144–5). I will set power and control aside because an adequate discussion of them is too ramified for the present context.

Chouliaraki and Fairclough claim that orders of discourse are associated with fields à la Bourdieu. As features of large phenomena of this alleged type, orders of discourse themselves qualify as a kind of large discursive formation. On my account, accordingly, they are features of constellations of practices and arrangements. To simplify matters, I will henceforth bracket images and non-verbal forms of communication and focus on types of language alone.

Types of language encompass various elements, which for simplicity's sake I will summarise as words, ways of using words and ways of constructing discourses qua strings of words and sentences. Examples of types of language are eyewitness accounts, storytelling and literary narrative (1999: 56–7). Types of language – that is, combinations of words, ways of using words and ways of constructing discourses – presumably enable communication in providing both the terms and the techniques for putting together spoken and written texts. I doubt, however, that specific sets of language types, as opposed to language types at large, enable acts of speaking and writing in particular bundles and constellations (e.g. those of education), including any that constitute fields (e.g. the educational field). In the first place, types of language are mobile and circulate among bundles and constellations, both through lines of communication and by virtue of people participating in different bundles. This especially holds of language types that employ non-technical words, but it also holds of some types that utilise technical ones (e.g. 'vocational learning', 'active learning techniques'). The elements of types, moreover, can circulate within and among bundles independently of types. Non-technical words, for instance, are remarkably mobile, as are some technical ones (e.g. 'inflation' and 'neurotic'). In addition, both within and across bundles, words, ways of using them and ways of constructing discourses can (re)combine and form a multitude of types. And the distribution of, especially, natural language types and their elements is contingent and often haphazard; sayings anytime can, and occasionally do, import types or elements thereof into bundles or constellations where they have not hitherto appeared. Consequently, it is not distinct sets of language types that enable speaking, writing and communicative interaction in particular constellations such as those of education. Rather, language types *in general* achieve this.[3] Finally, it is true that bundles and constellations sometimes exhibit 'typical' language types (cf. Bakhtin's speech genres). Typicalities, however, enable nothing: they are simply patterns in language use laid down in past usage.

Now, nothing can be spoken or written that is not spoken or written in words, in a certain way, and as part of some discourse. When, consequently, a person speaks or writes, s/he must employ some type of language, either an existing one or a revised (or even new) one for whose development the existing spectrum of types was the starting point. Either way, she is constrained by the current spectrum. Again, however, the mobility of words (especially those of natural language) and of ways of using words or constructing discourses suggests that language types in general, and not distinct collections thereof, constrain speaking and writing in particular bundles and constellations. Likewise again, the repetition (typicality) of certain language types in particular bundles and constellations constrains nothing, in this case not just because typicalities are just patterns, but also because some sayings in many, if not most, bundles and constellations fail to use typical words or to exemplify typical ways of using words or constructing discourses – simply too many things go on in any bundle. This is even true in highly regulated environments such as missile control rooms and courts of law. In sum, specific sets of language types do not order particular constellations – e.g. fields, if they exist – by enabling and constraining acts of communication in them.

Another, possibly more promising way of construing how collections of language types (along with images and non-verbal forms of communication) order and regulate bundles is to ascribe them normative force. Normativity is a contested notion, but under one interpretation for types of language to carry normative force is for combinations of words, ways of using them, and ways of constructing discourses to be acceptable for or enjoined (prescribed, required, expected) of people. On this interpretation, such combinations enjoy this status by virtue of people knowing about them, unreflectively using or exemplifying them and sanctioning activity that conforms or fails to conform. This is how teleoaffective structures possess normative force on my account. I do not know whether Fairclough accepts that discourse orders regulate bundles normatively or, if he does, whether he affirms that their normative regulation can be construed thus (see, however, Fairclough, 2015: 68). Regardless, when normativity is so understood, some bundles and constellations *are* governed by distinctive sets of (normative) language types. It is true that the mobility of language types as well as the mobility and re-combinability of their elements, together with the fact that most of what people say is acceptable in the bundles in which they say it, indicate (1) that broad ranges of language types are acceptable in most bundles (this has only become truer in the modern world) and (2) that an indefinitely large common range of types is acceptable in the bundles and constellations where a given dialect of some natural language predominates. At the same time, bundles and constellations vary in the language types acceptable or enjoined in them in so far as, for example, they utilise technical vocabulary or slang (as in professional or subcultural bundles), embrace official procedures (as in governmental or religious bundles), exhibit command structures (as in military bundles) or are associated with particular localisable ethnic groups (cf. Gumperz's 1982 communication styles). These bundles are all contexts in which peer pressure, control by rule or command or the situations in which people act require the use of particular types. Thus, although the bundles in which a given dialect of some natural language holds sway more or less share an indefinitely large set of normative discourse orders, some of these bundles possess additional orders of technical, slang, official, ritual or ethnic discourse alongside this large set. These latter bundles – but these alone – carry distinct semantic spaces (Taylor, 1985a) that are tied, *inter alia*, to the languages used in them. Note, however, that these additional distinct orders that govern certain less extensive constellations do not thoroughly regulate speaking and writing in them. This contrasts with the indefinitely complex orders of natural language that comprehensively, although weakly, regulate speaking and writing in bundles dominated by particular dialects of natural language.

In sum, language types and discourse orders, like sayings and texts, travel and are distributed throughout bundles and constellations. This holds of many technical or specialised types and orders, too. Types and orders also (1) govern the linguistic articulation of the intelligibility of human activity and the world in which it proceeds and (2) make intertextuality possible. Meaning, however, suffuses bundles. Although sayings and texts are weakly regulated semantically wherever a given natural language dialect dominates, only in certain bundles and constellations are sayings and texts semantically regulated – sometimes strongly, but always incompletely – by distinct language types and discourse orders. So distinct orders do exist in the practice plenum but lack the comprehensive structuring significance that Chouliaraki and Fairclough attribute to them. Grammar and syntax are different matters.

To conclude, discursivity pervades the plenum of practices in two ways. First, sayings and texts, and thus language and concepts, exist throughout and constantly circulate through the plenum. They thereby connect and thread through bundles and constellations. Certain bundles and constellations are also incompletely ordered normatively by distinct sets of language types and discourse orders. Second, sayings and texts give human life linguistic conceptual content. Through such content, sayings and texts are intertextually linked and the practice plenum is suffused by articulated significance. Language is an immensely important and in some sense omnipresent part of social existence. Its structuring significance for social life lies partly in contributing to the hanging together of bundles and constellations and partly in providing an articulatory and intertextual potential for social life generally and overall.[4]

Notes

1 Note also that Scollon and Gee, on the one hand, and Fairclough, on the other, take up opposed positions on the further issue of whether practices are regularities or manifolds.

2 Abstract discursivities can take many possible forms, including Saussure's (1966) systems of differences, the textuality that Derrida (1976) claimed pervades being and human being-in-the-world and the rule systems that some social theorists (e.g. Parsons, 1968) have attributed to sectors of human life (where rules are unformulated contentful instructions or directions). Some discussion of Derrida can be found in Schatzki (2002). This book also extensively engages Laclau and Mouffe's (1985) notion of discourses as totalities of systematically and inter-relatedly meaningful actions, words and things. Note that textuality à la Derrida must be distinguished from the unformulated understandings that Taylor (1985b) believes pervade large domains of practice: these understandings are not discursive in nature. An idea closely related to Taylor's is discussed in the essay by Welch and Warde in this volume. For criticism of rules as unformulated contents see Schatzki (1997).

3 Chouliaraki and Fairclough recognise the mutability and mobility of language types and their elements, but they do not see that these features undermine the idea that such types enable and constrain communication.

4 I would like to thank the contributors to this volume for comments and suggestions on an earlier draft of this chapter at the workshop in Lancaster in October 2015. For incisive remarks I am particularly indebted to the commentators on my chapter, Davide Nicolini and Alan Warde. Nicolini also provided detailed written comments, which proved very useful when revising.

10

REFLEXIVE KNOWLEDGE IN PRACTICES

Robert Schmidt

Practice theory has until now stood out primarily through the sensitivity that its analyses show to the material conveyors, carriers and elements of social practices (things, artefacts, technologies, bodies). Social practices might – to put it concisely – be defined as processing activities that are conveyed, situated, materially embedded, distributed and interconnected through cultural knowledge and skilled body movements. Definitions of this sort are closely linked to praxeological critiques of mentalistic and cognitivistic approaches and have led practice theory to neglect mental elements of practices as well as the reflexive or theoretical forms of knowledge that are integrated into practices.[1] Practice theorists, therefore, still need to uncover precisely *how* reflexive, theoretical and analytical activities are enmeshed in and contribute to both practical processes and the dynamics and transformations of practices.

In this chapter, I will pick up the thread of this ambition and begin by proposing a praxeological re-conceptualisation of reflexive, analytical and theoretical activities and elements of practices. In particular, I will suggest that these activities and elements should be conceived of neither as individual and exclusive competences of a subject, nor as unobservable internal events inside the heads of human agents, but instead as observable features of practices (part 1). I shall then develop this perspective and render it plausible using an instructive case study, namely, the new analysis and knowledge practices adopted in professional football (part 2). Drawing on this example, I will close with more general reflections on the observability and publicness of reflexive activities (thinking, analysing, reflecting, etc.) and on the praxeological decentring of the subject (part 3).

Praxeologisation

The majority of the (new) approaches that are currently discussed under the heading of the *practice turn* have evolved in very close connection with empirical research: this is true of ethnomethodology (Garfinkel, 1967), of Goffman's (1967) naturalistic observations and analyses of interactions and not least of Bourdieu's ethnography and his praxeology of Kabyle (1977) and later French society (1984). The practice turn, in other words, is at the same time a turn that develops theories based on empirical research. Notwithstanding this fact, especially in the German debate, practice theory approaches are seen mainly as new developments in theory formation. This trivialises the critical and reflexive arguments that such approaches articulate against the conventional understanding of theory, in particular, against what one might call with Bourdieu (2000) the 'scholastic' understanding of theory.[2]

'Scholastic' theories tend to universalise the social experiences of theoreticians and intellectuals and to impute these experiences to the members and practitioners that they study. This creates a picture (or rather: caricature) of a social world that consists entirely of talking heads without bodies, which are exclusively engaged in mental activities, i.e. in thinking, arguing and communicating with each other. Thus, according to Bourdieu, 'scholastic' understandings of theory are hallmarked by a predisposition to mentalism.

'Scholastic' theories also tend to confuse the theoretical models of reality that they have constructed with the foundations of that reality. This categorical 'scholastic' fallacy is found especially in social theories that are marked by realistic and substantialist understandings of underlying social structures, systems, rules, norms or other analytical concepts. The normativist functionalism of Talcott Parsons may serve as an instructive example here. Parsons substantialises norms and values and depicts them as discrete and independent entities juxtaposed with social action.[3]

By critiquing such 'scholastic' perspectives and confusions, praxeological approaches focus squarely on analysing the relationships between practices of researching and theorising on the one hand, and the practices studied on the other; that is the methodological twist that they give to 'questions of social theory'. Theory is not explained so much by reference to relations between socially situated theoreticians and their objects. Rather, theory is conceptualised as the outcome and product of empirically accessible and more or less self-contained theoretical practices and their relations to the practices they study and theorise, i.e. whose practical logic they at the same time discern and necessarily fall short of. Accordingly, the praxeological programme aims at a specific, reflexive and revised relationship between theory and empirical research (Schmidt, forthcoming a).

Implementation of this programme takes place via a process of praxeologisation – an epistemic and methodological process that can create interesting tensions and interactions between empirical perspectives and theoretical tools of perception (Schmidt, 2016). Praxeologisation involves describing objects, phenomena, processes and connections of interest as effects and consequences of social practices, thereby interpreting them in a new way. This methodological understanding of praxeologisation contrasts praxeology with realist views of social practices. Views that claim that the social is really composed of practices (and not of social actions, social structures, networks of humans and non-humans, etc.) tend to incite unproductive ontological debates. Praxeologisation proposes to replace the definitional, declarative, anthropological, ontological or normative assumptions that are inevitable in such debates with a methodological procedure. This procedure at once sets up a contrast with realism and secures a realness strength of the praxeological constructs (Schmidt, 2016).

The praxeological critique of 'scholastic' and inherently mentalistic approaches has nonetheless also brought about a certain skewedness or one-sidedness in practice theory: for the reverse side of the sensitivity shown by praxeological analyses to the material carriers, conveyors and elements of social practices is a neglect (typical of many empirical studies in practice sociology) of mental features that are bound up with practices. These phenomena include sense-making and reflexive, analytical and theoretical forms of knowledge, which I will elaborate on in more detail below.

Inasmuch as these aspects are explored at all, they are usually treated as irreducible capabilities that reside in a private mental interior of a subject and cause visible external behaviour. This assumption is in tension with praxeological epistemology, since it implies that 'the subject' and its subjectivity (and not practices or the situational interplay of practice components) are sources of reflexivity and sense, creativity and transformation.[4] Praxeologising and empiricising (1) the mental, cognitive and reflexive components of practices, (2) reflexive practices (i.e. theorising, analysing, reflecting, etc.); and (3) theoretical modes of knowledge, amounts to treating them as overtly public and shared activities not unique to an individual subject. A desideratum in praxeology is making both the practical uses of theoretical knowledge and the production of analytical models – i.e. theoretical and analytical practices – the object of empirical-praxeographic research. This perspective aims to clarify *precisely how* reflexive, analytical and theoretical knowledge processes contribute to practices. In what follows, I will explain and develop this perspective using an instructive case: the new analysis and knowledge practices that have been adopted in professional football.[5]

Changing practices in professional football

As comparison of historical and current recordings of televised football matches shows, the cultural practice of football has greatly changed since the 1950s. The game is played more quickly today; players appear much more athletic and the game more intense; and the formations and patterns made by teams on the pitch are fundamentally different.

From a sociological and practice theoretical point of view, these changes derive from innovations in all the core elements of the bundle of practices that is professional football – in other words, changes in materials, in cultural meanings and in forms of knowledge and knowing-how (Shove et al., 2012). New materials (shoes, clothing, lawns, training and playing devices, medical technology, physiologically optimised bodies, but also – as we shall see – GPS-supported tracking systems and thermal imaging cameras, software, etc.) combine with new cultural meanings (such as the currently dominant image of the team as a flexible work group that is adapted to the contingencies of the market place and consists of team players who can be freely substituted) and, not least, with new developments in forms of knowledge and know-how.

The bodily practice of game-playing is at the heart of professional football as well. What 22 players do during a match can hardly be described using conventional sociological conceptions of social action of a methodological individualist sort. Such concepts reduce game-playing to a mere aggregate result of the actions, choices and mentalities of individual players. Playing a match, however, does not involve planned reflexive action or rational choice, but rests on a practical embodied form of knowing-how. The players are not authors of individual moves that they mentally devise in advance.[6] Instead, movements develop out of the continually changing match figuration created by all the players on the pitch.[7] What dominates, in other words, is the physical practice of playing; analytical distance from events and the forms of knowledge and reflexivity associated with this are secondary.

Nevertheless, in the last 30 years, the cultural practice of football has developed a cognitive and epistemic dimension and its own analytical reflexivity: quantification, digital match analysis and associated forms of knowledge have fundamentally changed the practice. These innovations in practice-specific thought and analysis have had an impact not only on how the game is played, but also on how it is understood, interpreted and commented on. These new forms of knowledge have influenced the critical sense-making of coaches, journalists and audiences. They have led to football being examined, discovered and analysed anew.

Strategies and techniques in data generation: scouting, writing and tracking

The production of match analysis data in German professional football has increased rapidly since the 1990s in connection with the increasing importance of sports reporting. This can be seen in longer broadcast times, the development of special-interest programmes on private TV stations and Pay TV and greater coverage of sports in all national newspapers. Match data supplemental to audio-visual and print reporting increases the newsworthiness and accountability of football matches and enhances the marketing opportunities for professional football.

In the 2011–12 season, the German Football League commissioned a private service provider to produce match data for all matches of the first and second Bundesliga leagues.[8]

These data are made available to the clubs. The service provider is also allowed to market the data and sell them to online, TV and print media, as well as to sports betting providers.

Match data are mainly generated by a process known as scouting and writing: several scouts watch a match on television and in the stadium. They are linked by headset to a writer, who codes the match events verbally described by the scouts through mouse clicks or through briefly touching a touch screen containing the most important pre-defined event categories. Collaborative classification and coding thus takes place while the match is played. Because of the time pressure involved, it requires practised, routine understanding and skill, rather than much cognitive weighing up.

This method analyses or translates the match into a sequence of countable events. It sets aside team play and team behaviour and mainly focuses on passes, tackles, shots on goal and dead ball situations, i.e. events that can be assigned to individual players in order to record their performance. This practice of gathering statistics thus yields a specific interpretation of, and distinctive perspective on, the match. What is remarkable here is that many decisive aspects and dimensions of the play *cannot* be captured. For instance, the way in which the defenders' coordinated legwork ensures that the ball *cannot* be passed to the opposing forward necessarily escapes this analytic practice: it cannot register that, owing to careful and anticipatory playing behaviour, something has *not* happened.

Event-orientated coding creates and works with classifications whose relation to the game-as-played is necessarily arbitrary – despite the pre-defined catalogue and despite the training of scouts and writers – because in football, a sport which is comparatively short on cleanly demarcated events, most of the incidents requiring coding are not clearly delimited from each other or classified within the game itself.[9] Rather, they blend into each other in the ongoing process of playing. But although identifying and differentiating meaningful units is a difficult task, it must be carried out in real-time practice.

Club managers and competent fans in particular tend to be critical of the methods used in these scouting and writing processes and in the production of event data. Above all, they critically point to the 'subjectivity' of such processes (meaning their arbitrariness), relying as they do on the football competence of scouts and coders. Within this ethnotheory of subjectivity, tracking processes[10] are considered 'more objective'. These processes are designed to reduce the contribution of human observers (and their 'subjectivity') and rely instead on the technical-visual registering of play and players' movements that turns them into data and quantifies them.

Tracking processes transpose the problem of identifying and interpreting meaningful units from match observation to the processing and analysis of data. These analytic processes, for example, automatically calculate the distances covered by players and their positions and distances from each other and they determine and visualise the top and average speeds of the teams and individual players. These data on movement and positioning must then be interpreted. In spite (or because) of the sometimes elaborate graphics – for instance, the widely used *heat maps*, which show the distribution of a given player's presence on the pitch throughout an entire match – new ways of reading the displays so that they make sense in match and player analysis are constantly being explored and discussed.

At the same time, the search continues for data-mining algorithms that are capable of automatically recognising patterns in the large volumes of data generated by tracking and that are therefore capable of extracting analytically relevant knowledge. The main purpose here is to produce new techniques for long-term monitoring of the athletic and tactical abilities of squads and individual players (Schlipsing, 2014).

Contexts and practices of using match analysis data

While there are, as yet, no empirical observations or studies of precisely how match analysis data are practically generated or of how they figure in analytical, reflexive and knowledge processes,[11] some typical contexts and practices of their use in professional football can be described.

Online, TV and print media are among the most important clients of match analysis data producers, because match data provide a basis for reporting (for instance, in live broadcasts of football matches). However, the typical media use of match data goes far beyond this, for instance, in setting discrete data-related topics and thus increasing the accountability of professional football. An early use of this kind of data led to the controversial headline 'Podolski found guilty of being laziest runner in Bundesliga' (Muras, 2011), a claim which served to draw attention at the start of the 2011–12 season to the work of the match analysis company commissioned by the German Football League. This announcement successfully turned the novel match analysis data into a news item and provoked a public debate. It was repeatedly pointed out that a high total distance covered in one match does not prove anything about the player's quality, since good players run effectively and therefore the shortest distances.[12]

Data-based reporting receives a decidedly critical response from fans and audiences interested in methods of match analysis. Methodological questions concerning the reliability of the measurements or the validity of the measured parameters are debated in public. What does the variable 'overall performance', which is applied to individual players and sometimes also to whole teams, actually mean? How valid is this measurement? Are these and other similar measurements of any relevance to success or to the nature of the game? The media, furthermore, typically use match analyses to construct their own parameters and statistical artefacts. For instance, the special interest channel Eurosports has developed the so-called player performance index (PPI), which statistically measures the part a player takes in his team's success and expresses it as an index number.[13]

An additional context for the use of match analysis data is provided by the producers of football simulation video games and sports betting providers. The performance values of individual players serve as the basis for modelling game avatars in video games that are controlled, substituted, bought and sold by gamers. Analytic processes also become significant in real-time online betting: teams' chances of success can be calculated continuously by referring to match data and the values generated for various success variables (which also include index numbers for bets that have already been placed).

The unpredictability of football play, the very limited calculability of success in sport and the economic risks involved in signing players that are evaluated in terms of these performance ratings, condition the use of analytical processes and player and match data by the clubs' athletic management teams. Managers utilise match and player data – supported by sports science and medical expertise – to monitor their own organisational targets, for instance, checking and evaluating the overall performance of individual players over long periods of time. The corresponding analytical data facilitate decision-making, for example, to minimise risks associated with player transfers.

Sports accounting and match data also enable coaches to verify whether players have followed the tactical instructions they have been given or to corroborate their impression of how individual players or parts of the team have performed. However, clubs also use match analysis data in public relations to 'prove' their representations and readings of the team's success or failure or to defend individual players against public criticism.

(How) do match analyses change the game?

These new forms of analysis, reflection and knowledge contribute in different ways to the bundle of practices that constitute professional football. Their impact on the match and match strategies, on the practice-specific reasoning characteristic of football, on the development of competing expertise and discourses and on links with other practices (of betting, video gaming, etc.) can be determined on various levels and across different time scales.

For instance, when the coaches' bench reacts to the real-time data delivered by the analysis software about distances between players in the backline, ball-passing statistics or the number of tackles won by individual players by changing tactics or by making a substitution, one can say that the match analyses 'join the game' and 'play along' in real time.[14] Other modes of 'contributing' result from the performativity and reactivity of the analytical process that occurs once the match is over.

In his readable book *Die Fußballmatrix*, the German sports journalist Christoph Biermann (2009) attributes all important tactical innovations of the present day – such as ball-orientated defending (dissolution of man-to-man marking), maintaining ball possession ('tiki-taka'), strengthening the centre (two defensive midfielders) and shrinking the play area by moving lines and formations – to such statistical, software-supported analyses of the success rate of certain tactical variants.

This thesis can be corroborated by considering the specific performativity of the analysis and accounting processes. Software-supported analyses of the performances of individual football players and whole teams continuously construct and evaluate characteristics that they seem merely to register and measure. These include not only players' own aptitudes (accuracy of passes, goal-scoring ability, willingness to run, etc.), but also aspects of play that have only come to count as relevant, important and strategically significant by virtue of the existence of software-supported match analysis. Examples are the speed at which players 'switch' from defence to offence after winning the ball and 'domination in midfield'.

In other words, analytical practices do not merely record events on the pitch, they also have a tautological character – as do police crime statistics, for instance. Just as crime statistics never simply record what happened, but rather document organisational behaviour of police departments and reflect the crime-control activities of the police authorities (Meehan, 1986), so match analyses relate, report and respond to how professional football organisations, managers and coaching staff orient themselves toward certain aspects of the game. However, the indicators and parameters involved nonetheless provide a 'real' representation of actual events. The analysis software thus helps to produce new match truths. If, for instance, the assertion that the team's defenders lose more than 70 per cent of all headers is regarded as a revelation of a hidden fact, which lies behind the team's defeat, software-supported analysis will be credited with having compellingly uncovered that *in truth* the defence lost the game.

The best way to think of the 'new truths' or 'realities' of football matches is to think of them as the continuously produced results of a circular process of reflexivity between play and match analysis. The analytical data are, of course, indexical, meaning that they can only be understood in the context of play. For example, the expression 'distance covered in first half: 6.7 km' only makes sense against the background of the actual activities of a player in the match. We understand that she covered this distance while playing. Conversely, however, the analytical data can also be used as a context or 'background' for understanding play. In this case, for instance, a player's visible exhaustion can become a sign (or index) of the distance already covered by her in the game, which has been documented statistically and expressed as a number. Such circular reflexivity (in which the analytical data act both as sign and as context) brings out and secures the intelligibility both of the analytical data and the play. It creates an 'augmented reality' that is hidden from spectators in the stadium (who may detect a player's exhaustion but not know the distance she has covered) and is manifest only in the process of reflexivity between play and analytical data.

The match analyses and data generation I have described, the various uses to which player and match analyses are put and their far-reaching impact, create forms of reflexivity within the practices of professional football. The fact that comparable forms of reflexivity have evolved in many other practice bundles and organisations[15] indicates that activities of reflection, and reflexive knowledge, are specific (and at the same time general) features of practices. I have shown for professional football that these are activities and processes of doing analysis (i.e. classifying, coding, counting, calculating, correlating, visualising, identifying, interpreting, reasoning, etc.) in which different sorts of participants (scouts and writers, match data producers, coaches, managers, advisors, journalists, fans, competent spectators and artefacts like algorithms, monitors, cameras, etc.) are involved. Within the framework of a praxeological epistemology, these social instances of reflection, analysis and feedback can themselves be understood and examined as practices, i.e. as empirically accessible, observable sets of organised *doings and sayings* (Schatzki) that are intertwined with artefacts and technologies. Practices of analysing and reflecting are widely dispersed throughout social life. They contribute – as I have made clear for professional football – in quite different ways to changes in bundles of practices.[16]

With software-supported match and player analyses proliferating in football, new football-specific forms of knowledge and communicative practices that critique these techniques are evolving. The game is examined in new ways and thereby transformed: the new analytical practices become an important element of coaching and athletic performance. They are therewith related to other practices such as those of organising, recruiting, education and training; they initiate changes in the discourses associated with professional football (media, marketing, advertising, etc.); they institute links to new practices and groups (e.g. video gaming and gamer communities); and through their performativity, reactivity and circular reflexivity, they set in motion all sorts of interactions within and between the bundle of practices that constitute football.

Decentring the subject

These considerations have given us an empirical-praxeological understanding of analytic activities and knowledge that distances itself from pervasive mentalistic concepts of reflexivity and the reflecting subject. Reflexivity can be described as practice-specific wholes of public and fundamentally observable practices of analysing, reflecting, theorising, etc. These are practical activities that express mental activities and to whose performers mental activities are ascribed.

We can even go a step further and claim that using mentalist concepts of the subject and ethnotheories of subjectivity in the conceptualisation of reflexive or analytic practices and reflexivity in practices only complicates efforts to grasp social practices and bundles of practices in their procedural logic and transformational dynamics. To clarify this, I would like to outline a few moves that praxeology makes to distance itself from such an understanding of the subject. These moves ultimately enable a transition from a subjectivist to a praxeological epistemology.[17]

According to Elisabeth Anscombe (1975), a student of Wittgenstein's, we must consider 'the subject' (which knows itself as 'I') as an illusion that is deeply rooted in the Indo-Germanic languages. This illusion becomes problematic from an epistemological perspective when, as so often happens, the subject is cited as a *cause* in sociological descriptions of sequences of events or processes (on this point, see also Elias, 1984). Praxeological epistemology emphasises that it is not necessary to posit acting subjects as causes, authors or conceptual points of departure in the attempt to describe and apprehend the meaningfulness, reflexivity and dynamics of change of social practices. This epistemological orientation is the result of various conceptual praxeological moves that remove the subject from the focus of analytical attention. This decentring is needed – so the consensus argues – because when 'the subject' occupies the centre of attention, it blocks analytical access to collective structures of meaning, shared implicit knowledge systems, public patterns of meaning and the logics of implementation of social processes.

From methodological individualism to methodological situationalism

The first distancing move leads from the socio-phenomenological subject and its intentional consciousness to situated participants and thus from the late writings of Alfred Schütz (1973) to Harold Garfinkel (1967) and Erving Goffman (1967). This move is underscored by one of Goffman's most quoted passages. According to him, the real object of situated interactions is 'not the individual and his psychology, but rather the syntactical relations among the acts of different persons mutually present to one another … Not, then, men and their moments. Rather moments and their men' (1967: 2ff).

This methodological-situationalist perspective shifts attention from the acting subject and its situational definitions toward interactional situations and the interplay of actions. For – so the thesis goes – we do not understand social situations (as a distinct area or social reality) and their inner logics and dynamics as long as we think of them from the perspective of the acting subject. Situated sense-making must be conceptualised as situated participants' joint, observable, embodied behaviour of interaction, representation and interpretation. It cannot be treated as internal mental process. Additionally, situated sense-making always draws on collective transsituational knowledge systems, framings and – last but not least – reflexive forms of knowledge in a situated manner. Goffman's analyses of interactions thus focus not only on moments and their men, but also on collective frames of meaning and their situated modulations. In other words, this first distancing move, accentuated by Goffman, replaces the acting subject with 'decentred' situated participants.

From social actions to situated social practices

A second epistemological distancing move takes us from the acting subject and its subjective attributions of meaning and sense to a practical sense or feel for the game, thus from individual social actions to situated social practices. This shift originates in the critical realisation that the conceptual centrality of the acting subject obscures acknowledgement of the independent momentum and ongoing local and translocal accomplishments of social processes. Bourdieu, among others, emphasised this again and again. His concept of *sens pratique* (Bourdieu, 1990) exposes the antagonistic cooperation and interconnection of participants, the mute physical dimensions of social events and their characteristic temporality and the role of shared forms of knowing-how and knowledge.

This is immediately obvious in football: the course of match events goes beyond the individual match actions of individual players. As participants in the match, players continuously enact practical performances of interpretation and comprehension. They are required to make their individual actions legitimate acts of football-playing by reference to the practice's explicit and implicit criteria (committing a foul is playing football too!). This is accomplished through continuous socialisation: the game, or rather the practice, which is always already running, continuously appropriates individual players, continuously teaches them practical know-how and makes them into competent co-players and carriers of the *sens pratique* specific to football (at the same time continuously ejecting other participants).

As the example of football also shows, practices and moves in practices are more than routines or habits. They always display obstinacy, creativity and variability. However, to conceptualise such characteristics of the *sens pratique*, it is neither necessary nor useful to assume an acting subject. For the individual player is no acting subject devising his or her moves in advance. Instead, brilliant passes, surprising dribbles, precise crosses or low-risk square balls emerge from the continuously changing match figuration created by 22 mutually relating players. In sum, the second epistemological distancing move (or decentring) makes the acting subject into a co-player and carrier of collective complexes of knowing-how, comprehension and knowledge. In football, as I have shown, the latter increasingly includes analytical practices and reflexive modes of knowledge generation as well.

From subjective meaning to the public nature of meaning

A third distancing move criticises the fundamental assumption connected with the idea of an acting subject, namely the existence of a subjective private interior, a mental sphere, which is treated as the cause of visible external behaviour. This criticism is, of course, already implied in the first two distancing moves. The decentring of the subject is achieved as a renunciation of mentalism, which describes the social world as a meaningful correlate of the intentions of conscious subjects. Participants in social practices, who have replaced the acting subject via the distancing moves I have outlined, are regarded as carriers of collective patterns of knowledge and meaning. These patterns are not found privately 'in the head' of the acting subject, but always also in things, acting bodies and – as in the case study I have summarised – in artefacts such as catalogues of definitions, algorithms and software programmes. They are publicly mobilised, expressed, observed and interpreted.

Practice theory considers all components of practices to be public. For these components to be public is for them to be accessible to observation and interpretive perception on the part of participants and observers of practices. From this, it follows that activities and processes of reflection, doing analysis and knowledge production, are public social practices and components of more integrated practice bundles; they do not have a separate autonomous existence in some internal, unobservable mental sphere. Consequently, practice-theory approaches do not simply negate mental states of affair. Rather, they revise their traditional epistemological status: practices express the mental 'publicly' (Schmidt and Volbers, 2011), and interpreters attribute it (Reckwitz, 2000a) to participants or persons. A person is a participant in practices, to whom mental states *inter alia* are attributed. This briefly outlined view repudiates the traditional idea that the subject's mental reflexive ability and knowledge are causes of its physical actions and behaviours.

From subjectivism to a critique of theoretical/scholastic reason

A fourth distancing move describes the idea of the acting subject as a variant of the scholastic fallacy. A reflexive, cultural-analysis perspective strives to illuminate not only the phenomena studied, but simultaneously the scientific practices of observing, describing, classifying and interpreting them. It thus seeks to reveal the effects that result from the specific relations of scientific practices to the practices they examine.

A contemplative distance is constitutive of this relationship with examined phenomena and occurrences. If such a distanced scientific view, which has been released from the urgencies and pressures to act at the object level, is not self-reflexive and left unanalysed, it invites intellectualist projections. As noted above, Bourdieu (2000) drew up a typology of such projections and scholastic fallacies. Subjectivism features prominently in this typology. What is meant by 'subjectivism' here is essentially a non-reflexive generalisation of the theoretician's particular world view in which the theoretician 'project[s] his theoretical thinking into the heads of acting agents' (Bourdieu, 2000: 51) and constructs an acting subject that corresponds to his own imaginary self-image. This subject reflects non-stop, thinks before it acts, possesses stores of intellectual (but not physical or practical) knowledge and cultivates a free and creative relationship with the world's pressures. Such an intellectualist projection is an obstacle to understanding the logic of practice and thus also, and not least, to understanding the practical contribution that analytical processes and reflexive knowledge make to practices.

To decipher the contribution that analytical practices make to integrated bundles of practices and their dynamic processes of change, we require an understanding of reflexivity that does not treat 'analysing', 'reflecting', 'theorising', etc. as subjective activities, but rather – as the example of professional football shows – as observable practices of analysing, reflecting and theorising and their collective modes of knowing-how and knowledge. Treating reflection and analysis as public and observable practices leads to further distancing moves that decentre 'the subject', opens analytical access to reflexive forms of knowledge and the mental elements of social practices and by doing so advances practice theory.

Acknowledgements

I am grateful to the editors of this volume for their lucid and valuable comments on an earlier version of this chapter.

Notes

1 To be sure, this does not apply to the pioneering works of the first wave of practice theory. So, e.g. Schatzki (1996) elaborately dissects the presence and nature of mind in social practices. For a further elaboration on this, see also Schatzki (2016a).

2 The methodological problem that most interests practice theory is the difference between practical and theoretical logic, with which Bourdieu (1977; 1990; 2000) dealt at length in his epistemological reflections. Bourdieu's praxeology discovers misrepresentations of practical processes in theoretical models that are designed to represent them and reveals these misrepresentations and deformations with critical intent. However, bound up with this epistemological programme is a further desideratum that Bourdieu does *not* work

on. As Luc Boltanski (2011), for instance, has criticised, Bourdieu largely construes practices as the opposite of scholasticism. This contrasting between practice and scholasticism results in 'scholastic' or 'theoretical reason' (as Bourdieu calls it) being understood and described merely as a projecting and self-misunderstanding perspective, but *not* as a set of theoretical practices. Theoreticians are portrayed as mistaken holders of a 'scholastic' position and view, but not as practically involved in the social world of science.

3 For a critique of Parson's approach, see Garfinkel (1967). Criticisms of scholastic views also often cite Levi-Strauss and his realistic understanding of structures. Levi-Strauss equates cultural and social structure with unconscious structures of the human mind. For a critique of Levi-Strauss, see Bourdieu (1990).

4 For such an attempt to integrate into practice theory the concept of subjectivity with its critical-reflective competences and potentials for changes as a structure that is formed in practices, see Alkemeyer and Buschmann in this volume.

5 This illustration is drawn from an ongoing research project at the Catholic University Eichstätt on the new analysis and knowledge practices of professional football (see Schmidt, 2016).

6 More precisely, the players might be considered authors only in the sense their performances of moves are attributed to them by others. That is, they figure as persons in the practice of game playing. This praxeological understanding of the concept of person will be elucidated below.

7 Norbert Elias coined the concept of 'figuration' – which explains the emergence of social orders – to capture this priority of the match over individual players and their moves: 'The concept of figuration draws attention to people's interdependencies. What actually binds people together into figurations? Questions like this cannot be answered if we start by considering all individual people on their own, as if each were a *Homo clausus*. That would be to stay on the level of psychology and psychiatry which study the individual person… There is a tacit assumption that societies – figurations formed by interdependent people – are fundamentally no more than congeries of individual atoms. The examples of card-game and football matches may help to make the shortcomings of this hypothesis more apparent' (Elias, 1984: 132).

8 As an employee of the company explained, this catalogue of definitions – which is not publicly available – was drawn up 'supported by sports science' and is used as the basis for training the scouts and writers who classify and log match events in real time in accordance with this catalogue of definitions. The employee made it clear that the catalogue is above all intended to 'make sure there are no questions left open' while at the same time ascribing a performative aspect to it: with the help of media reporting, its definitions have been successfully taught to spectators and fans – 'everyone now shares our idea of a successful tackle'.

9 Here, football is different from, e.g. baseball or basketball. In baseball in particular – a game for which quantifying match and player analyses based on coding evolved much earlier (Schwarz, 2004) – play consists of successive individual situations that are delimited from each other.

10 In tracking, different technical processes are used. Alongside tracking using the stadiums' fixed thermal imaging cameras, cheaper methods have recently been developed that calculate an overall real-time picture of all on-pitch agents of play based on match recordings from only two cameras (Schlipsing, 2014).

11 The first and very promising exception is the yet unpublished dissertation by René Tuma (2015), which used videography and participant observation for its empirical examination of, among other things, practices of video-supported match analysis in football training.

12 'The fact that we don't run much could just mean that we position ourselves well as a team', FC Schalke 04 goalkeeper Ralf Fährmann commented on this debate (as quoted in Kupfer, 2011).

13 The English Premier League has commissioned the video games company EA Sports – a division of the US video games company Electronic Arts – to determine and market this index. It advertises the index thus: 'the EA Sports PPI is the official player rating index of the Barclays Premier League. It measures a player's contribution to the success of his team using six key indices. The intention is to remove any opinion bias and only work with proven statistical measurements which become more accurate as the season progresses' (Barclays Premier League, 2015). EA Sports also uses the index in the football simulation game FiFa.

14 In this connection, match analysis in football raises interesting questions about the relationship between analytical processes and the events being analysed: what does it mean if, for instance, the results of passing statistics, which are continuously made available during the match, lead to changes in tactics or to substitutions? Does match analysis therefore encounter its own classifications and operationalisations on the pitch? Are there parallels here to the so-called 'social studies-scientification' of sectors of society (Beck and Bonss, 1989)? This expression captures the fact that sociology can encounter socio-techno operationalisations of its own concepts and theories in the phenomena it studies – it encounters itself. The developments in football that I have outlined can be understood as a transformation of match analysis in match technology that parallels the transformation of sociological analysis in social technology.

15 For example, the review and accounting processes used by companies and educational institutions (Vormbusch, 2004).

16 From this perspective, practices of analysing, reflecting and theorising can be understood as 'dispersed practices' that can be a part of different 'integrated practices'. The latter are bundles of practices – like those of professional football – which are linked not only through shared forms of knowledge and understanding, but additionally through institutionalisations, infrastructures and organisational aspects such as explicit rules, provisions and teleo-affective structures, i.e. goals, tasks, projects, plans, etc. (Schatzki, 1996: 91–110).

17 The following line of decentring the subject primarily refers to approaches in sociology. There are other related lines in philosophy and social theory that, e.g. lead from Friedrich Nietzsche through Martin Heidegger and Ludwig Wittgenstein to Charles Taylor.

11

MATTERS OF PRACTICE

Elizabeth Shove

It is obvious that the lives of things and practices are mutually constituted and densely interwoven. It is also obvious that really significant trends like the massive increase in carbon dioxide emissions over the last few decades are outcomes of what Schatzki (2010a) describes as 'practice-arrangement' nexuses. Situated in the space between these two opening sentences, the purpose of this chapter is to develop a practice theoretically compatible account of material relations that helps conceptualise rapid increases in per capita energy demand.

The grand scale of this ambition is in part a critical response to those who contend that theories of practice are especially and perhaps only good for analysing daily routines and localised patterns of consumption (Welch and Warde, 2015; Geels, McMeekin, Mylan and Southerton, 2015). For the moment, and particularly in the environmental field, empirical work inspired by practice theory tends to focus on end consumers: on those who do the cooking, have daily showers or twiddle with heating systems. However, this is *not* a necessary feature of taking practices to be the central topic of enquiry. As I hope to show, systematic consideration of the matters of practice provides a means of connecting otherwise separate realms of producing, manufacturing, making and doing. Moving in this direction has the further advantage of demonstrating the relevance of practice theory for understanding processes that are commonly taken to be the preserve of disciplines that deal with resource economics, environmental politics, world trade and global energy demand.

In other respects, the chapter is deliberately limited in scope. The methodological decision to think about how energy demand is constituted informs the way in which I characterise and slice material-practice relations and the examples I use. Although many of the issues discussed below are of wider relevance, what follows is not designed as an all-purpose exercise in mapping the many routes and processes through which practices are materialised, and vice versa. Accepting that materials and practices *are* interwoven, and that humans, artefacts, organisms and things of nature are variously but unavoidably enmeshed in social life (Schatzki, 2010a), I focus on the problem of understanding the emergence of configurations and practices that are distinctly resource intensive. This depends on developing a more detailed account of how specific flows of 'matter-energy' are formed.

With this challenge in mind I start by considering three *roles* that things can play in practice.[1] Some things are necessary for the conduct of a practice, but are not engaged with directly. I suggest these have an 'infrastructural relation' to practice. A second category includes things that are directly mobilised and actively manipulated. I count these as 'devices'. Third, there are things which are used up or radically transformed in the course of practice and that figure as 'resources'. This way of thinking about things is distinctively practice-centric. It is so in that identical objects can have different roles and thus fall into different categories, depending on how they are positioned within and in relation to different practices.

The main business of the chapter is to explore the relevance of such an approach and to show what it might have to offer within practice theory and beyond.

More specifically, can this three-part classification help in disentangling and describing the packaging of material-practice relations across sequences and chains of production and consumption? I write about house building, home heating and watching television as a means of detailing relevant processes of connecting and prefiguring.

A second ambition is to use this scheme to think about how the status of things changes in practice. For example, when and how do device-oriented relations become infrastructural and vice versa? As I show, the shifting status of things like larders, fridge-freezers and frozen food chains is part of making and reproducing multiple distinctions and flows. I suggest that transitions of this kind are relevant for understanding how resources, including forms of energy, circulate and how 'demands' are built. In the third part I comment on how things which tend to have infrastructural, object-oriented or resource-based roles figure in the spatial and temporal patterning of practices and vice versa.

I finish by taking stock of what this method of dissecting material practice relations allows us to see and to say. Before getting into these cases and questions, I briefly introduce the lines of thinking on which this approach draws and from which it departs.

Material relations in practice

Although there have been careful and detailed expositions of things within and as part of social practices (Reckwitz, 2002b; Schatzki, 2002), there is rather less analysis of the range and variety of material relationships involved or of precisely how material entities figure in what people do.

To date, the most significant difference is between discussions of material *elements* which are treated as being integral to the conduct of a practice (Shove *et al.*, 2012) and material *arrangements* amidst which practices transpire (Schatzki, 2010a). For Shove, Pantzar and Watson, the material elements of car driving might reasonably encompass the road network, a system of petrol stations and the steering wheel itself. All are accorded the same material status. Meanwhile, Schatzki's concept of material *arrangements*, amidst which practices transpire, does not distinguish between things which are directly, routinely or only distantly and occasionally implicated in the conduct of a practice. This is not in itself a problem. In both cases broad brush representations of 'material' are sufficient and consistent with the similar but not equivalent ambitions of the authors involved.

However, this language of elements and arrangements is of limited value if we want to know how and why specific patterns of production and demand arise and are engendered by correspondingly specific conjunctions of practice. Warde's (2005) observation that things, including energy and other resources, are consumed in the course of practice provides the starting point for a more differentiated account. The statement that 'the enactment of any one practice (for example, cooking a meal or travelling to work) typically depends on the prior existence and availability of a range of energy sources (gas, electricity, oil), infrastructures (grids, pipes, roads) and devices (cookers, cars, bicycles)' suggests that objects can be classified, in advance, under one or another of these ready-made headings (Shove and Walker, 2014: 50). This is a rather literal account.

A more subtle approach, and one that I develop here, is to distinguish between *the roles* that materials play in the enactment of any one practice. This is in keeping with those who view objects not as isolated entities, but as always integrated within and always inseparable from more extensive assemblages (Appadurai, 1986; Ingold, 2007; Introna, 2013; Shove, Walker and Brown, 2014). It is also consistent with Rinkinen *et al.*'s (2015) method of characterising 'object relations' in daily life. Rather than taking objects to have a fixed status, Rinkinen, Jalas and Shove adopt a relational approach, distinguishing between the various ways in which people describe and engage with the materials involved in keeping warm in winter. Although I work with a more bounded and also more pragmatic view of things, the shared proposition is that materials are defined, constituted and positioned with respect to each other through their role within specific practices.

This method makes it possible to show how things switch between roles and to recognise that things which have a background or infrastructural relation to certain practices may be more directly engaged in the conduct of others. These theoretical moves are important, but they do not prevent me from appropriating concepts and insights from disciplines and fields which define resources, artefacts and infrastructures in other ways and which focus on them for different reasons. As well as picking out useful points of connection, the next few paragraphs provide a reminder both of the complexity of the material world and the specialisation of academic research dealing with infrastructures, devices and artefacts or resources.

Writing about things in the background

Defining things which have an *infrastructural relation* to a practice as those which are necessary but that are not interacted with directly, results in a situationally specific but potentially extensive list of possibilities. Depending on the practices at stake, homes, kitchens and a good supply of oxygen would be as likely to qualify as 'infrastructure' as power grids, harbours or pylons. There are no hard-and-fast rules about what to count as necessary background: as is usually the case, this is a matter of judgement and purpose. In the examples discussed later in the chapter, an interest in conceptualising escalating energy demand provides one filter.

Although many things can have an infrastructural relation to practice, the systems and arrangements through which power, data and water are provided and distributed often figure in this role. As such, sociological and historical literature on infrastructures provides a useful point of reference. Classic contributions to this field including Hughes (1993), Nye (1992), and Hård and Misa (2008) focus on the social, technical and institutional processes involved in establishing what are typically complicated, geographically distributed, relatively expensive and often relatively durable networks. Coming at similar issues but from a different angle, writers like Coutard, Hanley and Zimmerman (2005), Bulkeley, Castan Broto, Hodson and Marvin (2012) and Graham and Marvin (2001) focus on institutional actors (cities, utilities, etc.) and the political interests involved in the (re)development of networked and decentralised forms of provision. Writing of this kind tends to consider infrastructures-in-the-(re)making as distinct from infrastructures-in-use. This is intriguing and also ironic. When infrastructures become invisible in daily life, that is when they are functioning normally, academic interest in them seems to wane. While there is widespread agreement that electricity, communication and data systems constitute an essential backdrop to contemporary life – breakdowns and failure provide tangible evidence that this is so (Nye, 2010) – questions about how different practices become and remain electrified, or internet-dependent, and about what these processes mean for resource consumption, currently fall between the cracks of established disciplines and debates.

Grand observations about '[t]he growing dependence of modern societies on technological systems … [and] the steady increase of systemic vulnerabilities and risks due to the growing complexity of these systems' (Silvast, Hänninen and Hyysalo, 2013: 4) indicate what appears to be a collective transformation in the material relations of many practices at once. By implication, infrastructural transitions do not occur in isolation. As Edwards *et al.* note, 'the actual infrastructures of people's real work lives always involve particular configurations of numerous tools used in locally particular ways' (Edwards, Bowker, Jackson and Williams, 2009: 370). In other words, networks of water, power or data are only of value and only develop and expand when they connect with and enable a proliferation of devices and appliances that are in turn enmeshed in practice. Things in the background are of necessity tied to things in the foreground and to the ongoing mobilisation of things in action.

Writing about things in action

It is fairly straightforward to identify things which have a device-oriented role in relation to the conduct of a practice and that are visibly and actively used in the process of doing. The more complicated task is to conceptualise the conjunctions of human and non-human competence and capacity that follow.

Giard and de Certeau's discussion of the 'instrumentation relationships' that exist between practitioners and things, and through which practices are configured, highlights a number of features that are picked up in related literatures and that are especially relevant for a discussion of energy demand. They write about how an influx of appliances 'born of an intensive use of work in metals, plastic materials and electrical energy has transformed the interior landscape of the family kitchen' (Giard, de Certeau and Mayol, 1998: 210), modifying the skills of the cook and his/her gestures and actions in practice along with the relation between bodily and other forms of energy.

Going into a bit more detail, there are clearly different ways of representing the relation between cook and appliance. One option is to view such combinations as hybrid entities: part cook, part appliance. From this point of view, cooking is done not by the cook alone but by what Wallenborn describes as an 'extended' body (Michael, 2000; Wallenborn, 2013). A related but slightly different approach, also rooted in actor network theory, is to consider the manner in which the appliance and its designers script the cook, defining a programme of action that he or she may find difficult to resist (Akrich, 1992).[2] As well as bringing product and tool designers into view, this strategy raises further questions about how aspects of knowing and doing are integrated, delegated and divided and how aspects of practice become 'black boxed'.

The common point is that things which are mobilised in practice are not merely 'used'. Rather, such things are implicated in defining the practice itself. In this role, things-in-action matter for the division of labour in society, for the extent to which practices depend on human or other forms of power and related patterns of resource consumption.

One feature of the instrumentation relationship which is largely overlooked by Giard and de Certeau and in much other writing about scripts, hybrids and consumption in general is that many, although certainly not all, practices involve making, repairing, adapting or somehow intervening in the lives and flows of things. Acknowledging the material outputs of practices, including the uses of objects and infrastructures in the reworking of resources opens the way for a more dynamic account of material transformation, circulation and exchange.

Writing about things that are used up

It is again not too difficult to itemise things that are consumed, in the sense of being used up, in the course of a practice. Staying with examples from the kitchen, making bread requires a predetermined list of ingredients: yeast, flour, water, etc., along with fuel to power the oven. Although sociologists of consumption have had relatively little to say about the unglamorous world of consumables or the materially trans-formative outcomes of practice (Gronow and Warde, 2001; Shove and Warde, 2002), such topics are of greater interest to those who write about waste.

Key themes here have to do with the changing status of things as they are con-sumed, used and reconfigured. For example, Strasser (1999) writes about how the (low value) by-products of certain practices figure as (high value) inputs to oth-ers (O'Brien, 2012). As well as drawing attention to the ways in which practices are linked by material interdependencies and by chains of waste and want, this literature underlines the persistence of the material world. Although constantly transformed, there is a sense in which materials are not literally used 'up'. This is also true for energy: technically defined as the capacity to do work, it is the quality and not the quantity of energy that changes through 'use' (Funtowicz and Ravetz, 1997).

Alongside but detached from these detailed representations of using and trans-forming and far from any social theory of practice, economists often treat resources, including things like oil, steel, sugar, coffee, etc., as unchanging commodities the circulation of which reflects seemingly abstract political and economic processes. In the environmental field, increasingly elaborate methods have been developed to quantify and allocate carbon emissions (relating to the use of energy) associ-ated with increasingly complicated supply chains in which ready-made compo-nents are exported, assembled and shipped on as 'resources' and as input to sub-sequent stages of production (Daudin, Rifflart and Schweisguth, 2011). Building on previous efforts to describe international or cross-regional flows of trade, such techniques record inputs and outputs across various units/scales in an attempt to track the spatial/institutional location of emissions associated with the produc-tion and assembly of materials, parts, components and finished goods (Tukker and Dietzenbacher, 2013). Although critical for allocating national and sectoral responsibility for carbon emissions and for showing how these patterns are shaped by and also part of world trade, analyses like these concentrate on flows of mate-rial but without reference to the roles that resources or end products play in daily life or to the history of these arrangements. Economic historians with an interest in culture and consumption pay more attention to the mutual making of 'needs' and markets and to the emergence of use and not just exchange value (Mintz, 1986; Fernández-Armesto and Sacks, 2012). However, these accounts are rarely matched by parallel discussions of accompanying devices, forms of knowledge or related infrastructures.

Although analysed and conceptualised in different ways and within different disciplinary traditions, infrastructural, device-oriented and resource-based rela-tions are thoroughly inseparable, being welded together in various combinations across a myriad of different practices. As the preceding paragraphs indicate, aspects of these relations have been selectively addressed by a range of academic interests, each driven by distinctive preoccupations and paradigms. In borrowing from across this repertoire of ideas and fitting them into an account of the roles things play in practice, the next parts of the chapter are haphazardly interdisciplinary. Organised around the same basic question – Do distinctions between infrastructural, device-oriented and resource-based relations help in detailing material-practice relations that matter for energy demand, and if so, how? – each section focuses on a different theme. The first examines the sequential packaging and prefiguring of material relations, the second considers the fluid status of things within and between practices and the third comments on spatial and temporal configurations of infrastructures, devices and resources.

Material relations in combination and in sequence

In his 2010 article entitled *Materiality and social life*, Schatzki writes about how materials prefigure practices. In his words, prefiguration should be 'understood as a qualification of possible paths of action on such registers as easy and hard, obvious and obscure, tiresome and invigorating, short and long and so on'. He goes on to say that 'the particulars of material arrangements prefigure the course of practices in indefinitely complex ways' (2010a: 140). The question for me is whether there are methods of narrowing this complexity down, not in general, but in relation to the specific issue of how such prefiguring matters for energy demand.

One method of exploring this question is to use the distinctions introduced above – that is, to consider things which have an infrastructural, device-oriented or resource-based relation to practice – as a means of detailing connections between house building, keeping a house warm and watching television.

Table 11.1 outlines some of these possibilities. Predictably enough, each practice – building, warming, watching – is defined by its own combination of infrastructural, device-oriented and resource-based relations. A more interesting and also less obvious feature is that some of these material relations are sequentially linked and shared in common.

For example, reading down from the top of Table 11.1,[3] we see that house building today requires a power supply and scaffolding in the background. These infrastructural features enable the safe operation of an armoury of power tools (devices) that are used in linking and transforming resources and components through the construction process. This is not the end of the story in that the finished house, including features of size, layout, insulation, etc., acquires an infrastructural role with respect to the practices of heating. In this context, the boiler counts not as a resource to be installed and 'consumed' in the construction process, but as a device that is directly engaged with. The nicely heated living room then combines with the national broadcast network in constituting an infrastructure that enables occupants to watch TV in comfort.

This method of distinguishing between different yet connected material relations suggests that paths of action are *successively* and *repeatedly* qualified. This is relevant in that certain sequences of prefiguring may turn out to be self-reinforcing, potentially combining in ways that channel overall patterns of resource use. Although Akrich (1992) does not discuss unfolding or cumulative series of 'scripts', nor does Latour

TABLE 11.1 Material relations in combination and in sequence

Examples of material relations	Practices
Infrastructural: electric power network, scaffolding	House building
Device-oriented: power tools, drills, mixers, etc.	
Resource-based: electricity, cable, gas pipe, bricks, insulation and complicated ready-made components like boilers	
	↓↓↓↓↓↓↓↓
Infrastructural: electric power network, the fabric of the home (see above)	Heating the home
Device-oriented: boilers (see above)	
Resource-based: gas and electricity	
	↓↓↓↓↓↓↓↓
Infrastructural: a warm room (see above), a broadcasting system	Watching television
Device-oriented: television, sofa	
Resource-based: electricity	

(1992) consider how 'programs of action' might be partly shaped or 'written' by those which precede them, these diachronic relations are evidently important.

Taking a more lateral or synchronic view, what Giard and de Certeau (1998) refer to as 'instrumentation relationships' feature in each of the practices described above. And in each case, electricity is involved. This is not just a matter of recognising that energy is embodied in the materials of which homes are made and in the process of their construction. Rather, the point is that powered devices (which bridge between infrastructural relations and resources) have transformed the extent and the division of human labour on the part of the building contractors *and* of the future homeowners for whom they build. From this point of view, practices like those of building, heating and watching TV are collectively involved in establishing and reproducing the 'need' for networks of power.

Figure 11.1 works with similar ideas but extends them, incorporating processes of manufacturing (especially of appliances) together with resource manufacture and power generation, this time indicating how these might variously constitute cooking, laundering and watching TV.

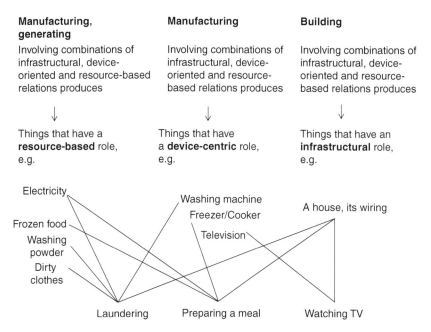

Manufacturing, generating	Manufacturing	Building
Involving combinations of infrastructural, device-oriented and resource-based relations produces	Involving combinations of infrastructural, device-oriented and resource-based relations produces	Involving combinations of infrastructural, device-oriented and resource-based relations produces
↓	↓	↓
Things that have a **resource-based** role, e.g.	Things that have a **device-centric** role, e.g.	Things that have an **infrastructural** role, e.g.

FIGURE 11.1 Patterns of making and doing

This more elaborate image implies that domestic, professional and manufacturing practices interact in concert. It is an obvious point but what is involved in doing the laundry depends, in part, on what the washing machine can do. And what the machine can do in turn depends on how and of what it is made. In this way, the skills and practices of washing machine making are quite directly tied to those of washing.

Second, while the specialisation of devices is also evident (TVs are not used in laundering), some of the manufacturing and resource-related relations that lie behind these objects overlap. For example, small electric motors and other components – light-emitting diodes, switches, etc. – are embedded in a range of otherwise diverse appliances. This is relevant in that the development and use of standardised parts has widespread and not practice-specific implications.

Third, and as is increasingly evident, energy demand is constituted right across the map. Electrified instrumentation relationships occur in factories as well as in kitchens; appliance designs matter for the relation between human and other forms of power (as in cooking and laundry); and with electrical wiring in place, new practices (TV watching) are enabled. More than that, forms both of automation and delegation (to machines and non-human forms of power) collectively reconfigure the distribution, definition and constitution of competence (Shove et al., 2007).

Categorising and defining things in terms of their *role* in a practice helps bring these topics to the fore and provides a means of thinking about forms and types of interconnection and of prefiguration. However, it is important to remember that material roles are often ambiguous and always provisional.

Material relations in flux

How do things come to have the roles they do, and how do these relations vary and change? In this section, I comment on instances in which things switch status, for example between device-oriented and infrastructural roles and in which they flip between background and foreground depending on the practices within which they are situated.

Some of these movements are extensions of processes discussed above. For example, the 'full' automation of heating or lighting systems removes the possibility of direct interaction, meaning that these services are actively provided by building managers and designers, but passively encountered by building occupants. Distinctions between things that have an appliance or device-related role and those that figure as background infrastructure quite often mirror other boundaries, including institutional roles of management and responsibility.

One currently controversial example concerns the status and hence the design, ownership and provisioning of electric vehicle charging points (Grandclement, Pierre and Shove, 2015). Should these be conceptualised as part of the background and as something which enables the use of an electric car, but which is not in itself 'used'? Alternatively, does the charging point figure as a discrete device that is actively used as part of a new practice, namely that of charging the vehicle? It is not yet clear how the material politics will evolve, but it is evident that whatever the outcome, it will be an expression of a shuffling of practices between households, car manufacturers and utilities. More subtly, concepts of state and market, and of consumption and production, are made real through interactions of this kind.

A second insight, again arising from this exercise in thinking about how things figure in practice, is that certain entities simultaneously occupy different roles. The fridge-freezer is one such item. To elaborate, the entire frozen food sector and the systems of agriculture, manufacturing and distribution of which it is comprised depend on the background co-existence of millions of home freezers. From an industry point of view, these appliances have an infrastructural role in relation to practices of producing and distributing frozen food. Meanwhile, each individual freezer has a more localised and also a more foreground status within a specific complex of shopping, cooking and eating practices. Recognising that the freezer's device-oriented role (in the home) defines and depends on the freezer's infrastructural roles within practices of production and distribution enables us to detect the interpenetration of material relations threading through the complexes of practices that together constitute frozen food systems – and the forms of global trade associated with them.

In brief, tracking material roles as they span and flip between practices and across supply chains helps explain how large technical systems are multiply sustained and how such infrastructures become embedded across different areas of daily life. Moves like these promise to counter what remains a rather lopsided emphasis on the social and institutional processes involved in establishing and reconfiguring networks of provision and power. As mentioned above, energy demand is constituted right across the map. Paying attention to the ways in which material relations (infrastructural, and device-oriented) are arranged and bundled promises to reveal the contours of this map as formed both by flows of energy through sequences of practice, as discussed in the previous section, and by the demarcation and switching of material roles, as considered here.

Material relations in time and space

Given that consumption occurs in the course of social practices, the spatial organisation and timing of such practices matters for the spatial organisation and timing of consumption and for the circulation, distribution and storage of the many materials involved. What this means, in detail, again depends on the various parts things play in practice. For example, consumables which are 'used up' need storing and replenishing. By contrast, things which stand in a background or infrastructural relation to practice, or which have a device orientation are rarely depleted in the same way.[4] Such things are, however, crucial for the range and extent of resources involved, for how these are distributed and for when and where they are consumed.

Systems that often have an infrastructural role, like gas and electricity grids along with networks of roads, railways or of data and communication, are typically designed to meet present and sometimes future 'needs': the common logic being that of 'predict and provide'. Since the scale of energy/resource demand depends on the number and the type of devices in use at any one time, infrastructures have to cope with daily and seasonal fluctuations related to *when* and also *where* multiple practices are enacted. Systems are consequently sized for moments when lots of people are simultaneously engaged in travelling, exchanging data or in doing things that draw energy/resources through the system.

In terms of practice theory, understanding how peaks and troughs of energy demand come to be as they are depends on thinking not about one practice at a time, but about how complexes of practice relate to each other and how sequences and rhythms are formed. From this point of view, the sociology of time has a potentially central role in understanding and explaining patterns of energy consumption and in characterising relations between resources, devices and infrastructures at different spatial and temporal scales. Although not written with such questions in mind, Zerubavel's (1979) sophisticated account of the ebb and flow of people and practices in hospital life is, at the same time, an account of organisational and societal synchronisation. Since practices often depend on, and are in part defined by, co-existing infrastructures (electricity and data; water and gas, etc.), their coming together and their separation in space and time is felt across different systems of provision (Shove, 2009). This is significant in that the strategy of designing systems to cope with the peaky-ness of rhythms and complexes of practice depends on building in redundancy and on systematically 'over' sizing. By implication, energy use, in aggregate, is not only an outcome of the enactment of specific practices: it also relates to spatial and temporal relations between practices.

Doing any one practice typically depends on the coming together of devices, infrastructures and resources. However, things which figure in one or another of these roles are often distributed differently, in social as well as geographical terms. This is relevant in that uneven patterns of ownership and access are significant for discussions of social inequality and of what some refer to as 'fuel poverty' (Sovacool, 2015). For example, the fact that infrastructural arrangements and necessary background features are in place is of limited value if potential practitioners lack either the devices or the resources/consumables required. Also important, certain infrastructural arrangements are designed to prevent the use of certain devices and thereby to exclude specific practices/practitioners. For example, motorways exclude the safe, comfortable or legal use of bicycles, and as in Winner's (1985) classic example, bridges can be constructed to keep buses and bus passengers at bay.

As these few examples indicate, disaggregating material roles promises to be of value in analysing the social-spatial qualities of arrangements that make certain practices harder or easier to enact. Realising that potential depends on developing methods of accounting for the separate spatial-temporal 'coordinates' of devices, resources and infrastructures, while recognising that practices reflect and depend on their conjunction and active integration in space and time.

Discussion and conclusion

Theories of practice have made important contributions to the analysis and understanding of social life and will continue to do so *without* distinguishing between different material roles. However, this chapter suggests that it may be useful to tease the world of things apart as a means of developing a practice theoretical approach to problems like those of understanding patterns of resource consumption. The series of thought experiments outlined above highlights the possibilities and limitations of such an exercise and draws attention to a handful of themes that deserve further attention within practice theory.

One is the point that many of the things that people do – at work, in design, in manufacturing and in the home – involve making or modifying materials that feature in other practices. Following sequences of material conjunctions and transformations represents a fresh way of conceptualising consumption and production and the threads of matter and inter-practice relationships that bind these seemingly separate spheres together. As described above, capturing and characterising these connections depend on recognising the fluid status of things and their role in the foreground, in the background and in spanning between different practices.

Second, there is something intriguing about how material relationships are implicated in bounding what count as separate practices and in related processes of merger and hybridisation. The margin between device-oriented and infrastructural roles appears to be especially critical in this respect. For example, the 'line' between device and infrastructure is sometimes subtly, sometimes dramatically repositioned through processes of automation and delegation.

Third, the approach outlined in this chapter makes it plain that the production and circulation of goods and commodities is thoroughly and unavoidably embedded in the ongoing conduct and transformation of social practices around the world. In so far as energy use and patterns of consumption are consequences of what it is that people do (Shove and Walker, 2014), theories of social practice could and should occupy a central and not a marginal place in explaining international trade and the carbon emissions that follow.

To put this more concretely, the 9.6 billion tons of stuff that was transported in container ships in 2013 along with the estimated 93 million barrels of oil and liquid fuels that are on average consumed each day (United Nations Conference on Trade and Development, 2014; International Energy Agency, 2016) should not be interpreted as expressions of macro-economic and political forces or the circulation of capital or outcomes of multilevel or any other kinds of transition, as if these were somehow detached from the realm of social practice. Instead, these flows of goods and transformations of energy are expressions and consequences of the multiply materialised character of what Schatzki (2002) describes as the 'plenum' of practice. This argues for a re-reading of input-output models, particularly if these are used as methods of quantifying and characterising the 'responsibility' for carbon emissions (whether directly or in the form of embodied energy) or of informing policy on this topic (Daly, Scott, Strachan and Barrett, 2015). If we take a step or two back, it becomes obvious that such methods focus on the 'symptoms' – that is the flows of goods and of energy – and in so doing fail to enquire further into the different registers, scales and dynamics of practice on which the global choreography of material (infrastructures, devices, resources) actually depends.

Established methods of modelling, accounting and policy making have the further disadvantage of overlooking the extent to which infrastructures[5] and systems of provision interlock with the uses of devices and hence the consumption of resources. Following the account of material-practice relations developed here, energy demand is made at multiple sites and moments: it is certainly not an outcome of consumer 'need' as if this had an independent life of its own. At a minimum, this argues for a more joined-up form of policy analysis that acknowledges the co-constitution of supply and demand.

Two other observations point to new ways of thinking about how energy demand increases and how it might reduce. I have argued that infrastructures have a background role and that because of this they have what seems to be a distinctive part to play in configuring, prefiguring and multiply enabling many different practices *and* relations between them. In this context it is important to notice the escalatory effect of the concept of predict and provide. In many cases the idea that infrastructures should be capable of meeting foreseeable forms of demand constitutes what amounts to a self-fulfilling prophecy. This is not the only option.

Since practices are always on the move, the material configurations associated with them, and on which they depend, are not fixed in stone. Following the argument developed here, intervention at the level of infrastructural relations represents a form of intervention that matters for many practices at once. Current infrastructures will not last forever and how they are repaired, re-shaped or renewed over the next few decades will have a major impact on other aspects of material-practice relations and hence on future energy demand, whether for good or ill.

In conclusion, the strategy of characterising things *in relation* to practices makes sense theoretically and is analytically productive, providing a means of revealing sequences of production and consumption and the different implications of these processes for things in the background, in action and that are 'used up'. As a methodological position, it is decidedly but perhaps necessarily slippery: in this analysis, things-in-relation-to-practice are always multiple, never stable and never fully defined. However, this is not the main problem. If the aim is to draw on the reach and power of social theories of practice and to exploit their potential in accounting for global transitions in resource consumption, trade and carbon emissions, the more pressing and more obvious challenge is that of engaging with, or acting alongside, incumbent models and theories of economics and of resource and carbon accounting which conceptualise materials and resources – whether in the role of consumables or as temporally embodied in devices and infrastructures – in terms that are abstracted from an understanding of their relative and fluid roles in multiple practices. For the moment, there is a basic theoretical divide between a relational account of things in practice (as developed here) and 'fixed' interpretations of goods and services of the kind that underpin discussions of resource economics and energy demand. Looking ahead, one way and perhaps the only way out is to develop forms of environmental policy analysis and intervention that do not take demand for granted and that are capable of confronting fundamental questions about what materials and related forms of energy are for.

Notes

1 Other roles are no doubt possible.
2 Infrastructures and things in the background also 'script' and make some programmes of action easier or more difficult to follow, but they do so in different ways.
3 There are other ways of defining top: the table illustrates just a few links in a series of more extensive chains.
4 Of course things in an infrastructural role often require ongoing maintenance and repair (involving resources and 'consumables') if they are to continue functioning in the background.
5 Here taken in a literal sense, meaning power grids, etc.

12

PLACING POWER IN PRACTICE THEORY

Matt Watson

Practice theory must be able to account for power. This imperative has two sides, one intellectual and the other pragmatic. The intellectual side of the imperative comes from the ubiquity of power as a part of social relations. For practice theory, all social relations are constituted and reproduced through practices. As Schatzki states, 'both social order and individuality... result from practices' (1996: 13). Therefore, practice theory must be able to account for how power works. The pragmatic side of the imperative may be less compelling, as it relies on a conviction that social theory should, in part, be valued for its capacity to make a positive difference in the world. For practice theory to inform future change meaningfully (or to account convincingly for past change), it must be able to account for power.

Power is a fundamental concern of social theory and I am writing about it for two reasons, the first being the difficulty of analytically grasping what we take for power in a way that is consistent with the ontological commitments of practice theory. The second is that the bulk of what comprises contemporary work identifying with practice theory, particularly in empirical application, is typically conservative in terms of its practical implications. Generally, applications of practice theory that seek to be relevant result in arguments against the technical or behavioural preoccupations of policy approaches. This is despite the intellectual radicalism of practice theory, which posits an understanding of the social and of human subjectivity which embodies a fundamental critique of the implicit theoretical foundations of dominant ways of conceiving and doing governing.

My ambition, then, is to work through ways in which power is already present in how practice theory has been developed and used and then to engage cognate fields of theory to look for an account of power which is coherent with practice theory. The chapter does not start from a premise that practice theory must have something distinctive to say about power and much less that practice theory is the best means of understanding power as an aspect of the social. Rather, it starts from a conviction that, to fulfil its potential, practice theory needs to be able to speak of power and so it is worth seeking a compatible account of power. I also aim to establish some grounds for thinking about whether practice theory may have something distinctive to say about power and consider to what good this might be put.

In all of this, there are many possible foundations to build on within the practice theory literature. For Barnes, to 'engage in a practice is to exercise a power' (2001: 28). For Nicolini, one of the five distinctive features of practice theory common across the full range of its expression by different scholars is that they 'foreground the centrality of interest in all human matters and therefore put emphasis on the importance of power, conflict, and politics as constitutive elements of the social reality we experience' (2012: 6). Key thinkers who have shaped contemporary understandings of power are also included in articulations of the intellectual heritage of contemporary practice theory, including Bourdieu and Foucault (Reckwitz, 2002b) and Marx (Nicolini, 2012). Along with this, current contributions have increasingly articulated concepts which promise to enable practice theory to move beyond the localism of a focus on performances of practices (Shove *et al.*, 2012; Nicolini, 2012; Schatzki, 2015a), opening up the means to engage with the sorts of social phenomena such as those of government or commerce that are commonly identified with the exercise of power.

There are then grounds for thinking that practice theory can meaningfully engage with questions of power and some foundations on which to build a discussion of that potential. The chapter moves towards this goal by framing the discussion with reference to fundamentally different understandings of power. It is impossible here fully to plumb the complexities of how power has been thought about and deployed in social theory (Lukes, 2005). It is nonetheless useful to scope out the relatively obvious poles of meaning and to outline the path taken through the relations between power and practice in the discussion that follows.

A first key distinction is between understanding power as an object or as an effect. In common sense usage power is an object, generally understood as a capacity of a person, institution or other social actor. Within such a framing, it is how both power and the effects of its exercise are profoundly unevenly distributed which motivates both deliberate political action and critical theoretical engagement. Understood as object, power still has different meanings. It can refer simply to the capacity to act with effect (essentially making power synonymous with agency, as that is conventionally understood). More distinctively, power can refer to the capacity to direct or purposively influence the actions of others. In this meaning, power can be identified as a property of an individual – say a monarch or corporate CEO – or collective social actor like the state. It is hard to escape understandings of power as object or capacity. The distinctions it brings with it – between the capacity to act with effect and capacity to shape the actions of others – also prove useful in organising the following discussion.

However, over the course of the chapter this discussion moves towards a position which repudiates understandings of power as an object or property. At least since

Foucault, it has been increasingly normal for people meddling with social theory to understand power as itself an effect. It is this way of thinking about power which is implicit within practice theory. Indeed, to be consistent with the ontological commitments of practice theory, power must be understood as an effect of performances of practices, not as something external to them. Power only has reality in so far as it is effected, and made manifest, in moments of human action and doing. This position has pleasing ontological consistency, but seems unlikely to enable practice theory to move from the political impotence which I claim above as impetus for this chapter. If power only has meaningful existence in moments of human action and interaction, how do we account for the apparent reality of enduringly powerful social agents such as corporations or governments?

In addressing this question, I engage with existing ways of thinking about power and consider how current formulations and applications of practice theory articulate with them. This provides a basis for exploring the complementarity of current expressions of practice theory with Foucauldian analytics of power relations and of governing. Bringing these together with aspects of other complementary intellectual traditions provides the basis for a concluding discussion of how power can be meaningfully engaged with and conceptualised through practice theory and for some reflection on what that means.

Is practice theory all about power?

If power is understood at the most basic level as acting with effect, then practice theory can be understood as essentially being all about power. Indeed, all of the relations comprising the social are constituted and reproduced through the actions of humans (amidst the many non-human entities also involved in those actions). All sorts of human action have effect in this way, whether in how the repetitive timing of eating reproduces fundamental shared social rhythms (Southerton, 2009) or in how the consequences of day traders' routinised actions (Schatzki, 2010b) cumulatively reshape financial markets. In accounting for both social change and the reproduction of social stability as the result of human action, practice theory is inherently about power, if power is seen as capacity to act with effect.

Of course, emphasising the power inherent in the actions of individual humans is only part of the story. Practice theory is perhaps best understood for its emphasis on the shaping of human action by relations and phenomena external to the person performing any such action. This is so to the extent that practice theory is sometimes cast as denying human agency or problematising the possibility of social change. While such claims reflect a profound misrepresentation on both points, they highlight the extent to which practice theory is centrally about the shaping as well as possibility of action.

With a focus on the shaping of action, we move closer to the second basic understanding associated with seeing power as object, that is, an interpretation of power as the capacity to direct or influence the actions of others. Understanding that action is always an effect of diverse relationships implies the shaping of action from elsewhere. This starting point for approaching the shaping of action remains rather one-sided, attending to the heterogeneous phenomena that share in how action is shaped, rather than how power is wielded to shape it. However, leaving aside the question of how to identify who or what wields influence, practice theory is replete with resources for understanding the shaping of (the possibilities for) human action. This is perhaps clearest in relation to the roles of rules.

An emphasis on the role of rules in the shaping of human action represents one of the most significant points of commonality between the range of scholars identified as key protagonists in the intellectual history of practice theory, reflecting shared roots in Wittgenstein's work. However, just what is encompassed by the concept of the rule varies. For Schatzki, rules are 'explicit formulations, principles, precepts and instructions that enjoin, direct or remonstrate people to perform specific actions' (Schatzki, 2010b: 79). Meanwhile for Giddens, what Schatzki refers to here as rules are *formulated* rules, 'codified interpretations of rules rather than rules themselves' (1984: 21). Rules – or more broadly the normativity of practices, however understood – are both the grounds for and limits upon the possibility of meaningful and practicable action by practitioners.

Among the ways in which the shaping of individual action is conceptualised, rules are easiest to grasp. Particularly in formalised or codified form, rules can look like means of exercising power in a conventional sense: after all, laws are prime examples of codified rules. Indeed, for Schatzki, rules 'are formulations interjected into social life for the purpose of orienting and determining the course of activity, typically by those with the authority to enforce them' (2010b: 79). However, rules as apparent means of power are situated amidst a great range of other ways in which action is constituted and influenced. In Reckwitz's (2002b) 'ideal type' practice theory, it is the conventionalised assembly of the diverse elements and their interconnections which constitute the pattern reproduced in the performance of a practice and in the action of individual practitioners. The routes through which power might be considered to be exercised are still more obscure in Shove, Pantzar and Watson's model of practices as composed by the relations between meanings, competences and materials, even if rules and other means of normativity run through accounts of how practitioners integrate these elements in moments of performance (2012). This model has provided the basis for attempts to reconceptualise possible targets for intervention (Shove *et al.*, 2012: 152–63), but it has little to say about the means through which power operates.

At first sight, other theorists' work appears more amenable to developing analyses framed in terms of power relations. Within Giddens' theory of structuration (1984), practices are the medium through which recursive relations between moments of human action and social structures constitute one another. Giddens invokes a vocabulary of power that is absent in more recent articulations of practice theory. For example, starting from his analysis of action, he identifies the role of allocative resources (capabilities) and authoritative resources ('types of transformative capacity generating command over persons or actors' (Giddens, 1984: 33)) leading to consideration of the structural dimensions of social systems, in signification, domination and legitimation.

While Giddens' work offered routes for articulating practices with the workings of power, Bourdieu (1984) provides the most compelling account of the systematic reproduction of unequal distributions in relation to practice, through the concepts of habitus, capital and field. The meanings of these concepts, their relations to each other and the relations of each and all of them to practice, are somewhat unfixed over Bourdieu's work. Moreover, the concepts – particularly that of habitus – cover aspects of what other theorists would consider part of practices, representing the socialised norms and tendencies of conduct guiding actions and dispositions, along with the ways in which social relations become embodied to persons in capacities, dispositions and ways of thinking. However, the concept of habitus enables an appreciation of social difference, which a focus on practices as the principal unit of analysis obscures, and it does so without resorting to individualism. While Bourdieu might be considered to hollow out the concept of practice and to omit relations which others take to be central to an understanding of practice, he draws out concepts which facilitate the conceptualisation of the production and reproduction of unequal distributions, including of those things which constitute the capacity to act. These differences, and the processes through which they come about and are maintained, constitute the grounds of systematic social differences, as reified into concepts of class, for example.

So, it is clear that practice theory can indeed be understood as being all about power. Practice theory demonstrably offers an understanding of how capacities to act with effect are constituted through its account of the relational, and profoundly social, grounds for action – understood as the performance of practice. However, it has not yet been shown to account for the ways in which some practices and practitioners are able deliberately to affect the conduct of practices and practitioners elsewhere. Yet, in enabling one to grasp the different phenomena and relations which shape and influence patterns of action, practice theory should be able to account for means of executing power which involve shaping or directing the action of 'others'. Practice theory must be in a position to cast distinctive light on, say, how inequality results from uneven distributions of the capacities to act, as explored by Walker (2013). However, it is harder to grasp how power is executed in the directing of another's action, in authority over others, or in the core of what it takes to understand and tackle the effects of power in the world.

This is unsurprising. The above discussion treads a line through various articulations of practice theory guided by a heuristic understanding of power as object. This understanding is in tension with the fundamental ontological commitments of practice theory. An account of action which shows it to be both enabled and shaped by a distributed and heterogeneous range of phenomena and relations has little or no space for recognising specific instruments of power which direct action. In its basic expression in action, power is rendered a relational, socially constituted effect. Yet, observable phenomena in the social world – powerful institutions, patterns of domination, the reproduction of social elites and of hegemonic ideologies – demand some means of understanding, if practice theory is indeed an account of the social. Developing such a position depends on looking for different ways of understanding power, as effect rather than object. In attempting to grapple with power while understanding it as an effect, the next step is to turn to Foucault.

Power as effect

Turning to Foucault to help theorise power is not an unusual move, but it is somewhat ironic. He disavowed both the analysis of the phenomenon of power and elaboration of the foundations of such analysis as the goal of his work (Foucault, 1982: 777). Fully comprehended as effect rather than object, power escapes analysis. What can be analysed are power relations, which are always agonistic. Some people and institutions are systematically advantaged by their position amidst these power relations and can use those relations to pursue their own ends, which can include shifting their location amidst power relations further to enhance relative advantage. But ultimately, no one person or entity has control of those relations. To understand those relations, we need to '[trace them] down to their actual material functioning' (Dreyfus and Rabinow, 1982: 186).

Questions of how institutions such as states or markets structure fields of action across space and time, far beyond the immediate reach of practitioners (including the situations that look most like the exercise of power conventionally understood), can be approached through the framing of *governmentality*. Foucault's own working through of governmentality is as an analytic representation of specific historical processes. In his 1978 lectures (Foucault, 1991), the concept is developed while accounting for the shift in governing he identifies in sixteenth century Europe, from defining the purpose of rule to be the retention of territory to it being the governing of population. Governmentality is initially an account of this specific process, of

> the ensemble formed by the institutions, procedures, analyses and reflections, the calculations and tactics that allow the exercise of this very specific albeit complex form of power, which has as its target population, as its principal form of knowledge political economy, and its essential technical means apparatuses of security.
>
> *(Foucault, 1991: 101)*

This characterises the rise and spread of government as the purpose of the state: a process of governmentalisation (Foucault, 1991: 101). However, numerous scholars have further developed Foucault's underlying ideas under a burgeoning field of governmentality studies (Burchell, Gordon and Miller, 1991; Dean, 2009).

This vein of work has done much to unpick the means – the rationalities, techniques and apparatuses – through which conduct is conducted (Gordon, 1991). But how is the conduct of conduct effected? That is, what is *distinctive* (rather than the same) about the practices of governing or of corporate influence? What characterises those practices which have influence over the performance of other practices?

How is the conduct of conduct practised?

If Foucault enables us to consider 'the conduct of conduct' in ways that are consistent with practice theory's ontological commitments, there could be a route for taking practice theory's engagement with power beyond accounting for capacities to act and the distributed range of relations which converge in shaping those capacities. Can we also understand how certain practices are distinctively capable of orchestrating, disciplining and shaping practices conducted elsewhere?

'Basically power is ... a question of government' (Foucault, 1982: 789). The potential of Foucault's account of how conduct is conducted here may seem limited given that his focus is not on power but on governing. Clearly, power operates in, on and through practices in many ways other than through the actions of government as formally understood. However, for Foucault, the term government is not restricted to formal institutions of state, but is used in a more general sense to mean shaping the conduct of others, to 'structure the possible field of action of others' (1982: 790). All scales of social phenomena are governed, from the self to the national and beyond. Governing can be understood as those actions and means through which the conduct of other people is more or less deliberately conducted, throughout social situations. With governing so understood, an account of how it is practised promises to fill out an account of power using resources already identified within practice theory literature.

However, for present purposes it makes sense to focus upon the power relations that act over space and time with the involvement of identifiable formal institutions – such as those of the state – that are in a position of relative dominance. Foucault himself acknowledges the value of such institutions as an empirical focus for an analytics of power relations, recognising that they 'constitute a privileged point of observation' (1982: 791). Institutions are sometimes considered something of a stretch for practice theory thanks to the putative difficulty it has in dealing with social phenomena which can be understood as large scale. However, the flat ontology of practice theory does not mean denying the scale of institutions or other large social phenomena. Rather, it entails recognition that such scale is produced and reproduced through practices. As Schatzki explains,

> all social phenomena... are slices or sets of features of the plenum of practices and arrangements, differing simply in the continuity, density and spatial-temporal spread and form of the practices, arrangements and relations that compose them. It follows that all social phenomena – large or small, fleeting or persistent, micro or macro – have the same basic ingredients and constitution.
>
> (2015b)

The observation that social phenomena have the same basic ingredients and constitution in whatever realm of the social or whatever apparent scale of social phenomena, means that the practices of ministerial offices, cabinet rooms and corporate board rooms mostly have the same characteristics as the practices of domestic life or leisure pursuits. They too are comprised of meanings, rules, competences, embodied knowledges, materials, spaces and more, brought together through largely routinised and mundane patterns of action. Increasingly, the lines of practice theory discussed above are being brought to bear upon institutional situations and into articulation with approaches which are well established in analyses of such settings.

Indeed, some lines of inquiry associated with practice theory, broadly defined, have been developed by authors who focus upon institutions and organisations. Much of this work is concerned with conceptualising learning and knowing as processes that are situated, ongoing and generally collective in character, even in work places that are thought to be highly rationalised. For example, questions about how someone becomes competent as a member of a profession or work place have been addressed with reference to concepts of shared engagement, enterprise, repertoires and histories of learning (Wenger, 1998). More broadly, the notion of a community of practice, associated with Lave and Wenger (1991), has been used to represent and influence the workings of more or less identifiable organisations and institutions such as schools or hospitals.

Orlikowski (2002) follows Lave (1988) and Suchman (1987) in understanding people comprising organisations as 'purposive and reflexive, continually and routinely monitoring the ongoing flow of action' (Orlikowski, 2002: 249). Whereas practice-based studies of organisations typically concentrate on particular individuals or spatially proximal work groups, Orlikowski writes about globalised processes of product development as necessarily collective arrangements distributed across geographically separated situations and moments of practices: in short, she focuses on 'organisational knowing' rather than individuals' knowledge.

She identifies practices that are part of belonging to and sustaining the group – of sharing identity and interaction, but also of the doing of the work, in spatially and temporally distributed locales, to common purpose. Orlikowski consequently develops an account of a corporate organisation's capacity to act as that is constituted through the widely distributed, ongoing and situated practices of people comprising the organisation. In accounts like these, institutions are shown to take form as distinctive social phenomena through shared, collective, predominantly tacit ways of shaping, enabling, disciplining and aligning a multitude of largely mundane practices.

While Foucault acknowledges the value of an empirical focus on institutions, he goes on to identify certain problems with such a method. These are problems which are typically associated with practice theory-informed studies of institutions, such as those discussed above. Key here is the risk that an analysis of the practices comprising institutions will focus upon practices which are essentially reproductive of that institution. While fundamental to understanding the phenomenon of an institution, reproductive practices – such as informal social interaction, bodily engagement with technologies and so on – often lack any direct relation to the ways in which institutions act external to themselves. That the practices comprising work, even in spaces of state or corporate power, are of essentially the same emergent, relational character as practices in more obviously 'everyday' situations, is another important corrective to conventional rationalist accounts of the workings of state or economy. However, while an understanding of the ways in which institutions reproduce themselves is clearly pertinent to an understanding of how institutions operate, stressing the sameness of the practices involved fails to account for how power is *done*.

Foucault's means of avoiding the problem of focusing too exclusively on the reproductive functions of institutions is to approach them from the standpoint of power relations, rather than vice versa (1982: 791). Rather than being distracted by the mass of institutional activity that is common to social life in institutions and elsewhere, his method is to follow the technologies and apparatuses of governing. These are the mechanisms – administrative, institutional and physical – which enable the exercise of power. This approach has been used to good effect. For example, Dean (2009) examines the distinctive 'technologies of performance' characterising neoliberal governance – the targets, audits and indicators through which the actions of agencies are shaped and policed. These complement parallel 'technologies of agency', which are the means through which responsibility is shifted from central government to increasingly fragmented and diverse agencies of governing.

However, in the context of this discussion, research that focuses on the technologies of governing is often limited in that it does not connect to an understanding of practices within institutions or show how these articulate with, constitute and operate relevant technologies and apparatuses. It therefore fails to characterise the practices which enable the conduct of conduct and the accumulation of the necessary resources to act in such ways. Governing over space, as is the case with institutions identified with the nation state or a multinational corporation, is only possible through the marshalling, coordination and harnessing of countless practices, which provide financial resources (e.g. through the multitude of practices that generate and gather taxes or profits), information (e.g. through census) or threat of force (e.g. through the armed forces and police).

This is because the embodied action at the core of all performances of practices can only be spatially and temporally immediate. As a result, the extension and amplification of action can only happen through intermediation. Such intermediation can rarely, if ever, be accomplished without depending on other practices as well as on technologies and more. Appreciating the ability of some practices to orchestrate and align others makes it possible to account for the appearance of institutional hierarchy and scale and for differential capacities to act, while retaining a flat ontology. Clearly, governing technologies must articulate with the practices of governing which rely upon them as means of influence and as means of shaping the conditions of possibility and thus the actions of others. It is this conjunction which is important and which helps specify what is distinctive about the practices of governing.

The sociology of translation provides further resources and means of developing connections between Foucauldian approaches to governmentality and practice theory-informed understandings of institutions. In recent years, a number of authors coming from different starting points, but often inspired by the work of

Bruno Latour, have sought to conceptualise practices and the properties of large organisations. Rose and Miller recognise the need, in investigating the problematics of government, to 'study the humble and mundane mechanisms by which authorities seek to instantiate government' (Rose and Miller, 1992: 183) from techniques of calculation and computation and devices like surveys and means of data presentation, to aspects of professions and details of buildings. While principally dealing with Foucauldian governmentality, Rose and Miller turn to Latour's account of power in pursuing this project. Latour (1987; 1984) sees power as an effect of the composition and alignment of heterogeneous relations, rather than seeing it as an explanation of an actor's successful composition of that network of relations. The power of a given social actor is an effect of its location in networks of relations through which that actor can shape the actions and calculations of others. In working with the sociology of translation as a means of interrogating modes of neoliberal governing, Rose and Miller (1992) focus on *inscription devices* as means of making stable, mobile, comparable and combinable vast ranges of data involved in governing; and the ways that modes of representation so achieved work in enabling *centres of calculation* – the nodes of networks which aggregate and re-represent the flows of inscriptions so produced, as a means of acting over distance.

In writing about action over distance, Nicolini (2012: 179) also introduces Latour's work, doing so as a means of overcoming the limits he identifies within practice theory – particularly the work of Schatzki. While recognising fundamental differences between Schatzki and Latour, Nicolini nevertheless sees the potential for linking the two approaches. Indeed, Schatzki (2015b) has himself engaged with Latour's work in the cause of better understanding the constitution of large social phenomena. While restating points of difference with actor-network theory (ANT) – whereas ANT sees the social as comprised only by associations, Schatzki sees it as comprised of practices and arrangements – Schatzki recognises commonalities in the flat ontologies underlying both approaches. Based upon such commonalities, he appropriates concepts from ANT to help illuminate how large social phenomena like governments, corporations or universities can emerge from the plenum of practices and arrangements.

The attraction of Latour's work and ANT more broadly, both for Rose and Miller (1992) coming from a governmentality tradition and in part for Schatzki (2015b) and Nicolini (2012), is ANT's capacity to account for large phenomena and action over distance without recourse to explanation at any level other than that defined by actions. Concepts like centres of calculation help move governmentality-oriented understandings of the technologies of neoliberal governance towards the practices comprising it. For Nicolini and Schatzki, such concepts offer ways of accounting for how practices have effect over time and space.

While Latour's ontology has no place for understanding practices as the basic stuff of the social, it is not difficult to see how practice-based accounts of the activity comprising institutions mesh with accounts of particular forms of association that appear to be crucial in enabling action in one locale to shape action over distance in another (or in many) locales. Inscriptions are outcomes of particular, normalised practices – practices of inscription. Similarly, the forms of calculation that characterise centres of calculation depend upon routinised and standardised processes of data storage and manipulation, which are performed and reproduced through more or less institutionalised practices of filing, archiving, etc. As Schatzki (2015b) indicates, it is not difficult to recast sites of association and alignment (as seen within ANT) as 'bundles' of practices. In turn, and as Rose and Miller (1992) discuss, particular modes of inscription and calculation are the stuff of technologies of governing in a Foucauldian sense. Latour's work consequently promises a means of developing connections between a focus on practices of governing and an understanding of the technologies and apparatuses through which governing is enacted.

In their engagements with Latour, neither Nicolini nor Schatzki directly addresses power. Indeed, Schatzki quickly moves to reduce any sense that one site has determinative influence, given that 'the progression of social affairs is thoroughly contingent' (Schatzki, 2015b: 8). Accepting this, there is nevertheless the problem that some sites, some organisations and some people are clearly situated in systematically advantageous positions amidst the associations, arrangements and alignments comprising social life, such that they have distinctive capacity to act purposively in ways which shape action over distance and across locales of action. The challenge is to develop concepts and methods that can help grasp how arrangements and associations of practices and the heterogeneous flows they are bound with are produced through, and reproduce, systematic inequities in capacities to act, including to act in ways which shape others' capacities to act.

One possibility is to consider the ways in which Latourian sites, such as centres of calculation, relate to the properties of organisations and institutions of governing. Such institutions comprise the ordering and stability necessary for the complex orchestration of practice that provides both the means and purpose of governing. They do so through aligning and disciplining the performance of key practices through other practices such as objective setting, managing, disciplining and incentivising. But perhaps more distinctively, such institutions are characterised by the extent to which capacities to accomplish governing are solidified and sedimented into relatively durable properties of the institution. Means and functions of practice are delegated to technologies and more or less codified procedures. Buildings, information infrastructures, divisions of labour and hierarchical institutional relationships between people and more are technologies for effectively aggregating the means of and the means to power. As Rose and Miller put it: 'powers are stabilised in lasting networks only to the extent that the mechanisms of enrolment are materialised in various more or less persistent forms – machines, architecture, inscriptions, school curricula, books, obligations, techniques for documenting and calculating and so forth' (1992: 183–4). Such materialised features of institutionalisation are part of the means through which practices are ordered and aligned, enabling those institutions to have effect, however constrained by the inescapable contingency of social life. These features also underpin an institution's capacity to accumulate the means of extending the capacity to act, for example, in the form of money or information.

At the same time, those features also underlie the obduracy of the practices of governing.

In sum, the conduct of conduct happens through practices which, while made of the same stuff as other practices, have distinctive characteristics not least resulting from the ways in which they are aligned over time. Concepts from both governmentality and ANT help to draw those working with practice theory towards a recognition that not all practices are 'the same' and that only some enable the aggregation and alignment of the resources necessary to assemble, maintain and exert some degree of control via technologies of governing. Practice theory is well equipped to describe and specify practices which have this potential, and in so doing address the missing links in understanding the processes of governing as constituted, reproduced and enacted through practices all of the way through.

Placing power in practice theory?

This chapter has not argued that practice theory provides the best or only way of understanding power. Much of power is performed through immediate interpersonal interaction, in the details of speech, bodily conduct and human interaction. Practice theory clearly can have things to say here, but power relations at this level are probably more amenable to analysis in terms of conversation analysis or through an ethno-methodological approach, with or without an underpinning in practice theory. The chapter has been more concerned with relating practice theoretical concepts to apparently powerful large scale phenomena, like corporations and governments. Practice theorists have repeatedly shown that such large phenomena are comprised through practices and the arrangements they produce and reproduce. But questions about the ability of a corporation to shape actions and accumulate resources or about the ways in which international tax laws shape trade are often better approached through other means. For better or worse, economic theory, or theories of political economy, could not do the work they do if they refused to reify power relations and if instead power relations were always analysed through the multiple practices from which they are an effect.

Like any other approach, practice theory is not going to be able to give an all-encompassing account of power. However, the discussion above has demonstrated that it has distinctive contributions to make as part of a range of related strategies that shed light on how power exists as an effect of collective activity and its consequences. Ultimately, power relations and their consequences only exist through connections between moments of the performance of practices. Showing how this works out with reference to the reality of large phenomena like companies, economies, states and ideologies calls for a wide range of conceptual tools. In identifying affinities between practice theory, Foucauldian governmentality and Latourian ANT, this chapter highlights what appear to be especially promising options.

But what does practice theory stand to gain in pursuing an understanding of power? To return to the imperatives noted at the start of this chapter, if practice theory can account for all aspects of the social, it should be able to account for power as a pervasive aspect of the social. Second, if practice theory is to make a difference, it must be able to provide an account of power with which it is consistent. Change is likely to entail and come through changes in power relations and purposive change will involve engaging in and with existing dominant power relations. In addition, engaging with questions of power provides a means of developing and advancing practice theory.

In summary, practice theory has within it a largely unspoken account of power. It is unspoken because within practice theory, power is ubiquitous. A practice (as entity) shapes human action (as performance). While the practice as entity is only the effect of performances, any one performance is substantially shaped by the practice as entity. Human action is therefore always influenced from elsewhere: it is the effect of relationships which are arguably always power relations (relations shaping action and the capacity to act), however diffused and distanciated. In turn, power relations are always and only the effect of the performance of practices, in concert with their arrangements. Further, power relations never result only from distinct, specifiable, moments of practice, but are effects of the ordering and the churn of innumerable moments of practices. This explains why practice theory does not tend to focus on power as a separate or distinct property of the social. As Barnes said: 'talk of practices is talk of powers' (2001: 28).

However, not much is gained by noticing that power is ubiquitous to practice. The more significant challenge is to understand power as integral to and an effect of distributed practices, while also accounting for distinct social phenomena which can be meaningfully understood as powerful. It is clearly relevant to point out that the practices taking place in a multinational's global HQ are shaped by embodied knowledge and tacit routine, just as much as the practices of a domestic kitchen or amateur sports club. But the further ambition is to be able to account for the qualities of the corporate HQ that make it distinct from those other sites of practice and for how these arise, while recognising that practices are made of the same basic stuff. The answers lie in understanding how practices are related to each other across different sites – hence the importance of conceptualising the connections and nature of relationships between practices (Shove *et al.*, 2012; Nicolini, 2012; Schatzki, 2015b). Tangling with questions about connections between practices takes on a sharper edge when the problem is that of explaining how some actors and sites come to be loci of a disproportionate capacity for shaping action elsewhere.

Existing thinking in cognate fields is of value in responding to this challenge. In most respects, an account of power that is compatible with practice theory can be fully encompassed by Foucault's account of governing and of power relations. Concepts from his work, not least in relation to governmentality, provide a means of ordering an analysis of practices in relation to the doing of governing (and being governed) which is sensitive to what it is in the flow of practices that is pertinent in understanding particular power relations. However, Foucault's own work and the work comprising more recent governmentality studies does not develop an account of how practices and their performance relate to and are anchored in the action of technologies and apparatuses of governing. In seeking to address this question, I turned to concepts from Latourian ANT that have already been used in describing how practices connect and act upon one another over distance (Nicolini, 2012). The processes of alignment and aggregation that characterise classic Latourian concepts like inscriptions, mobiles and centres of calculation come close to bridging between analyses of technologies and apparatuses of governing and accounts of practice. Working through these affinities and identifying tensions and gaps between practice theory and related approaches helps specify methods of revealing and showing how certain practices act upon others.

A practice theoretically compatible approach to power relations casts new light on the processes underpinning and effecting them. As outlined above, the challenge is in essence one of explaining exactly what flows between moments of performance, of revealing the dynamics within and between those flows and of showing how they are distinctively aggregated and aligned to serve distinct purposes. In taking up this challenge, practice theory can make a distinctive contribution to understanding the existence and operation of power in the social and can do so by focusing on how practices relate to and align with each other so as to enable and perpetuate the capacity to act and to act at a distance to shape conduct in other spaces and times.

Acknowledgements

Thanks to the book's editors and Torik Holmes for excellent advice and comments; to fellow contributors to this volume for discussion of an early draft at the Lancaster workshop. The ideas this chapter started from took the form of a manifesto which was productively taken apart at the Windermere workshop *Demanding ideas* in 2014.

13

HOW SHOULD WE UNDERSTAND 'GENERAL UNDERSTANDINGS'?

Daniel Welch and Alan Warde

Introduction

Practice theory is increasingly prominent in social scientific analysis. Hence, its virtues and its defects are being subjected to greater scrutiny. As part of that exercise, we examine the conceptualisation of widespread cultural understandings in the social scientific use of practice theory. Schatzki's (1996; 2002) schema of practice components has proved generative, particularly as adapted by Warde (2005) and Shove *et al.* (2012). However, virtually no attention has been paid to Schatzki's (2002) concept of 'general understandings', which is one potentially relevant instrument to address this challenge.[1] In *The site of the social*, Schatzki (2002) introduces the category of general understandings into his schema of components of practice, an addition to his earlier tripartite model of 'practical understandings', 'rules' and 'teleoaffective structures' (1996). In this chapter, we seek to open up issues posed by general understandings as a category within a schema of generic practice components. The concept of general understandings promises to deal with broad cultural conceptions which transcend the boundaries between 'integrative practices' (Schatzki, 2002).

General understandings might include such things as concepts, values and categories. Specific candidates might include: collective concepts, such as nation, state, economy or organisation; membership categories, such as ethnicity or gender; fundamental, culturally structuring concepts, such as animal\human or private\public and diffuse but culturally significant understandings, such as notions of convenience, cosmopolitanism or authenticity. Of course, many of these kinds of general understandings are the objects of whole fields of social scientific inquiry. Furthermore, we claim no originality in conceiving such objects of analysis in terms of practice. The movement away from substantialist ontologies in social science has seen the widespread reformulation of fixed social entities and collective concepts, such as nation or gender, as processes of enactment and (specific) categories of practice (e.g. Brubaker, 1996; Butler, 1993). We do not presume to add insight into the operations of specific kinds of general understandings (e.g. membership categories, values, etc.). This chapter, rather, aims to cast light on the theoretical issues posed by the concept of general understandings in the spirit of Schatzki's formulation.

The chapter proceeds by first examining Schatzki's use of the category of general understandings and its relation to 'teleoaffective structures' (section 2), 'practical understandings' and Schatzki's concept of 'practical intelligibility' (section 3). We explore how general understandings might serve cultural analysis or play a part in a model of culture-in-practice (section 4). In section 5, we identify three putative general features of the diffusion, persistence and actuation of general understandings through illustrative examples. First, they may have their origins either in discourse or in practices. Second, they may display intimately connected tacit and discursive elements. Third, they circulate between integrative practices through typical channels, processes and mechanisms. We conclude by summarising the core features and effects of general understandings and their potential explanatory power.

The category of general understandings

General understandings, in Schatzki's (2002) formulation, are common to many practices, condition the manner in which practices are carried out and are expressed in their performance. Schatzki gives the example of the Shaker view of labour as a sanctification of the earthly sphere, which conditioned how labouring practices were carried out, as well as being explicitly formulated in doings and sayings (2002: 86). The simplest way to approach general understandings, then, is as ideational elements common to multiple practices. That general understandings are formulated in *both* doings and sayings gestures towards a central feature of the category: that it sits across the boundary between the discursive and the non-discursive. The category thus immediately inveigles itself into two thorny problematics for practice theory: how to conceptualise the relation between practices and discourse (see Schatzki, this volume) and how to understand the tacit (see Collins, 2001; 2010; Rouse, 2001; 2007a).

Schemas which lack analytical differentiation between diffuse cultural understandings and practice-specific understandings risk obscuring important dynamics and processes (Welch and Warde, 2015). Pellandini-Simányi (2014) usefully suggests two different forms of change in ideational elements common to multiple practices, which we might think of as two ideal-typical processes.[2] One form of change is when an element, such as an ideal of masculinity, is affected by changes within one practice – for example a work practice – which in turn has knock-on effects on the ideal of masculinity in other practices, say, domestic cooking. A second form of change is when general understandings are connected as elements in a more or less coherent axiology, or 'cosmology' as Pellandini-Simányi (2014) has it. Schatzki (2010b) alludes to such configurations of general understandings in the context of his discussion of Eliade's work on ritual. Schatzki observes that cosmological general understandings establish, for Eliade, 'basic features of religious man's being-in-the-world' and that this 'complex of general understandings informs the teleological organisation of religious man's life (2010b: 151).[3] Changes in one element of such a complex of general understandings may trigger changes in other elements of that complex as well. The example Pellandini-Simányi (2014: 139) gives is that of the 'ethical vision of gentility', which contained (in our terms) the general understandings of masculinity and of luxury. As masculinity became increasingly defined in terms of rationality, previous notions of opulence were challenged and the ideal of luxury came to be redefined in rational terms, as a controlled expression of taste. A focus on general understandings thus foregrounds the issue of how to articulate analytically specific practices, say cooking, with wider configurations like domestic organisation.

Nicolini plausibly suggests general understandings constitute 'external understandings' of the overall project in which the practice is engaged (2012: 167). How should we think about that externality? *Where*, external to the focal practice, does the general understanding lie, or rather, come from? The *external* here hints at a supra-practice level which threatens to undo the 'high order ontological sameness' of Schatzki's flat ontology of the social (2011: 4). Thus Caldwell (2012) suggests that the notion of 'general understandings' potentially leads Schatzki back to the position from which his work aims to escape: 'the "social" conceived as "general understandings" may presuppose an object of enquiry that goes beyond the practices in which it is carried or enacted' (2012: 291). However, Caldwell evinces a widely held misunderstanding that Schatzki's general position amounts to a kind of 'Il n'y a rien en dehors du pratique'. Caldwell assumes either that general understandings presuppose a distinct ontological level (perhaps implied by the relative coherence that complexes of general understandings may assume) or that they are carried in discursive formations exhibiting forms of organisation other than that of integrative practices and therefore debarred from Schatzki's ontology. To take the latter possibility first, as Schatzki makes clear in his contribution to this volume, discursive formations exhibiting their own forms of organisation are entirely compatible with his ontology. Schatzki shows that various forms of discursive organisation intersect with integrative practices in the form of sayings and texts incorporated into and carried by them. It is an empirical matter how more or less integrated those discursive formations are with specific configurations of practices. As for the former, no distinct ontological level is necessarily implied by the category of general understandings. The 'external' or 'beyond' in which general understandings subsist simply *is* configurational, whether found specifically in discourse[4] or in heterogeneous assemblages of practice and discourse. A number of ontologically compatible concepts of such assemblages are already common conceptual currency, such as Foucault's 'dispositif', Boltanski and Thévenot's (2006) 'orders of worth' or Hajer's (1995) 'discourse coalitions'.

Schatzki (2002), however, offers a new configurational concept to 'illustrate' general understandings, although he does not develop it, that of 'teleoaffective regime'. This refers to something beyond the teleoaffective structure characteristic of specific practices. He gives three examples of teleoaffective regimes among the Shakers: a religious faith in salvation through Shaker existence and belief that the Shaker's lived order was the kingdom of God on earth, governing hierarchies through which Shaker life was administered and a commitment to communal property and living (2002: 28). Schatzki's (2002) fleeting deployment of teleoaffective regime in his account of the Shakers underscores how a focus on general understandings often foregrounds the configuration of sets of practices. General understandings are the property of integrative practices. But to articulate convincingly the role of these central beliefs in the Shakers' cultural life and social organisation, Schatzki has recourse to a configurational concept that expresses organisation beyond the integrative practices that subtend it. It seems that teleoaffective regime here does the conceptual work at the level of the sociocultural group that teleoaffective structures cannot, given the latter 'are not equivalent to collectively willed ends and projects (e.g. the general will or the we-intentions of a group)', but are the property of individual practices (Schatzki, 2002: 81). Teleoaffective regimes by contrast enjoin common ends. They articulate teleology and affect across practices, conditioning the teleoaffective structures of the practices they govern and subsequently becoming instantiated in situated activity through their performance. However, each of the Shaker teleoaffective regimes – belief in the Shaker order as the kingdom of God on earth and commitment to the hierarchical and communistic principles – could itself be conceptualised in terms of a general understanding. Hence the relation between general understandings and teleoaffective regimes as conceptual categories in Schatzki's (2002) account is therefore somewhat obscure.[5] Nevertheless, it might be profitable to specify further the category of teleoaffective regime even if the category of general understandings does much of the conceptual work.

General understandings, then, may inform the normative ordering of the teleoaffective structure of practices and may partake of axiologies which subtend the teleoaffective structures of multiple individual practices. General understandings may invoke or adjudicate normative controversy in the proper pursuit of practice, both in the sense of justifications and conventions discursively deployed in situations of contention (Boltanski and Thévenot, 2006) and in the broader sense in which the use of categories is both descriptive and normative (Bowker and Star, 2000; Jayyusi, 2013).

We now address how general understandings relate, first, to the practice component 'practical understandings' and second, 'practical intelligibility' (Schatzki, 2002). The former allows us to distinguish clearly between the pre-reflexive or tacit aspects of general understandings and the tacit aspects of practical understandings. The latter informs the role of general understandings in situated performance.

General understandings, practical understandings and practical intelligibility

Schatzki's (2002) category of 'practical understandings' refers to abilities germane to the practical procedures of practices, the sense of how to go on with an activity, identify it *as* such-and-such activity or respond appropriately: 'a skill or capacity that underlies activity' (Schatzki, 2002: 79). The most common forms of practical understandings are: 'knowing how to X, knowing how to identify X-ings, and knowing how to prompt as well as respond to X-ings' (Schatzki, 2002: 77). For example: 'Shaker medicinal herb production practices were linked by an inter-dependent pool of practical understandings of grinding, macerating, drying, storing, mixing, labelling, feeding, and printing labels' (Schatzki, 2002: 78).

While practical understandings are components of practice, 'practical intelli-gibility', for Schatzki, is a property of individuals, not practices: 'it is always to an individual that a specific action makes sense' (2002: 75). 'Practical intelligibility determines what it is that a person does next in the flow of conduct' (Schatzki, 2010b: 114). Practical understanding executes what practical intelligibility selects to do. In Schatzki's account, to the extent that practices determine practical intel-ligibility, they do so by moulding 'mental conditions' of individuals, such as those formed by the learning of practices or the ends and projects that individuals pur-sue, as well as affectivity (2002: 75 fn. 220, 81). General understandings inform practical intelligibility and govern activity by conditioning practical intelligibil-ity or the normative form that practical intelligibility can assume. For exam-ple, European tourists in, say, Mexico, may decide to forego eating at the local MacDonald's in favour of eating traditional Mexican food, because their general understanding of authenticity informs them that this accords with authentic cul-tural experience.

Practical understanding for Schatzki does not therefore mean a sort of general know-how lying behind most or all of human behaviour that exhibits sensitivity to context, such as Bourdieu's (1977) habitus or 'sens pratique' or Giddens's (1984) 'practical consciousness'. By contrast, practical understandings are the property of *particular* practices. For Bourdieu and Giddens, it is these *general* know-hows that determine what people do in specific contexts. For Schatzki (2002), however, prac-tical understandings do not *govern* activity or *determine* what it makes sense for people to do: that aspect of activity instead is governed by practical intelligibility.

It is far less common for general understandings directly to shape practical understandings. Think, for example, of the relationship between the Shakers' gen-eral understanding of the sanctification of labour and the practical understandings of their herb production practices, such as grinding, macerating or drying. While the general understandings inform the teleoaffectivity of herb production practices, it leaves their practical procedures undisturbed. The Shakers are highly atypical of commonplace contemporary social conditions, in the extent to which their core religious understandings suffused and orientated all their everyday practices. But even in this situation, unusually strongly governed by general understandings, it was only those specifically religious practices, where their religious general understand-ings were intrinsic, as it were, to the practice, that general understandings directly shaped practical understandings. By contrast, there is contingency between their general understandings and herb production practices, even in the light of the auto-telic imperative of the belief in the sanctification of labour.

We have to signal some disquiet with this account of practical intelligibility, which potentially has voluntaristic and individualistic implications for an account of social action which sit uneasily with stronger pragmatic and practice theoretical understandings of human activity. This potential is the more so, we suggest, in the context of an account of general understandings, where the latter might be misconstrued as anterior drivers of the subject's activity (Whitford, 2002). Having explicated the place of general understandings within Schatzki's schema, we now turn to the functions of the category for sociological analysis more broadly.

General understandings and culture

General understandings – all the more so when we invoke notions of *complexes* of general understandings, such as cosmologies or teleoaffective regimes – raise the question of how to understand the relation between culture and action. As noted above, the example of the Shakers is highly atypical of contemporary sociocultural milieu and thus of the place of general understandings within them. The Shakers were an unusually homogeneous sociocultural group, among whom foundational general understandings invested all practices. Furthermore, the sociocultural group was coextensive with a complex of practices: an orthopraxy animated by an orthodoxy of general understandings.

Despite the simplicity of the case, the question remains of how the Shakers' general understandings related to situated activity; or, how does this resolve the problem of, as it is commonly phrased, culture in action (Swidler, 1986). Schatzki invokes the Shakers' belief in the sanctification of labour in the context of evidence for the Shakers' propensity to toil hard for long hours. No doubt individual Shakers' engagement in their labours was invested with a sense of higher purpose and this served a strong motivating function. However, the danger would be to fall back into an account of social action where general understandings serve as anterior motivation for action and where declarative cultural commitments provide explanation (Whitford, 2002; Lizardo, 2012).

Instead, general understandings may contribute to a model of culture in practice: an alternative to both a Parsonian account of culture as internalised propositional knowledge or a Geertzian account of culture as externalised sign system (Biernacki, 2000; Lizardo and Strand, 2010; Warde, 2015). Biernacki argues that cultural meaning is generated by the ties between 'an order of representations *and* an order of practice that connects representation to a context of social exchange' such that 'we can concentrate analysis on variation in those types of ties' (2000: 302). That is to say, exploration of culture in practice might profitably proceed by addressing empirical questions regarding the relationships between general understandings and configurations of practice. We offer examples of such accounts below.

Invoking representation here suggests that we should specify the relation between the discursive and the non-discursive aspects of general understandings. General understandings sit across the discursive and the non-discursive divide and may exhibit pre-reflexive or tacit aspects. There is no need to establish a phenomenological boundary between the discursive and the tacit (Rouse, 2001; 2007a; Collins, 2001; 2010). As Biernacki argues, a pragmatics of the relation between representation and practice moves one away from 'a purely discursive notion of culture with-out... counterposing "corporeal" practice in a binary opposite that is inaccessible' (2000: 308). Furthermore, the notion of discursive practice holds that linguistic expression and understanding is integral to practical competence (Rouse, 2007a).

Sayer usefully articulates how values – a particular kind of general understand-ing – combine conceptual, pre-reflexive and affective components:

> Values are 'sedimented' valuations of things (including persons, ideas, behav-iours, practices, etc.) that have become attitudes or dispositions, which we come to regard as justified. They merge into emotional dispositions, and inform the evaluations we make of particular things, as part of our conceptual and affective apparatus.
>
> (*Sayer, 2012: 171*)

Values are both pre-reflexive 'moral intuitions' (Haidt, 2007; cf. Vaisey, 2009), which inform the cognitive and affective dispositions through which individuals respond to their environment, and they are deployed in discursive practice in justification and contention (Boltanski and Thévenot, 2006). The example of values illustrates how general understandings may combine the tacit and the discursive, the linkage of which we explore further in the following section.

General understandings in action

If we follow this line of reasoning, the category of general understandings does not, contra Caldwell (2012), suggest a model of the social that undermines the social ontology of practice. Rather, general understandings may inform a framework of culture-in-practice consistent with the social ontology of practice theories. The tight enmeshing of Shaker orthopraxy in teleoaffective regimes might be misleading when studying the functioning of general understandings in contemporary milieux with which sociological inquiry is commonly concerned. Let us therefore look to contrasting examples. Multiple existing examples of broadly practice theoretical accounts, even if not framed as such, address the emergence and entanglement of general understandings within contexts of practice. We will briefly examine three exemplary cases. In this section, we examine different examples of how general understandings are articulated with configurations of practice, or of culture in prac-tice, in order to identify some general processes and mechanisms which might sen-sitise future inquiry.

Central questions for sociology include where general understandings come from and what social processes and mechanisms convey them between different domains or configurations of practice. We begin with two ideal-typical processes concerning translation from discourse to praxis, on the one hand, and from praxis to discourse on the other.

Taylor (2004) offers examples of the first process in the emergence of the three 'modern social imaginaries': the public sphere, the market economy and the sovereign people. These imaginaries are fundamental cultural constituents of Western modernity: widely shared, pre-reflexive, background understandings that make possible certain common practices. Modern social imaginaries are congruent with secular 'meta-topical spaces' present to their members as 'framework[s] that exists prior to and independent of their actions' (Taylor, 2002: 115). However, the contents of the modern social imaginaries do not originate at this non-discursive level. Rather, they began life, in Taylor's account, as theory that gradually 'infiltrates and transmutes' an existing social imaginary, whose horizon they breach (Taylor, 2004: 109). Taylor is alert to 'the spectre of idealism', however, and thus grounds these processes in the practices that carry those general understandings (imaginaries), which 'are the essential condition of the practice making the sense that it does to the participants' (2004: 31–2). As Taylor has it, 'if the understanding makes the practice possible, it is also true that it is the practice that largely carries the understanding' (2004: 25).

Taylor suggests two kinds of processes through which transference comes about: first, a 'theory may inspire a new kind of activity with new practices, and in this way form the imaginary of whatever groups adopt these practices' (2004: 109). An example is the theological innovation that the first Puritan churches formed around the notion of covenant, which came to influence the civil structures of the American colonies. Second, a change may come about with a reinterpretation of a practice. The novel concept of popular sovereignty in the American Revolution found a propitious home in the existing institutions of elected legislatures in the colonies, such that: 'older forms of legitimacy are colonized ... with new understandings of order, and then ... transformed ... without a clear break' (Taylor, 2004: 110).

This latter example draws our attention to how, as Brubaker puts it when discussing ethnonational identities, general understandings 'need ecological niches in which to survive and flourish' (Brubaker, 2002: 185). Also, as Biernacki (2000) notes, in the context of Communist ideology in Eastern Europe, the life world may prove barren ground for ideological innovations: while some aspects of state ideology, such as production as the creator of value, became 'natural givens among working populations', other ideological aspects, such as collective authority over the generation of wealth 'were never accepted as genuine or taken for granted' (Biernacki, 2000: 306). A belief, furthermore, 'may appear specious if it is not an implicit organising principle of practice' (Biernacki, 2000: 308).

In the second, reverse, process, general understandings arise unbidden from practice. Swidler (2001) draws on an analysis of the formation and unification of the gay community in San Francisco from the early 1970s onward, and asks how, in the space of just a few years, did the adoption of one of a proliferating number of 'identities' become a crucial feature of membership in the wider lesbian and gay community? Notably, the community's diversity was enacted in the Lesbian/Gay Freedom Day Parade 'with floats, contingents, and marchers representing a panoply of more or less flamboyant identities' (Swidler, 2001: 91). From this condition, without any discursive coordination, a general understanding was formulated

> that diverse identities did not split the community, but united it; that organisers should not aspire to create a single unified organisation to represent the community; that the discovery and public assertion of new identities was part of the community building project.
>
> (*Swidler, 2001: 91*)

In the parade itself, 'groups apply to have a float included in the parade … and the more diverse their identity displays the more successful, exciting, and newsworthy the parade is' (Swidler, 2001: 92), anchoring the general understanding that the 'community' was composed of multiple identity groups. Swidler (2001) argues that the general understanding was precipitated from the practices involved in setting up the parade.

Our second illustrative case concerns issues of national identity. Anderson (1991) famously saw nations as imagined communities. Imagined communities exemplify the mutual dependency of representation and practice in the successful establishment of a general understanding of national belonging, including their pre-reflexive and affective aspects. In Anderson's account, the discursive and symbolic aspects of nationality are not sufficient in themselves to anchor the understanding of national membership or citizen obligation. Rather, he finds the basis of perceived solidarity in the practice of reading the morning newspaper, a routine shared by anonymous millions within the national boundaries, which enacts the core principle of that community. However, such diffuse general understandings of the existence of a nation – or, indeed of the public sphere, economy, society or authenticity – extend beyond the immediate background understanding that makes sense of particular practices. In such vein, Taylor speaks not just of modern social *imaginaries* but of *the* social imaginary, the 'inarticulate understanding of our whole situation' (2004: 25). This 'background' does not have clear limits, but nor is it limitless and despite being largely unstructured, it is neither inaccessible nor in-articulable.

Billig's (1995) analysis of nation and nationalism gives some substance to a claim that the broad background transcends the boundary between the articulated-discursive and the pre-reflexive, tacit, diffused and habituated. Billig's concern is not with expressly nationalist mobilisation, but with the sentiments lying behind and within the political arrangements of well-established Western polities which require no regular appeals for positive commitment or support for activities promoting national consciousness. How can a mostly dormant idea, with which most members of the population are not engaged, be credibly and effectively mobilised on occasion for political purposes by Western governments? Billig's answer is that national identity is reproduced in a habitual and mundane fashion as a type of nationalism specific to the West: *banal* nationalism. Billig writes:

> [T]he ideological habits which enable the established nations of the West to be reproduced… are not removed from everyday life… Daily, the nation is indicated, or 'flagged', in the lives of its citizenry. Nationalism, far from being an intermittent mood in established nations, is the endemic condition.
>
> (*Billig, 1995: 6*)

It is an ideological form which grounds an effective call to action or sacrifice when circumstances require it. But it is not consciously, intentionally, mindfully present in the populations affected by it. Rather, it lies in the background, signalled by cues in the environment, in commentaries on sport and cultural performances, in newspaper columns and stories. It is present and perceptible, but beneath the threshold of conscious attention. As Billig puts it:

> [N]ationhood provides a continual background for political discourses, for cultural products, and even for the structuring of newspapers. In so many little ways, the citizenry are reminded of their national place in a world of nations. However, this reminding is so familiar, so continual, that it is not consciously registered as reminding. The metonymic image of banal nationalism is not a flag which is being consciously waved with fervent passion; it is the flag hanging unnoticed on the public building.
>
> (*Billig, 1995: 8*)

The un-waved flag, a symbolic object to which no attention is paid, is yet the means by which nationhood is 'constantly flagged'. Billig employs an analysis of the sports pages which 'day after day, invite "us", the readers, to support the national cause' (Billig, 1995: 11). The regular and routine use of 'we' and 'us' – in international sports coverage or news broadcasts is a form of banal appeal to a political identity which mostly exists at the preconscious level, presuming an acceptance of allegiance and obligation upon which people neither reflect nor meditate. Nations, nationhood and national identity are sometimes topics attracting deliberate and discursive attention, as explanations and justifications of behaviour, general understandings expressed and contested in an explicit manner. However, they are probably much more often present and effective as tacit background to understandings and experience of other practices like spectatorship at sports events, listening to radio reports on issues of international relations or encountering people with a different coloured skin on the bus to work. Traces of them are all around in the environment. Their taken-for-granted ubiquity is the source of their strength. In Billig's terms, banal nationalism has 'the powers of an ideology which is so familiar that it hardly seems noticeable' (1995: 12). Thus, nation stands as an exemplary instance of a general understanding which operates across the divide between the discursive on the one hand, and the pre-reflexive, dispositional and affective on the other.

A third illustrative case of general understandings in circulation concerns the cultural understanding of *authenticity*. The concept of authenticity plays a prominent role in modern Western cultural history and we have a number of authoritative accounts of its translations. Lindholm notes:

> [T]here are two overlapping modes for characterising any entity as authentic: genealogical or historical (origin) and identity or correspondence (content). Authentic objects, persons and collectives are original, real, and pure; they are what they purport to be, their roots are known and verified, their essence and appearance are one.
>
> (*Lindholm, 2007: 2*)

Such understandings of authenticity are carried in diverse practices. Tourists seek authentic cultural experiences. Food connoisseurs seek authentic dishes. Brand managers regard the authenticity of their brands as of foremost importance. The commonality among this diversity is that these disparate practices all in some way relate to identity, whether cultural, organisational or personal.

The concept of authenticity demonstrates how general understandings may both subtend and precipitate from broad cultural shifts and become instantiated in diverse practices thus creating novel configurations. It is possible to follow various translations of the idea of authenticity: from Protestant religiosity to Romantic literary innovation, to a pre-reflexive, background condition of modern identity (Taylor, 1989); from a value of the Modernist artistic avant-garde to a commonplace of modern consumer culture (Trilling, 1972; Orvell, 1989; Holt, 2002) and from the ideal of the anti-bourgeois individual to a buzzword of contemporary work place 'employee engagement' (Berman, 1970; Honneth, 2004). Space does not allow a detailed exposition but instances of authenticity illustrate several social processes and mechanisms by means of which general understandings may be conveyed from domain to domain, from the extra-mundane to the mundane and between the discursive and pre-reflexive. Its progress poses the always empirical questions of to what extent, and in what ways, do the general understandings condition those practices in which they are taken up and in what ways are they conditioned by them?

One feature of this story involves mediation by new *material* modes of communication. For example, the development in the eighteenth century of printing technology and the emergence of 'print capitalism' saw secular literary genres develop, disseminating Romanticism to a new reading public and a novel cultural concern with 'the authenticity of the selves who wrote such works' (Sinanan and Milnes, 2010: 2). In addition to material affordances, the diffusion of general understandings requires space or need for novel cultural understandings, a 'demand for intelligibility' which exerts 'pressure for greater explanation' (Boltanski and Chiapello, 2005: 103). Cultural dislocation is one regular explanation given for the fertility of the idea of authenticity, for example in the association of authenticity with commodities in the context of the cultural dislocations of nineteenth century urbanisation and industrialisation (Orvell, 1989). Another push comes from specific groups of cultural innovators and intermediaries who are often the *Träger* of general understandings and the translators of understandings across domains. Thus, as well as artistic avant-gardes, practitioners of commercial communications have played a key role in the translation of authenticity from, for example, 1960s counterculture to mainstream consumer and commercial culture (Frank, 1997; Welch, 2012).

To conclude our excursion into authenticity, the above cited genealogies demonstrate historical translations of authenticity from explicit discursive and symbolic articulation to pre-reflexive background understanding and back again. For example, the radical reflexivity of the modern self becomes ground for the Romantic cult of the artist; Modernism gives explicit voice to the notion of authenticity, which is diffused into wider culture by novel forms of media, finding receptive cultural niches at anomic moments of social and economic transformation.

As with Billig's 'banal nationalism', authenticity figures as diffuse background understanding, sedimented in cognitive and affective dispositions and activated and transmitted by diverse discursive, symbolic and material elements of popular and consumer culture. It became a pre-reflexive background understanding to the concept of identity, which itself came under intense scrutiny in the scholarship of the later twentieth century. It is central to commonplace modern axiology and informs the teleoaffective structures of diverse practices across multiple domains, from the religious to the artistic to the commercial; and from cultural production to technologies of the self (Foucault, 1988). Its ubiquitous taken-for-granted-ness enables its transposition into novel practical and discursive contexts, as for example with the *prima facie* unlikely instance of the identity of brands and organisations (Holt, 2002; Welch, 2012).

These examples have highlighted the point that general understandings may be implicated across diverse domains and illustrated the diverse processes and dynamics through which general understandings are translated, diffused and instantiated. A genealogy of general understandings will necessarily trace a contingent historical path where understandings are articulated within different institutional contexts.

Conclusion

We have drawn attention to how general understandings operate both discursively and pre-reflexively. Thus, for example, contemporary seekers of authentic experience do not have to resort to discursive articulations in order to recognise and embody authenticity. The same claim could be made for nationality. Also, general understandings may be articulated in the 'sayings' of various practices and in their discursive form link practices together in ways unachievable through non-discursive performances. They may partake of teleoaffective formations that reign over complexes of practice, sociocultural groups, professions, cultural domains or other slices of praxis and thus offer insight into larger configurational phenomena. The concept potentially therefore contributes to the practice theoretical analysis of larger scale social and cultural phenomena; it might stretch beyond local phenomena or situated activity to which analysis practice theory is all too often relegated (see Nicolini, this volume; Schatzki, 2016b). It offers the analytical affordances of practice theory without debarring traditional sociological concerns with 'macro' phenomena, providing a route through which the characteristics of the 'macro' can be generated from a flat ontology of practice. Common to the illustrations above is the articulation of macro-sociological concerns (regarding modernity and nationalism, for example) with micro-sociological contexts, or put in other ways, of the level of discursive formation with that of situated activity or of the level of the institutional with that of affective, embodied dispositions.

We suggest that general understandings exhibit at least three functions. First, general understandings may have an integrating or organising function, as is demonstrated by Schatzki's (2002) analysis of the Shakers, for whom general understandings integrated practice into an overarching cultural formation or by Swidler's (1986) case of the organisation of the San Franciscan gay and lesbian community through diverse identities. Billig's (1995) 'banal nationalism' demonstrates a second possible function – justification, which sits across the pre-reflexive responses of affective disposition and discursive contention. Third, general understandings have a function of enabling intelligibility, as when general understandings animated the everyday practice of the Shakers or when the quest for authentic self-expression motivates and orientates artistic endeavours. General understandings inform practical intelligibility, which governs individual conduct (Schatzki, 2002), albeit always through the 'normative accountability' of practices (Rouse, 2007a: 529). They are among the shared presuppositions which ground the intelligibility of social practices (Rouse, 2007a: 517).

There are several things that a theory of practice might want to do with a notion of general understanding. First, general understandings permit the analysis of large scale phenomena. Second, the concept presents a way to explicate the role of culture in practice, accounting for how very general ideas are incorporated into practice; it captures how such understandings are transmitted, translated and appropriated by practices, how they inform and shape practices and in turn how they are themselves conditioned by practices. General understandings are experienced, articulated and negotiated in situated and embodied activity and thereby transpose the cultural to situated activity. They encompass the pre-reflexive and thus help us understand forms of transmission of practice *without* discursive articulation as well as the actuation of dispositions and orientation of action through environmental cues. Third, the concept might also show how adjacent and distant practices might borrow from and change one another. As general understandings inform multiple practices, they could also help us to answer questions about the role of cultural intermediaries in transferring meanings and understandings and about the effect of intermediation on practices. Lastly, general understandings mediate discursive formations and practices, linking a focal practice to the discourses which inform and condition it and in the process become practical categories of identification, justification and evaluation.

Notes

1   The only exceptions we are aware of are Caldwell (2012), Jarzabkowski *et al.* (2015), and Keller and Vihalemm (2015).
2   Pellandini-Simányi's (2014) concern is with the nature of 'consumption norms', the extrapolation to general understandings is our own.
3   Such a complex, its manner of organisation and its modes of instantiation, are therefore central objects of study. The extent to which general understandings were more common in the past, as Schatzki (2010b: 151) intuits, how we might characterise such complexes (for example, in relation to sign modalities), whether general understandings play a different role, or are more or less integrated, in different times and places, and so forth, are fundamental questions of social science. We do not attempt to address any such fundamental questions here.
4   We are quite capable of articulating in talk and text relatively coherent world views, ideologies, etc.
5   Schatzki notes: 'General understandings combine with teleology in the determination of human activity. They specify ends and purposes, stipulate forms of activity, and inform how objects and events can be used in the pursuit of particular ends and purposes...' (2010b: 152).

REFERENCES

Abbott, A. (1988) *The system of professions: an essay on the division of expert labor.* Chicago: University of Chicago Press.

Akrich, M. (1992) 'The de-scription of technical objects', in Bijker, W. E. and Law, J. (eds.) *Shaping technology/building society.* Cambridge: MIT Press, 205–24.

Alkemeyer, T. (2006) 'Lernen und seine Körper. Habitusformungen und -umformungen in Bildungspraktiken', in Friebertshäuser, B., Rieger-Ladich, M. and Wigger, L. (eds.) *Reflexive Erziehungswissenschaft. Forschungsperspektiven im Anschluss an Pierre Bourdieu.* Wiesbaden: VS-Verlag, 119–42.

Alkemeyer, T. (2013) 'Subjektivierung in sozialen Praktiken. Umrisse einer praxeologischen Analytik', in Alkemeyer, T., Budde, C. and Freist, D. (eds.) *Selbst-Bildungen. Soziale und kulturelle Praktiken der Subjektivierung.* Bielefeld: Transcript, 29–64.

Alkemeyer, T. and Brümmer, K. (2016) 'Körper und informelles Lernen', in Harring, M., Witte, M. D. and Burger, T. (eds.) *Handbuch informelles Lernen. Interdisziplinäre und internationale Perspektiven.* Weinheim/Basel: Beltz Juventa, 493–509.

Alkemeyer, T. and Buschmann, N. (2016) 'Praktiken der Subjektivierung –Subjektivierung als Praxis', in Schäfer, H. (ed.) *Praxistheorie. Ein soziologisches Forschungsprogramm.* Bielefeld: Transcript, 115–36.

Alkemeyer, T. and Michaeler, M. (2013) 'Die Ausformung mitspielfähiger "Vollzugskörper". Praxistheoretisch-empirische Überlegungen am Beispiel des Volleyballspiels', *Sport und Gesellschaft – Sport and Society*, 10(3), 213–39.

Alkemeyer, T., Brümmer, K. and Pille, T. (forthcoming) 'Intercorporeality at the motor block: on the importance of a practical sense for social cooperation and coordination', in Meyer, C., Streek, J. and Jordan, J. S. (eds.) *Intercorporeality: emerging socialities in interaction.* Oxford: Oxford University Press.

Alkemeyer, T., Schürmann, V. and Volbers, J. (eds.) (2015) *Praxis denken. Konzepte und Kritik.* Wiesbaden: VS-Verlag.

Anderson, B. (1991 [1983]) *Imagined communities: reflections on the origin and spread of nationalism.* Rev. ed. London: Verso.

Andrews, G. J., Chen, S. and Myers, S. (2014) 'The "taking place" of health and wellbeing: towards non-representational theory', *Social Science & Medicine*, 108(May), 210–22.

Anscombe, E. (1975) 'The first person', in Guttenplan, S. (ed.) *Mind and language: Wolfson College lectures 1974*. Oxford: Clarendon Press, 45–64.

Appadurai, A. (1986) *The social life of things: commodities in cultural perspective*. Cambridge: Cambridge University Press.

Austin, J. L. (1975 [1962]) *How to do things with words*. 2nd edn. Edited by J. O. Urmson and M. Sbisà. Cambridge: Harvard University Press.

Bachmann-Medick, D. (2006) *Cultural Turns. Neuorientierungen in den Kulturwissenschaften*. Reinbek: Rowohlt.

Bakhtin, M. M. (1986) *Speech genres & other late essays*. Translated by V. W. McGee. Edited by C. Emerson and M. Holquist. Austin: University of Texas Press.

Balzer, N. (2014) *Spuren der Anerkennung. Studien zu einer sozial- und erziehungswissenschaftlichen Kategorie*. Wiesbaden: VS-Verlag.

Barad, K. (2003) 'Posthumanist performativity: toward an understanding of how matter comes to matter', *Signs*, 28(3), 801–31.

Barad, K. (2007) *Meeting the universe halfway: quantum physics and the entanglement of matter and Meaning*. Durham: Duke University Press.

Barad, K. (2013) 'Ma(r)king time: material entanglements and re-memberings: cutting together-apart', in Carlile, P. R., et al. (eds.) *How matter matters: objects, artifacts, and materiality in organization studies*. Oxford: Oxford University Press, 16–30.

Barclays Premier League (2015) *What is the EA SPORTS Player Performance Index?* Available at www.premierleague.com/en-gb/players/ea-sports-player-performance-index/what-is-the-ea-sports-ppi.html (accessed 8 August 2015).

Barnes, B. (2001) 'Practice as collective action', in Schatzki, T. R., Knorr Cetina, K. and Von Savigny, E. (eds.) *The practice turn in contemporary theory*. New York: Routledge, 25–36.

Beck, U. and Bonss, W. (1989) 'Verwissenschaftlichung ohne Aufklärung? Zum Strukturwandel von Sozialwissenschaft und Praxis', in Beck, U. and Bonss, W. (eds.) *Weder Sozialtechnologie noch Aufklärung?* Frankfurt am Main: Suhrkamp, 7–45.

Bedorf, T. (2015) 'Leibliche Praxis. Zum Körperbegriff der Praxistheorien', in Alkemeyer, T., Schürmann, V. and Volbers, J. (eds.) *Praxis denken. Konzepte und Kritik*. Wiesbaden: Springer VS, 129–50.

Bennett, J. (2007) 'Edible matter', *New Left Review*, 45(May–June), 133–45.

Bennett, J. (2010) *Vibrant matter: a political ecology of things*. Durham: Duke University Press.

Berman, M. (1970) *The politics of authenticity: radical individualism and the emergence of modern society*. New York: Atheneum.

Biermann, C. (2009) *Die Fußball-Matrix: Auf der Suche nach dem perfekten Spiel*. Köln: Kiepenheuer & Witsch.

Biernacki, R. (2000) 'Language and the shift from signs to practices in cultural inquiry', *History and Theory*, 39(3), 289–310.

Billig, M. (1995) *Banal Nationalism*. London: Sage.

Bird, A. (2007) 'Perceptions of epigenetics', *Nature*, 447(7143), 396–8.

Blue, S., Shove, E., Carmona, C. and Kelly, M. P. (2016) 'Theories of practice and public health: understanding (un)healthy practices', *Critical Public Health*, 26(1), 36–50.

Böhme, G. (2000) *Atmosphäre: Essays zur neuen Ästhetik*. Frankfurt am Main: Suhrkamp.

Böhme, G. (2001) *Aisthetik. Vorlesungen über Ästhetik als allgemeine Wahrnehmungslehre*. München: Wilhelm Fink.

Böhme, H. (2006) *Fetischismus und Kultur: Eine andere Theorie der Moderne*. Reinbek: Rowohlt.

Boltanski, L. (2010) *Soziologie und Sozialkritik*. Frankfurt am Main: Suhrkamp.

Boltanski, L. (2011) *On critique: a sociology of emancipation*. Cambridge: Polity Press.

Boltanski, L. and Chiapello, E. (2005) *The new spirit of capitalism*. London: Verso.

Boltanski, L. and Honneth, A. (2009) 'Soziologie der Kritik oder Kritische Theorie? Ein Gespräch mit Robin Celikates', in Jaeggi, R. and Weche, T. (eds.) *Was ist Kritik?* Frankfurt am Main: Suhrkamp, 81–116.

Boltanski, L. and Thévenot, L. (2006) *On justification: economies of worth.* Princeton: Princeton University Press.

Boltanski, L. and Thévenot, L. (2011) 'The sociology of critical capacity', *European Journal for Social Theory*, 2(3), 359–77.

Borch, C. and Stäheli, U. (eds.) (2009) *Soziologie der Nachahmung und des Begehrens: Materialien zu Gabriel Tarde.* Frankfurt am Main: Suhrkamp.

Bourdieu, P. (1977) *Outline of a theory of practice.* Cambridge: Cambridge University Press.

Bourdieu, P. (1990) *The logic of practice.* Cambridge: Polity Press.

Bourdieu, P. (1984) *Distinction: a social critique of the judgement of taste.* Cambridge: Harvard University Press.

Bourdieu, P. (1991) *Language and symbolic power.* Translated by G. Raymond. Edited by J. Thompson. Cambridge: Polity Press.

Bourdieu, P. (2000) *Pascalian meditations.* Stanford: Stanford University Press.

Bourdieu, P. (2005) 'Habitus', in Hillier, J. and Rooksby, E. (eds.) *Habitus: a sense of place.* 2nd edn. Harts: Ashgate Publishing Ltd, 43–9.

Bourdieu, P. and Wacquant, L. (1992) *An invitation to reflexive sociology.* Chicago: University of Chicago Press.

Bowker, G. C. and Star, S. L. (2000) 'Invisible mediators of action: classification and the ubiquity of standards', *Mind, Culture and Activity*, 7(1–2), 147–63.

Braidotti, R. (2006) 'Posthuman. All too human: towards a new process ontology', *Theory, Culture & Society*, 23(7–8), 197–208.

Braidotti, R. (2013) *The Posthuman.* Cambridge: Polity Press.

Brake, A. (2016) 'Theorie der sozialen Praxis und informelles Lernen', in Harring, M., Witte, M. D. and Burger, T. (eds.) *Handbuch informelles Lernen. Interdisziplinäre und internationale Perspektiven.* Weinheim/Basel: Beltz Juventa, 86–104.

Bröskamp, B. (2015) 'Bildungspraktiken der frühen Kindheit', in Alkemeyer, T., Kalthoff, H. and Rieger-Ladich, M. (eds.) *Bildungspraxis. Körper, Räume, Objekte.* Weilerswist: Velbrück, 37–70.

Brubaker, R. (1996) *Nationalism reframed: nationhood and the national question in the new Europe.* Cambridge: Cambridge University Press.

Brubaker, R. (2002) 'Ethnicity without groups', *Archives of European Sociology*, 43(2), 163–89.

Brümmer, K. (2015) *Mitspielfähigkeit. Sportliches Training als formative Praxis.* Bielefeld: Transcript.

Brümmer, K. and Alkemeyer, T. (forthcoming) 'Practice as a shared accomplishment. Intercorporeal attunement in acrobatics', in Meyer, C. and Von Wedelstaedt, U. (eds.) Moving bodies in interaction - interacting bodies in motion. Intercorporeal and interkinesthetic enaction in sports. Amsterdam: John Benjamins.

Brümmer, K. and Mitchell, R. (2014) 'Becoming engaged. Eine praxistheoretisch-empirische Analyse von Trainingsepisoden in der Sportakrobatik und dem Taijiquan', *Sport und Gesellschaft – Sport and Society*, 11(3), 156–85.

Bruni, A. (2005) 'Shadowing software and clinical records: on the ethnography of non-humans', *Organization*, 12(3), 357–78.

Bruni, A., Gherardi, S. and Parolin, L. (2007) 'Knowing in a system of fragmented knowledge', *Mind, Culture and Activity*, 14(1–2), 83–102.

Bulkeley, H., Castan Broto, V., Hodson, M. and Marvin, S. (2012) *Cities and low carbon transitions.* London: Routledge.

Burchell, G., Gordon, C. and Miller, P. (eds.) (1991) *The Foucault effect: studies in governmentality.* Chicago: Harvester Wheatsheaf.

Burkitt, I. (1999) *Bodies of thought: embodiment, identity, modernity*. London: Sage.

Butler, J. (1993) *Bodies that matter: on the discursive limits of "sex"*. New York/London: Routledge.

Butler, J. (1997) *The psychic life of power: theories in subjection*. Stanford: Stanford University Press.

Caldwell, R. (2012) 'Reclaiming agency, recovering change? An exploration of the practice theory of Theodore Schatzki', *Journal for the Theory of Social Behaviour*, 42(3), 283–303.

Callon, M. and Latour, B. (1981) 'Unscrewing the big Leviathan: how actors macrostructure reality and how sociologists help them to do so', in Knorr Cetina, K.D. and Cicourel, A. V. (eds.) *Advances in social theory and methodology: toward and integration of micro- and macrosociologies*. Boston: Routledge and Kegan Paul, 277–303.

Caysa, V. (2016) *Empraktische Vernunft*. Frankfurt am Main: Peter Lang.

Cecez-Kecmanovic, D., Galliers, R. D., Henfridsson, O., Newell, S. and Vidgen, R. (2014) 'The sociomateriality of information systems: current status, future directions', *MIS Quarterly*, 38(3), 809–30.

Chouliaraki, L. and Fairclough, N. (1999) *Discourse in late modernity: rethinking Critical Discourse Analysis*. Edinburgh: Edinburgh University Press.

Christensen, W., Sutton, J. and McIlwain, D. J. F. (2016) 'Cognition in skilled action: meshed control and the varieties of skill experience', *Mind & Language*, 31(1), 37–66.

Ciompi, L. (1997) *Die emotionalen Grundlagen des Denkens: Entwurf einer fraktalen Affektlogik*. Göttingen: Vandenhoeck & Ruprecht.

Clough, P. T. and Halley, J. (eds.) (2007) *The affective turn: theorizing the social*. Durham: Duke University Press.

Code, L. (1987) *Epistemic responsibility*. Hanover: University Press of New England.

Collins, H. M. (2001) 'What is tacit knowledge?', in Schatzki, T. R., Knorr Cetina, K. and Von Savigny, E. (eds.) *The practice turn in contemporary theory*. London: Routledge.

Collins, H. M. (2010) *Tacit and explicit knowledge*. Chicago: Chicago University Press.

Collins, R. (1981) 'On the microfoundations of macrosociology', *American Journal of Sociology*, 86(5), 984–1014.

Coole, D. and Frost, S. (2010) 'Introducing the new materialisms', in Coole, D. and Frost, S. (eds.) *New materialisms: ontology, agency, and politics*. Durham: Duke University Press, 1–46.

Corradi, G., Gherardi, S. and Verzelloni, L. (2010) 'Through the practice lens: where is the bandwagon of practice-based studies heading?', *Management Learning*, 41(3), 265–83.

Corvellec, H. and Czarniawska, B. (2014) Action nets for waste prevention. Available at https://gupea.ub.gu.se/handle/2077/35329 (accessed 30 May 2016).

Coutard, O., Hanley, R. and Zimmerman, R. (2005) *Sustaining urban networks: the social diffusion of large technical systems*. London/New York: Routledge.

Cowan, R. S. (1989) *More work for mother: the ironies of household technology from the open hearth to the microwave*. London: Free Association Books.

Crary, J. (2002) *Aufmerksamkeit. Wahrnehmung und moderne Kultur*. Frankfurt am Main: Suhrkamp.

Crompton, R. and Sanderson, K. (1986) 'Credentials and careers: some implications of the increase in professional qualifications amongst women', *Sociology*, 20(1), 25–42.

Crossley, N. (1995) 'Merleau-Ponty, the illusive body and carnal sociology', *Body and Society*, 1(1), 43–63.

Czarniawska, B. (2004) 'On time, space, and action nets', *Organization*, 11(6), 773–91.

Daar, A. S., Singer, P. A., Persad, D. L., Pramming, S. K., Matthews, D. R., Beaglehole, R., …Bell, J. (2007) 'Grand challenges in chronic non-communicable diseases', *Nature*, 450(7169), 494–6.

Dale, K. (2005) 'Building a social materiality: spatial and embodied politics in organizational control', *Organization*, 12(5), 649–78.

Daly, H. E., Scott, K., Strachan, N. and Barrett, J. (2015) 'Indirect CO2 emission implications of energy system pathways: linking IO and TIMES models for the UK', *Environmental Science & Technology*, 49(17), 10701–9.

Daudin, G., Rifflart, C. and Schweisguth, D. (2011) 'Who produces for whom in the world economy?', *Canadian Journal of Economics – Revue canadienne d'économique*, 44(4), 1403–37.

Dawkins, R. (1978) *The selfish gene*. Oxford: Oxford University Press.

Dean, M. (2009) *Governmentality: power and rule in modern society*. London: Sage.

Deleuze, G. and Guattari, F. (1987) *Thousand plateaus: capitalism and schizophrenia*. Minneapolis: University of Minnesota Press.

Delitz, H. (2009) *Architektursoziologie*. Bielefeld: Transcript.

Derrida, J. (1976) *On grammatology*. Translated by G. C. Spivak. Baltimore: Johns Hopkins Press.

De Wit, O., Van den Ende, J., Schot, J. and van Oost, E. (2002) 'Innovative junctions: office technologies in the Netherlands, 1880–1980', *Technology and Culture*, 43(1), 50–72.

Diprose, R. (2002) *Corporeal generosity: on giving with Nietzsche, Merleau-Ponty and Lévinas*. Albany: State University of New York Press.

Doucet, A. (2013) 'A "Choreography of Becoming"', *Canadian Sociological Association – La Société Canadienne de Sociologie*, 50(3), 284–305.

Dreier, O. (2003) 'Learning in personal trajectories of participation', in Stephenson, N., et al. (eds.) *Theoretical psychology: critical contributions*. Concord: Captus University Publications, 20–9.

Dreier, O. (2008) *Psychotherapy in everyday life*. Cambridge: Cambridge University Press.

Dreyfus, H. L. and Rabinow, P. (1982) *Michel Foucault: Beyond structuralism and hermeneutics*. 2nd edn. Chicago: University of Chicago Press.

Durkheim, É. (1912) *Les formes élémentaires de la viereligieuse*. Paris: Félix Alcan.

Düttmann, G. A. (1997) *Zwischen den Kulturen: Spannungen im Kampf um Anerkennung*. Frankfurt am Main: Suhrkamp.

Eaton, S. C. and Bailyn, L. (2000) 'Career as life path: tracing work and life strategies of biotech professionals', in Peiperl, M. A., et al. (eds.) *Career frontiers: new conceptions of working lives*. Oxford: Oxford University Press, 177–98.

Edwards, P. N., Bowker, G. C., Jackson, S. J. and Williams, R. A. (2009) 'Introduction: an agenda for infrastructure studies', *Journal of the Association for Information Systems*, 10(6), 364–74.

Elgin, C. Z. (forthcoming) 'The epistemic normativity of knowing-how', in Dirks, U. and Wagner, A. (eds.) *Abel im Dialog: Perspektiven der Zeichen- und Interpretationsphilosophie*. Berlin: De Gruyter.

Elias, N. (1976) *Über den Prozeß der Zivilisation: Soziogenetische und psychogenetische Untersuchungen*. Frankfurt am Main: Suhrkamp.

Elias, N. (1984) *What Is Sociology?* Translated by S. Mennell and G. Morrissey. New York: Columbia University Press.

Elkjaer, B. (2009) 'Pragmatism. A learning theory for the future', in Illeris, K. (ed.) *Contemporary theories of learning*. London/New York: Routledge, 74–89.

Elliott, A. (1992) *Social theory and psychoanalysis in transition: self and society from Freud to Kristeva*. Oxford: Blackwell.

Emirbayer, M. (1997) 'Manifesto for a relational sociology', *American Journal of Sociology*, 103(2), 281–317.

Essbach, W. (2001) 'Antitechnische und antiästhetische Haltungen in der soziologischen Theorie' in Lösch, A. (ed.) *Technologien als Diskurse: Konstruktionen von Wissen, Medien und Körpern*. Heidelberg: Synchron, 123–36.

Ettinger, B. (2006) *The matrixial borderspace*. Minneapolis: University of Minnesota Press.

Evans, B. (2006) '"Gluttony or sloth": critical geographies of bodies and morality in (anti) obesity policy', *Area*, 38(3), 259–67.

Evans, K. (2009) *Learning, work and social responsibility. Challenges for lifelong learning in a global age.* Dordrecht: Springer.

Evetts, J. (1994) 'Career and motherhood in engineering: cultural dilemmas and individualistic solutions', *Journal of Gender Studies*, 3(2), 177–85.

Fairclough, N. (1992) *Discourse and social change.* Cambridge: Polity Press.

Fairclough, N. (2005) 'Peripheral vision discourse analysis in organization studies: the case for critical realism', *Organization Studies*, 26(6), 915–39.

Fairclough, N. (2013) *Critical discourse analysis: the critical study of language.* Abingdon: Routledge.

Fairclough, N. (2015 [1989]) *Language and power.* 3rd edn. London: Routledge.

Falzon, M. A. (ed.) (2012) *Multi-sited ethnography: theory, praxis and locality in contemporary research.* Farnham: Ashgate Publishing Ltd.

Feldman, M. and Orlikowski, W. (2011) 'Theorizing practice and practicing theory', *Organization Science*, 22(5), 1240–53.

Fernández-Armesto, F. and Sacks, B. (2012) 'The global exchange of food and drugs', in Trentmann, F. (ed.) *The Oxford handbook of consumer history.* Oxford: Oxford University Press, 127–44.

Ford, M. (2015) *Rise of the robots: technology and the threat of a jobless future.* New York: Basic Books.

Fotaki, M., Metcalfe, B. D. and Harding, N. (2014) 'Writing materiality into management and organization studies through and with Luce Irigaray', *Human Relations*, 16(10), 1239–63.

Foucault, M. (1976) *The archaeology of knowledge.* Translated by A. M. Sheridan-Smith. New York: Harper and Row.

Foucault, M. (1980) 'The confession of the flesh', in Gordon, C. (ed.) *Power/Knowledge.* Translated by C. Gordon. New York: Pantheon, 194–228.

Foucault, M. (1982) 'The subject and power', *Critical Inquiry*, 8(4), 777–95.

Foucault, M. (1988) 'Technologies of the self', in Martin, L. H., Gutman, H. and Hutton, P. H. (eds.) *Technologies of the self.* Amherst: University of Massachusetts Press, 16–49.

Foucault, M. (1991) 'Governmentality', in Burchel, G., Gordon, C. and Miller, P. (eds.) *The Foucault effect: studies in governmentality.* London: Harvester Wheatsheaf, 87–104.

Fox, N. J. (2011) 'The ill-health assemblage: beyond the body-with-organs', *Health Sociology Review*, 20(4), 359–71.

Fraga, M. F., Ballestar, E., Paz, M. F., Ropero, S., Setien, F., Ballestar, M. L., …Estellar, M. (2005) 'Epigenetic differences arise during the lifetime of monozygotic twins', *Proceedings of the National Academy of Sciences of the United States of America*, 102(30), 10604–9.

Frank, T. (1997) *The conquest of cool.* Chicago: University of Chicago Press.

Fuller, A. (2007) 'Critiquing theories of learning and communities of practice', in Hughes, J., Jewson, N. and Unwin, L. (eds.) *Communities of practice: critical perspectives.* New York: Routledge, 17–29.

Funtowicz, S. and Ravetz, J. (1997) 'The poetry of thermodynamics: energy, entropy/exergy and quality', *Futures*, 29(9), 791–810.

Garfinkel, H. (1967) *Studies in ethnomethodology.* Englewood Cliffs: Polity Press.

Gebauer, G. (1998) 'Sport – die dargestellte Gesellschaft', *Paragrana. Internationale Zeitschrift für Historische Anthropologie*, 7(1), 223–40.

Gebauer, G. (2009) *Wittgensteins anthropologisches Denken.* München: Beck.

Gee, J. P. (1999) *An introduction to discourse analysis. Theory and method.* New York: Routledge.

Gee, J. P. (2014) *An introduction to discourse analysis. Theory and method.* 4th edn. Abingdon: Routledge.

Geels, F. W., McMeekin, A., Mylan, J. and Southerton, D. (2015) 'A critical appraisal of sustainable consumption and production research: the reformist, revolutionary and reconfiguration positions', *Global Environmental Change*, 34, 1–12.

Gherardi, S. (2006) *Organizational knowledge: the texture of workplace learning.* Oxford: Blackwell.

Gherardi, S. (2008) 'Situated knowledge and situated action: what do practice-based studies promise?', in Barry, D. and Hansen, H. (eds.) *The SAGE handbook of new approaches in management and organization.* Los Angeles: Sage, 516–25.

Gherardi, S. (2012a) *How to conduct a practice-based study: problems and methods.* Cheltenham: Edward Elgar Publishing.

Gherardi, S. (2012b) 'Why do practices change and why do they persist? Models of explanations', in Hager, P., Lee, A. and Reich, A. (eds.) *Practice, learning and change. Practice-theory perspectives on professional learning.* Dordrecht: Springer, 217–31.

Gherardi, S. (2015) 'How the turn to practice may contribute to working life studies', *Nordic Journal of Working Life Studies,* 5(3), 13–25.

Gherardi, S. (2016) 'To start practice-theorizing anew: the contribution of the concepts of agencement and formativeness', *Organization,* 23(5), 680–98.

Gherardi, S. and Nicolini, D. (2002) 'Learning in a constellation of connected practices: canon or dissonance?', *Journal of Management Studies,* 39(4), 419–36.

Gherardi, S. and Rodeschini, G. (2016) 'Caring as a collective knowledgeable doing: about concern and being concerned', *Management Learning,* 47(3), 266–84.

Gherardi, S. and Strati, A. (2012) *Learning and knowing in practice-based studies.* Cheltenham: Edward Elgar Publishing.

Giard, L., de Certeau, M. and Mayol, P. (1998) *The practice of everyday life: living and cooking. Volume 2.* Minneapolis: University of Minnesota Press.

Gibson, J. (1979) *The ecological approach to visual perception.* Boston: Psychological Press.

Giddens, A. (1979) *Central problems in social theory. Action, structure, and contradiction in social analysis.* Berkeley/Los Angeles: University of California Press.

Giddens, A. (1984) *The constitution of society: outline of the theory of structuration.* Cambridge: Polity Press.

Gieryn, T. F. (2002) 'What buildings do', *Theory and Society,* 31(1), 35–74.

Gilligan, C. (1982) *In a different voice: psychological theory and women's development.* Cambridge: Harvard University Press.

Glynos, J. and Howarth, D. (2007) *Logics of critical explanation in social and political theory.* Abingdon: Routledge.

Goffman, E. (1967) *Interaction ritual.* New York: Anchor Books.

Goffman, E. (1971) *Relations in public: microstudies of the public order.* New York: Basic Books.

Goffman, E. (1974) *Frame analysis. An essay on the organization of experience.* New York: Harper & Row.

Goffman, E. (1979) 'Gender display', in Goffman, E. *Gender Advertisements.* London/ Basingstoke: HarperCollins, 1–8.

Goffman, E. (1981) *Forms of talk.* Philadelphia: University of Pennsylvania Press.

Gordon, C. (1991) 'Governmental rationality', in Burchell, G., Gordon, C and Miller, P. (eds.) *The Foucault effect: studies in governmentality.* Chicago: University of Chicago Press, 1–51.

Graham, S. and Marvin, S. (2001) *Splintering urbanism: networked infrastructures, technological mobilities and the urban condition.* London: Routledge.

Grandclement, C., Pierre, M. and Shove, E. (2015) 'How infrastructures and consumers interact: insights from the interface', *Proceedings of the ECEEE Summer Study on Energy Efficiency.* Toulon, 1–6 July 2015.

Greco, M. and Stenner, P. (eds.) (2008) *Emotions: A social science reader.* London: Routledge.

Greenhough, B. (2011) 'Assembling an island laboratory', *Area,* 43(2), 134–8.

Gronow, J. and Warde, A. (2001) *Ordinary consumption.* New York: Routledge.

Grosz, E. (2011) *Becoming undone: Darwinian reflections on life, politics, and art.* Durham: Duke University Press.

Gumperz, J. (1982) *Discourse strategies.* Cambridge: Cambridge University Press.

Guzman, G. (2013) 'The grey textures of practice and knowledge: review and framework', *European Business Review*, 25(5), 429–52.

Hager, P. (2012) 'Theories of practice and their connections with learning: a continuum of more and less inclusive accounts', in Hager, P., Lee, A. and Reich, A. (eds.) *Practice, learning and change. Practice-theory perspectives on professional learning*. Dordrecht: Springer, 17–32.

Hager, P., Lee, A. and Reich, A. (2012) 'Problematising practice, reconceptualising learning and imagining change', in Hager, P., Lee, A. and Reich, A. (eds.) *Practice, learning and change. Practice-theory perspectives on professional learning*. Dordrecht: Springer, 1–14.

Hägerstrand, T. (1996) 'Diorama, path and project', in Agnew, J., Livingstone, D. N. and Rogers, A. (eds.) *Human geography: an essential anthology*. Oxford: Blackwell, 650–74.

Haidt, J. (2007) 'The New Synthesis in Moral Psychology', *Science*, 316(5827), 998–1002.

Hajer, M. (1995) *The politics of environmental discourse: ecological modernization and the policy process*. Oxford: Oxford University Press.

Hall, S. (1997) 'The spectacle of the "other"', in Hall, S. (ed.) *Representations. Cultural representations and signifying practices*. London: Sage, 223–79.

Halliday, M. (1994) *Introduction to functional grammar*. 2nd edn. London: Edward Arnold.

Hand, M. and Shove, E. (2007) 'Condensing practices: ways of living with a freezer', *Journal of Consumer Culture*, 7(1), 79–104.

Hand, M., Shove, E. and Southerton, D. (2005) 'Explaining showering: a discussion of the material, conventional, and temporal dimensions of practice', *Sociological Research Online*, 10(2). Available online at www.socresonline.org.uk/10/2/hand.html.

Handel, A. and Ramagopalan, S. (2010) 'Is Lamarckian evolution relevant to medicine?', *BMC Medical Genetics*, 11(1), 73.

Hanks, W. F. (1996) *Language and communicative practices*. Boulder: Westview.

Hara, N. (2009) *Communities of practice. Fostering peer-to-peer learning an informal knowledge sharing in the workplace*. Berlin/Heidelberg: Springer.

Haraway, D. (1991) *Simians, cyborgs and women: the Reinvention of nature*. London: Free Association Books.

Haraway, D. (1997) *Modest_Witness@Second_Millennium. FemaleMan©_Meets_Oncomouse™*. London/New York: Routledge.

Haraway, D. (2008a) 'Otherwordly conversations: terran topics, local terms', in Alaimo, S. and Hekman, S. (eds.) *Material Feminisms*. Bloomington: Indiana University Press, 157–87.

Haraway, D. (2008b) *When species meet*. Minneapolis: University of Minnesota Press.

Hård, M. and Misa, T. (2008) *Urban machinery: inside modern European cities*. Cambridge: MIT Press.

Harding, J. and Pribram, D. (eds.) (2009) *Emotions. A cultural studies reader*. London: Routledge.

Harré, R. (ed.) (1986) *The social construction of emotions*. Oxford: Blackwell.

Hatsukami, D. K., Stead, L. F. and Gupta, P. C. (2008) 'Tobacco addiction', *The Lancet*, 371(9629), 2027–38.

Healy, S. (2008) 'Air-conditioning and the "homogenization" of people and built environments', *Building Research & Information*, 36(4), 312–22.

Heidegger, M. (1986 [1927]) *Sein und Zeit*. Tübingen: Niemeyer.

Heilbroner, R. L. (1967) 'Do machines make history?', *Technology and Culture*, 8(3), 335–45.

Heuts, F. and Mol, A. M. (2013) 'What is a good tomato? A case of valuing in practice', *Valuation Studies*, 1(2), 125–46.

Hillebrandt, F. (2014) *Soziologische Praxistheorien. Eine Einführung*. Wiesbaden: Springer VS.

Hinchliffe, S. (2009) 'Scalography and worldly assemblies'. *Unpublished paper presented at the summer workshop "From Scale to Scalography"*. Oxford, 8 July 2009.

Hochschild, A. R. (1983) *The managed heart: commercialization of human feeling*. Berkeley: University of California Press.

Holloway, M., Adamson, S., Argyrou, V., Draper, P. and Mariau, D. (2013) '"Funerals aren't nice but it couldn't have been nicer".The makings of a good funeral', *Mortality*, 18(1), 30–53.

Holt, D. B. (2002) 'Why do brands cause trouble?', *Journal of Consumer Research*, 29, 70–90.

Holzkamp, K. (1978) *Sinnliche Erkenntnis. Historischer Ursprung und gesellschaftliche Funktion der Wahrnehmung*. 4th edn. Königstein im Taunus: Athenäum.

Holzkamp, K. (1995) *Lernen. Subjektwissenschaftliche Grundlegung*. Frankfurt am Main/New York: Campus.

Hommels, A. (2005) 'Studying obduracy in the city: toward a productive fusion between technology studies and urban studies', *Science, Technology & Human Values*, 30(3), 323–51.

Honneth, A. (1992) *Kampf um Anerkennung: Zur moralischen Grammatik sozialer Konflikte*. Frankfurt am Main: Suhrkamp.

Honneth, A. (2004) 'Organized self-realization', *European Journal of Social Theory*, 7(4), 463–78.

Hopwood, N. (2014) 'Four essential dimensions of workplace learning', *Journal of Workplace Learning*, 26(6–7), 349–63.

Hopwood, N. (2015) *Professional practice and learning: times, spaces, bodies and things*. Cham: Springer International.

Howson, A. and Inglis, D. (2001) 'The body in sociology: tensions inside and outside socio-logical thought', *Sociology*, 49(3), 297–317.

Hsu, E. (2007) 'The biological in the cultural: the five agents and the body ecologic in Chinese medicine', in Parkin, D. and Ulijaszek, S. (eds.) *Holistic anthropology. Emergence and convergence*. New York/Oxford: Berghahn Books.

Hughes, T. (1993 [1983]) *Networks of power: electrification in Western society, 1880–1930*. Baltimore: Johns Hopkins University.

Hui, A. (2012) 'Things in motion, things in practices: how mobile practice networks facilitate the travel and use of leisure objects', *Journal of Consumer Culture*, 12(2), 195–215.

Hui, A. (2013) 'Moving with practices: the discontinuous, rhythmic and material mobilities of leisure', *Social & Cultural Geography*, 14(8), 888–908.

Hui, A. (2015) 'Networks of home, travel and use during Hong Kong return migration: think-ing topologically about the spaces of human-material practices', *Global Networks*, 15(4), 536–52.

Iedema, R. (2001) 'Resemiotization', *Semiotica*, 37(1), 23–40.

Iedema, R. (2003) *Discourses of post-bureaucratic organization*. Philadelphia: John Benjamins Publishing Company.

Ihde, D. (1990) *Technology and the lifeworld: from garden to earth*. Bloomington: Indiana University Press.

Ihde, D. (1993) *Postphenomenology: essays in the postmodern context*. Evanston: Northwest University Press.

Illich, I. (1973) *Tools for conviviality*. London: Calder and Boyars.

Ingold, T. (2000) *The perception of the environment*. London: Routledge.

Ingold, T. (2007) 'Materials against materiality', *Archaeological Dialogues*, 14(1), 1–16.

International Energy Agency (2016) *Oil*. Available at www.iea.org/aboutus/faqs/oil/ (accessed 2 January 2016).

Introna, L. (2013) 'Epilogue: performativity and the becoming of sociomaterial assemblages', in De Vaujany, F. and Mitev, N. (eds.) *Materiality and space: organizations, artefacts and practices*. London: Palgrave Macmillan, 330–43.

Jalas, M. and Rinkinen, J. (2013) 'Stacking wood and staying warm: time, temporality and housework around domestic heating systems', *Journal of Consumer Culture*, 16(1), 43–60.

James, W. (1979 [1909]). *The meaning of truth, a sequel to 'pragmatism'*. Cambridge: Harvard University Press.

Januar, V., Saffery, R. and Ryan, J. (2015) 'Epigenetics and depressive disorders: a review of current progress and future directions', *International Journal of Epidemiology*, 44(4), 1364–87.

Jarzabkowski, P., Bednarek, R. and Spee, E. (2015) *Making a market for acts of God*. Oxford: Oxford University Press.

Jayyusi, L. (2013 [1984]) *Categorisation and the moral order*. London: Routledge.

Jones, M. (2014) 'A matter of life and death: exploring conceptualizations of sociomateriality in the context of critical care', *MIS Quarterly*, 38(3), 895–925.

Jullien, F. (1999) *Über die Wirksamkeit*. Berlin: Merve.

Karlic, H. and Baurek, P. (2011) 'Epigenetics and the power of art', *Clinical Epigenetics*, 2(2), 279–82.

Keller, M. and Vihalemm, T. (2015) 'Struggling with the euro: practical adaptation versus ideological resistance', in Strandbakken, P. and Gronow, J. (eds.) *The consumer in society: a tribute to Eivind Stø*. Oslo: Abstrakt Forlag, 229–49.

Kemmis, S. (2005) 'Knowing practice: searching for saliences', *Pedagogy, Culture & Society*, 13(3), 391–426.

Kemmis, S. (2010) 'Research for praxis: knowing doing', *Pedagogy, Culture & Society*, 18(1), 9–27.

Kemmis, S., Edwards-Groves, C., Wilkinson, J. and Hardy, I. (2012) 'Ecologies of practices', in Hager, P., Lee, A. and Reich, A. (eds.) *Practice, learning and change. Practice-theory perspectives on professional learning*. Dordrecht: Springer, 33–49.

Kemmis, S., Wilkinson, J., Edwards-Groves, C., Hardy, I., Grootenboer, P. and Bristol, L. (2014) *Changing practices, changing education*. New York: Springer.

Kemmis, S. and Mutton, R. (2012) 'Education for sustainability (EfS): practice and practice architectures', *Environmental Education Research*, 18(2), 187–207.

Kenny, K. and Fotaki, M. (2015) 'An ethics of difference: the contribution of Bracha Ettinger to management and organization studies', in Pullen, A. and Rhodes, C. (eds.) *The Routledge companion to ethics, politics and organizations*. London: Taylor and Francis, 494–505.

Keverne, E. B. and Curley, J. P. (2008) 'Epigenetics, brain evolution and behaviour', *Frontiers in Neuroendocrinology*, 29(3), 398–412.

King, A. (2000) 'Thinking with Bourdieu against Bourdieu: A "practical" critique of the habitus', *Sociological Theory*, 18(3), 417–33.

Klawetter, S. (2014) 'Conceptualizing social determinants of maternal and infant health disparities', *Affilia*, 29(2), 131–41.

Kline, S. J. (2003 [1985]) 'What is technology', in Scharff, R. C. and Dusek, V. (eds.) *Philosophy of technology: the technological condition: an anthology*. Oxford: Blackwell Publishers, 210–12.

Knorr Cetina, K. (1981) 'The micro-sociological challenge of macro-sociology: towards a reconstruction of social theory and methodology', in Knorr Cetina, K. D. and Cicourel A. V. (eds.) *Advances in social theory and methodology: toward and integration of micro- and macro- sociologies*. Boston: Routledge and Kegan Paul, 1–48.

Knorr Cetina, K. (2001) 'Objectual practice', in Schatzki, T. R., Knorr Cetina, K. and Von Savigny, E. (eds.) *The practice turn in contemporary theory*. London: Routledge, 175–88.

Knorr Cetina, K. (2005) 'Complex global microstructures: the new terrorist societies', *Theory, Culture & Society*, 22(5), 213–34.

Knorr Cetina, K. (2009) *Epistemic cultures: how the sciences make knowledge*. Cambridge: Harvard University Press.

Knorr Cetina, K. D. and Cicourel, A. V. (eds.) (1981) *Advances in social theory and methodology: toward and integration of micro- and macro- sociologies*. Boston: Routledge and Kegan Paul.

Koschorke, A. (2003) *Körperströme und Schriftverkehr*. München: Fink.

Krais, B. and Gebauer, G. (2002) *Habitus*. Bielefeld: Transcript.

Kristeva, J. (1986) 'Word, dialogue and novel', in Moi, T. (ed.) *The Kristeva Reader*. Oxford: Blackwell, 34–61.

Kuhn, T. S. (1970) *The structure of scientific revolutions*. Chicago: University of Chicago Press.

Kuhn, T. S. (1982) 'Commensurability, comparability, communicability', *PSA: Proceedings of the Biennial Meeting of the Philosophy of Science Association*, 2, 669–88.

Kupfer, O. (2011) 'Podolski war der Faulste – wie Impire den gläsernen Fußballer erschafft', *Westdeutsche Zeitung*, 10 August. Available at www.wz.de/home/sport/fussball/podolski-war-der-faulste-wie-impire-den-glaesernen-fussballer-erschafft-1.735362 (accessed 30 May 2016).

Kwa, C. (2002) 'Romantic and baroque conceptions of complex wholes in the sciences', in Law, J. and Mol, A. (eds.) *Complexities: social studies of knowledge practices*. Durham: Duke University Press, 23–52.

Laclau, E. and Mouffe, C. (1985) *Hegemony and socialist strategy: toward a radical democratic politics*. London: Verso.

Lande, B. (2002) 'Breathing like a soldier: culture incarnate', in Shilling, C. (ed.) *Embodying sociology: retrospect, progress and prospects*. Malden: Blackwell Publishing, 95–108.

Latour, B. (1984) 'The powers of association', *The Sociological Review*, 32(issue supplement), 264–80.

Latour, B. (1987) *Science in action: how to follow scientists and engineers through society*. Cambridge: Harvard University Press.

Latour, B. (1991a) *Nous n'avons jamais été modernes: essai d'anthropologie symétrique*. Paris: La Découverte.

Latour, B. (1991b) 'Technology is society made durable', in Law, J. (ed.) *A Sociology of monsters: essays on power, technology, and domination*, 103–31.

Latour, B. (1992) 'Where are the missing masses? The sociology of a few mundane artefacts', in Bijker, W. and Law, J. (eds.) *Shaping technology/building society: studies in sociotechnical change*. Cambridge: MIT Press, 225–58.

Latour, B. (2005) *Reassembling the social: an introduction to actor-network-theory*. Oxford: Oxford University Press.

Lave, J. (1988) *Cognition in practice*. Cambridge: Cambridge University Press.

Lave, J. (1996) 'On learning', *Forum Kritische Psychologie*, 38, 120–35.

Lave, J. (1997) 'Learning, apprenticeship, social practice', *Journal of Nordic Educational Research*, 17(3), 140–51.

Lave, J. and Wenger, E. (1991) *Situated learning: legitimate peripheral participation*. Cambridge: Cambridge University Press.

Law, J. (1994) *Organizing modernity*. Oxford: Blackwell.

Law, J. and Hassard, J. (eds.) (1999) *Actor Network Theory and after*. Oxford: Blackwell/The Sociological Review.

Leader, D. (2002) *Stealing the Mona Lisa: what art stops us from seeing*. London: Faber.

Leder, D. (1990) *The absent body*. Chicago: University of Chicago Press.

Lefebvre, H. (1991) *The production of space*. Oxford: Blackwell.

Leontjew, A. N. (1973) *Probleme der Entwicklung des Psychischen*. Frankfurt am Main: Athenäum-Fischer.

Leontjew, A. N. (1979) *Tätigkeit, Bewußtsein, Persönlichkeit*. Berlin: Volk und Wissen.

Levinson, S. C. (2005) 'Living with Manny's dangerous idea', *Discourse Studies*, 7(4–5), 431–53.

Lindberg, K. and Czarniawska, B. (2006) 'Knotting the action net, or organizing between organizations', *Scandinavian Journal of Management*, 22(4), 292–306.

Lindemann, G. (2017) 'Leiblichkeit und Körper', in Gugutzer, R., Klein, G. and Meuser, M. (eds.) *Handbuch Körpersoziologie*, B. 1: Grundbegriffe und theoretische Perspektiven Wiesbaden: Springer VS, 57–66.

Lindholm, C. (2007) *Culture and authenticity*. Oxford: Wiley.

Lizardo, O. (2012) 'Embodied culture as procedure', in Warde, A. and Southerton, D. (eds.) *The habits of consumption*. Helsinki: HCAS, 70–86.

Lizardo, O. and Strand, M. (2010) 'Skills, toolkits, contexts and institutions: clarifying the relationship between different approaches to cognition in cultural sociology', *Poetics*, 38, 204–27.

Loenhoff, J. (2012) 'Einleitung', in Loenhoff, J. (ed.) *Implizites Wissen. Epistemologische und handlungstheoretische Perspektiven*. Weilerswist: Velbrück, 7–30.

Löw, M. (2001) *Raumsoziologie*. Frankfurt am Main: Suhrkamp.

Luhmann, N. (1994 [1982]) *Liebe als Passion. Zur Codierung von Intimität*. Frankfurt am Main: Suhrkamp.

Lukes, S. (1973) *Émile Durkheim: his life and work. A historical and critical study*. London: Penguin.

Lukes, S. (2005) *Power: a radical view*. 2nd edn. New York: Palgrave Macmillan.

Lyotard, J. (1988) *The differend: phrases in dispute*. Translated by G. van den Abbeele. Minneapolis: University of Minnesota Press.

McGinn, R. E. (1991) *Science, technology, and society*. Englewood Cliffs: Prentice Hall.

MacIntyre, A. (1981) *After virtue. A study in moral theory*. Notre Dame: University of Notre Dame Press.

McNeill, W. H. (1997) *Keeping together in time. Dance and drill in human history*. Cambridge: Harvard University Press.

Maller, C. (2015) 'Understanding health through social practices: performance and materiality in everyday life', *Sociology of Health & Illness*, 37(1), 52–66.

Maller, C. and Strengers, Y. (2013) 'The global migration of everyday life: investigating the practice memories of Australian migrants', *Geoforum*, 44, 243–52.

Maller, C. and Strengers, Y. (2014) 'Resurrecting sustainable practices: using memories of the past to intervene in the future', in Strengers, Y. and Maller, C. (eds.) *Social practices, intervention and sustainability: beyond behaviour change*. London: Routledge, 147–62.

Marcus, G. E. (1995) 'Ethnography in/of the world system: the emergence of multi-sited ethnography', *Annual Review of Anthropology*, 24, 95–117.

Marcus, G. E. and Saka, E. (2006) 'Assemblage', *Theory, Culture & Society*, 23(2–3), 101–6.

Markham, S. J. (2015) 'Winding down the workday: zoning the evening hours in Paris, Oslo, and San Francisco', *Qualitative Sociology*, 38(3), 235–59.

Massumi, B. (2002) *Parables for the virtual: movement, affect, sensation*. Durham: Duke University Press.

Meehan, A. J. (1986) 'Record keeping practices in the policing of juveniles', *Journal of Contemporary Ethnography*, 15(1), 70–102.

Merleau-Ponty, M. (1962) *The phenomenology of perception*. Translated by C. Smith. London: Routledge and Kegan Paul.

Merleau-Ponty, M. (1966) *Phänomenologie der Wahrnehmung*. Berlin: de Gruyter.

Michael, M. (2000) 'These boots are made for walking…: mundane technology, the body and human-environment relations', *Body & Society*, 6(3–4), 107–26.

Miettinen, R., Samra-Fredericks, D. and Yanow, D. (2009) 'Re-turn to practice: an introductory essay', *Organization Studies*, 30(12), 1309–27.

Milagro, F. I., Mansego, M. L., De Miguel, C. and Martínez, J. A. (2013) 'Dietary factors, epigenetic modifications and obesity outcomes: progresses and perspectives', *Molecular Aspects of Medicine*, 34(4), 782–812.

Mintz, S. (1986) *Sweetness and power: the place of sugar in modern history*. New York: Penguin.

Mitcham, C. (1994) *Thinking through technology: the path between engineering and philosophy*. Chicago: University of Chicago Press.

Mol, A. (2008) *The logic of care. Health and the problem of patient choice*. New York: Routledge.

Monteiro, P. and Nicolini, D. (2015) 'Recovering materiality in institutional work: prizes as an assemblage of human and material entities', *Journal of Management Inquiry*, 24(1), 61–81.

Moore, L. J. and Kosut, M. (2010) 'Introduction: not just the reflexive reflex: flesh and bone in the social sciences', in Kosut, M. and Moore, L. J. (eds.) *The body reader: Essential social and cultural readings*. New York: New York University Press, 1–30.

Mumford, L. (1934) *Technics and civilization*. London: Routledge.

Muras, U. (2011). 'Podolski als lauffaulster Bundesliga-Profi überführt', *Die Welt*, 9 August. Available at www.welt.de/sport/fussball/bundesliga/1-fc-koeln/article13534946/Podolski-als-lauffaulster-Bundesliga-Profi-ueberfuehrt.html (accessed 30 May 2016).

Musil, R. (1987 [1930–1932]) *Der Mann ohne Eigenschaften. Volume 1*. Reinbek: Rowohlt.

Nassehi, A. (2003) *Der soziologische Diskurs der Moderne*. Frankfurt am Main: Suhrkamp.

Nicolini, D. (2009) 'Zooming in and out: studying practices by switching theoretical lenses and trailing connections', *Organization Studies*, 30(12), 1391–418.

Nicolini, D. (2012) *Practice theory, work, and organization: an introduction*. Oxford: Oxford University Press.

Nicolini, D. and Monteiro, P. (2016) 'The practice approach: for a praxeology of organizational and management studies', in Langley, A. and Tsoukas, H. (eds.) *The SAGE handbook of process organization studies*. London: Sage, 103–20.

Nicolini, D., Mengis, J. and Swan, J. (2012) 'Understanding the role of objects in cross-disciplinary collaboration', *Organization Science*, 23(3), 612–29.

Nicolini, D., Mørk, B.-E., Masovic, J. and Hanseth, O. (2017) 'Expertise as trans-situated: the case of TAVI', in Sandberg, J., Roleau, L., Langley, A. and Tsoukas, H. (eds.) *Skilfull performance: enacting expertise, competence, and capabilities in organizations*. Oxford: Oxford University Press.

Nielsen, K. (2008) 'Learning, trajectories of participation and social practice', *Critical Studies*, 10(1), 22–36.

Nightingale, F. (1859) 'Notes on hospitals: being two papers read before the National Association for the Promotion of Social Science, at Liverpool in October, 1858', *with evidence given to the Royal Commissioners on the State of the Army in 1857*. London: John W. Parker and Son.

Noland, C. (2009) *Agency and embodiment. Performing gesture/producing culture*. Cambridge: Harvard University Press.

Nye, D. (1992) *Electrifying America: social meanings of a new technology, 1880–1940*. Cambridge: MIT Press.

Nye, D. (2010) *When the lights went out: a history of blackouts in America*. Cambridge: MIT Press.

O'Brien M. (2012) *A crisis of waste? Understanding the rubbish society*. Hoboken: Taylor and Francis.

Orlikowski, W. J. (2002) 'Knowing in practice: enacting a collective capability in distributed organizing', *Organization Science*, 13(3), 249–73.

Orlikowski, W. J. (2006) 'Material knowing: the scaffolding of human knowledgeability', *European Journal of Information Systems*, 15(5), 460–6.

Orlikowski, W. J. (2007) 'Sociomaterial practices: exploring technology at work', *Organization Studies*, 28(9), 1435–48.

Orlikowski, W. J. (2010) 'The sociomateriality of organizational life: considering technology in management research', *Cambridge Journal of Economics*, 34(1), 125–41.

Orlikowski, W. J. and Scott, S.V. (2008) 'Sociomateriality: challenging the separation of technology, work and organization', *The Academy of Management Annals*, 2(1), 433–74.

Ortner, S. B. (1984) 'Theory in anthropology since the sixties', *Comparative Studies in Society and History*, 26(1), 126–66.

Orvell, M. (1989) *The real thing: imitation and authenticity in American culture, 1880–1940*. Chapel Hill: University of North Carolina Press.

Ostrow, J. M. (1990) *Social sensitivity. A study of habit and experience*. Albany: State University of New York Press.

Ott, M. (2010) *Affizierung. Zu einer ästhetisch-epistemischen Figur*. München: Fink.

Pantzar, M. and Shove, E. (2010a) 'Temporal rhythms as outcomes of social practices', *Ethnologia Europaea*, 40(1), 19–29.

Pantzar, M. and Shove, E. (2010b) 'Understanding innovation in practice: a discussion of the production and re-production of Nordic walking', *Technology Analysis & Strategic Management*, 22(4), 447–61.

Parks, R. and Reed, G. (2000) *Quiet strength: the faith, the hope, and the heart of a woman who changed a nation*. Grand Rapids: Zondervan.

Parsons, T. (1968 [1937]) *The structure of social action. A study in social theory with special reference to a group of recent European writers*. New York/London: Free Press.

Patel, S., Choksi, A. and Chattopadhyay, S. (2015) 'Understanding interindividual epigenetic variations in obesity and its management', in Tollefsbol T. O. (ed.) *Personalized Epigenetics*. Boston: Academic Press, 429–60.

Pellandini-Simányi, L. (2014) *Consumption norms and everyday ethics*. London: Palgrave Macmillan.

Pille, T. (2013) *Das Referendariat. Eine ethnographische Studie zu den Praktiken der Lehrerbildung*. Bielefeld: Transcript.

Pille, T. and Alkemeyer, T. (2016) 'Bindende Verflechtungen. Zur Materialität und Körperlichkeit der Anerkennung', *Vierteljahresschrift für wissenschaftliche Pädagogik*, 91(1), 170–94.

Pink, S. (2009) *Doing sensory ethnography*. London: Sage.

Pink, S. (2012) *Situating everyday life: practices and places*. London: Sage.

Pink, S. and Leder Mackley, K. (2014) 'Flow and intervention in everyday life – situating practices', in Strengers, Y. and Maller, C. (eds.) *Social practices, intervention and sustainability: beyond behaviour change*. London: Routledge, 163–78.

Plessner, H. (1975 [1928]) *Die Stufen des Organischen und der Mensch*. Berlin/New York: Walter de Gruyter.

Poggio, B. (2006) 'Editorial: outline of a theory of gender practices', *Gender, Work and Organization*, 13(3), 225–33.

Porter, A. J. (2013) 'Emergent organization and responsive technologies in crisis: creating connections or enabling divides?' *Management Communication Quarterly*, 26(1), 6–33.

Prinz, S. (2013) *Die Praxis des Sehens. Über das Zusammenspiel von Körpern, Artefakten und visueller Ordnung*. Bielefeld: Transcript.

Prior, L. (1988) 'The architecture of the hospital: a study of spatial organization and medical knowledge', *British Journal of Sociology*, 39(1), 86–113.

Pullen, A. and Rhodes, C. (2014) 'Corporeal ethics and the politics of resistance in organizations', *Organization*, 21(6), 782–96.

Pullen, A. and Rhodes, C. (2015a) 'Introduction to the special issue: ethics, embodiment and organizations', *Organization*, 22(2), 159–65.

Pullen, A. and Rhodes, C. (eds.) (2015b) *The Routledge companion to ethics, politics and organizations*. London: Taylor and Francis.

Rammert, W. and Schulz-Schaeffer, I. (2002) 'Technik und Handeln. Wenn soziales Handeln sich auf menschliches Verhalten und technische Abläufe verteilt', in Rammert, W. and Schulz-Schaeffer, I. (eds.) *Können Maschinen handeln? Soziologische Beiträge zum Verhältnis von Mensch und Technik*. Frankfurt am Main/New York: Campus, 11–64.

Rawolle, S. (2010) 'Practice chains of production and consumption: mediatized practices across social fields', *Discourse: Studies in the Cultural Politics of Education*, 31(1), 121–35.

Reckwitz, A. (2000a) 'Der Status des Mentalen in kulturtheoretischen Handlungserklärungen: Zum Problem der Relation von Verhalten und Wissen nach Stephen Turner und Theodore Schatzki', *Zeitschrift für Soziologie*, 29(3), 167–85.

Reckwitz, A. (2000b) *Die Transformationen der Kulturtheorien. Zur Entwicklung eines Theorieprogramms.* Weilerswist: Velbrück Wissenschaft.

Reckwitz, A. (2002a) 'The status of the "material" in theories of culture: from "social structure" to "artefacts"', *Journal for the Theory of Social Behaviour*, 32(2): 195–217.

Reckwitz, A. (2002b) 'Toward a theory of social practices: a development in culturalist theorizing', *European Journal of Social Theory*, 5(2), 243–63.

Reckwitz, A. (2006) *Das hybride Subjekt. Eine Theorie der Subjektkulturen von der bürgerlichen Moderne zur Postmoderne.* Stuttgart: Velbruk Wissenschaft.

Reckwitz, A. (2008) 'Praktiken und Diskurse. Eine sozialtheoretische und methodologische Reflexion', in Kalthoff, H. (ed.) *Theoretische Empirie: zur Relevanz qualitativer Forschung.* Frankfurt am Main: Suhrkamp, 188–209.

Reckwitz, A. (2012) 'Affective spaces. A praxeological outlook', *Rethinking History: The Journal of Theory and Practice*, (16)2, 241–58.

Reckwitz, A. (2013) 'Die Materialisierung der Kulturtheorien', in Johler, R. (ed.) *Kultur_ Kultur. Denken. Forschen. Darstellen. 38. Kongress der Deutschen Gesellschaft für Volkskunde in Tübingen 2011.* Münster: Waxmann, 28–37.

Reckwitz, A. (2015) 'Sinne und Praktiken', in Prinz, S. and Göbel, H. K. (eds.) *Die Sinnlichkeit des Sozialen.* Bielefeld: Transcript, 441–55.

Reckwitz, A. (forthcoming) *The invention of creativity: how society has become like art.* Cambridge: Polity Press.

Reh, S. and Ricken, N. (2012) 'Das Konzept der Adressierung. Zur Methodologie einer qualitativ-empirischen Erforschung von Subjektivation', in Miethe, I. and Müller, H. (eds.) *Qualitative Bildungsforschung und Bildungstheorie.* Opladen/Farmington Hills: Barbara Budrich, 35–56.

Reich, A. and Hager, P. (2014) 'Problematising practice, learning and change: practice-theory perspectives on professional learning', *Journal of Workplace Learning*, 26(6–7), 418–31.

Rhee, K. E., Phelan, S. and McCaffery, J. (2012) 'Early determinants of obesity: genetic, epigenetic, and in utero influences', *International Journal of Pediatrics*, 1–9.

Riedel, M. (2012) 'Soziologie der Berührung und des Körperkontakts', in Schmidt, R. and Schetsche, M. (eds.) *Körperkontakt. Interdisziplinäre Erkundungen.* Wiesbaden: Psychosozial-Verlag, 77–105.

Rinkinen, J., Jalas, M. and Shove, E. (2015) 'Object relations in accounts of everyday life', *Sociology*, 49(5), 870–85.

Roberto, C. A., Swinburn, B., Hawkes, C., Huang, T. T.-K., Costa, S. A., Ashe, M., … Brownell, K. D. (2015) 'Patchy progress on obesity prevention: emerging examples, entrenched barriers, and new thinking', *The Lancet*, 385(9985), 2400–9.

Rodeschini, G. (2013) 'Bodywork practices on the elderly: the process of feeding and the biomedicalization of aging', in Wolkowitz, C., *et al.* (eds.) *Body/sex/work – intimate, embodied and sexualised labour.* London: Palgrave Macmillan, 207–22.

Røpke, I. (2009) 'Theories of practice – new inspiration for ecological economic studies on consumption', *Ecological Economics*, 68(10), 2490–7.

Rose, N. and Miller, P. (1992) 'Political power beyond the state: problematics of government', *British Journal of Sociology*, 43(2), 173–205.

Rouse, J. (2001) 'Two concepts of practice', in Schatzki, T. R., Knorr Cetina, K. and Von Savigny, E. (eds.) *The practice turn in contemporary theory.* London: Routledge, 189–98.

Rouse, J. (2007a) 'Practice theory', *Division I Faculty Publications. Paper 43.* Available at http://wesscholar.wesleyan.edu/div1facpubs/43 (accessed 31 May 2016).

Rouse, J. (2007b) 'Social practices and normativity', *Philosophy of the Social Sciences*, 37(1), 46–56.

Sarangi, S. and Roberts, C. (eds.) (1999) *Talk, work and institutional order: discourse in medical, mediation and management settings*. Berlin: Walter de Gruyter.

Saussure, F. (1966 [1916]) *Course in general linguistics*. Translated by W. Baskin. New York: McGraw-Hill.

Sayer, A. (2012) 'Power, sustainability and well-being', in Shove, E. and Spurling, N. (eds.) *Sustainable practices: social theory and climate change*. London: Routledge.

Schäfer, A. and Thompson, C. (eds.) (2010) *Anerkennung*. Paderborn: Ferdinand Schöningh.

Schäfer, H. (2013) *Die Instabilität der Praxis: Reproduktion und Transformation des Sozialen in der Praxistheorie*. Bielefeld: Transcript.

Schatzki, T. R. (1996) *Social practices: A Wittgensteinian approach to human activity and the social*. Cambridge: Cambridge University Press.

Schatzki, T. R. (1997) 'Practices and actions: a Wittgensteinian critique of Bourdieu and Giddens', *Philosophy of the Social Sciences*, 27(3), 283–308.

Schatzki, T. R. (2001a) 'Introduction: practice theory', in Schatzki T. R., Knorr Cetina, K. and Von Savigny, E. (eds.) *The practice turn in contemporary theory*. New York: Routledge.

Schatzki, T. R. (2001b) 'On sociocultural evolution by social selection', *Journal for the Theory of Social Behaviour*, 31(4), 341–64.

Schatzki, T. R. (2002) *The site of the social: a philosophical exploration of the constitution of social life and change*. University Park: Pennsylvania State University Press.

Schatzki, T. R. (2006) 'On organizations as they happen', *Organization Studies*, 27(12), 1863–73.

Schatzki, T. R. (2009) 'Timespace and the organization of social life', in Shove, E., Trentmann, F. and Wilk, R. (eds.) *Time, consumption and everyday life: practice, materiality and culture*. Oxford: Berg, 35–48.

Schatzki, T. R. (2010a) 'Materiality and social life', *Nature and Culture*, 5(2), 123–49.

Schatzki, T. R. (2010b) *The timespace of human activity: on performance, society, and history as indeterminate teleological events*. Lanham: Lexington Books.

Schatzki, T. R. (2011) 'Where the action is (on large social phenomena such as sociotechnical regimes)', *Sustainable Practices Research Group Working Paper 1*. Available at www.sprg.ac.uk (accessed 31 May 2016).

Schatzki, T. R. (2012) 'A primer on practices', in Higgs, J., et al. (eds.) *Practice-based education: perspectives and strategies*. Rotterdam: Sense Publishers, 13–26.

Schatzki, T. R. (2013) *The edge of change: on the emergence, persistence, and dissolution of practices. Sustainable practices: social theory and climate change*. London: Routledge, 31–46.

Schatzki, T. R. (2015a) 'Practices, governance and sustainability', in Strengers, Y. and Maller, C. (eds.) *Social practices, intervention and sustainability: beyond behaviour change*. Abingdon: Routledge, 15–30.

Schatzki, T. R. (2015b) 'Spaces of practices and of large social phenomena', *Espace Temps. net*. Available at www.espacestemps.net/articles/spaces-of-practices-and-of-large-social-phenomena/ (accessed 27 July 2015).

Schatzki, T. R. (2016a) 'Crises and adjustments in ongoing life', *Österreichische Zeitschrift für Soziologie*, 41(suppl. 1), 17–33.

Schatzki, T. R. (2016b) 'Keeping track of large phenomena', *Geographische Zeitschrift*, 104(1), 4–24.

Schatzki, T. R. (2016c) 'Practices and learning', *Praxeologie & Differenz im erziehungswissenschaftlichen Diskurs*, Flensburg, 28–29 January 2016. Available at www.uni-flensburg.de/tagung-praxeologie/news-room/news/detail/News/theodore-schatzki-practices-and-learning/ (accessed 31 May 2016).

Schatzki, T. R. (2016d) 'Practice theory as flat ontology', in Spaargaren, G., Weenink, D. and Lamers, M. (eds.) *Practice theory and research: exploring the dynamics of social life*. Abingdon: Routledge.

Schatzki, T. R. (forthcoming) 'Multiplicity in social theory and practice ontology', in Jonas, M. and Littig, B (eds.) *Praxeological Political Analysis*. Abingdon: Routledge.

Schatzki, T. R., Knorr Cetina, K. and Von Savigny, E. (eds.) (2001) *The practice turn in contemporary theory*. London: Routledge.

Scheffer, T. (2008) 'Zug um Zug und Schritt für Schritt. Annäherung an eine transsequentielle Analytik', in Kalthoff, H., Hirschauer, S. and Lindemann, G. (eds.) *Theoretische Empirie. Zur Relevanz qualitativer Forschung*. Frankfurt am Main: Suhrkamp, 368–98.

Schegloff, E. A. (1997) 'Whose text? Whose context?', *Discourse & Society*, 8(2), 165–87.

Schindler, L. (2011) 'Teaching by doing. Zur körperlichen Vermittlung von Wissen', in Meuser, M. and Keller, R. (eds.) *Körperwissen. Über die Renaissance des Körperlichen*. Wiesbaden: VS-Verlag, 335–50.

Schlipsing, M. (2014) *Videobasierte Leistungserfassung im Fußball*. Dissertation. Fakultät für Elektrotechnik und Informationstechnik at the Ruhr-Universität Bochum.

Schmidt, R. (2012) *Soziologie der Praktiken. Konzeptionelle Studien und empirische Analysen*. Berlin: Suhrkamp.

Schmidt, R. (2016) 'Neue Analyse- und Wissenspraktiken im Profifußball', *Sport und Gesellschaft – Sport and Society*, 11(4), 211–26.

Schmidt, R. (2016) 'The methodological challenges of practicising praxeology', in Spaargaren, G., Weenink, D. and Lamers, M. (eds.) *Practice theory and research: exploring the dynamics of social life*. Abingdon: Routledge.

Schmidt, R. (forthcoming) 'Notes on praxeological epistemology and method', in Jonas, M., et al. (eds.) *Methodological reflexions on practice-oriented theories*. Cham: Springer International.

Schmidt, R. and Volbers, J. (2011) 'Siting praxeology: the methodological significance of "public" in theories of social practices', *Journal for the Theory of Social Behaviour*, 41(4), 419–40.

Schmitz, H. (1998) *Der Leib, der Raum und die Gefühle*. Bielefeld: Edition Sirius.

Schumacher, E. (1989) *Small is beautiful: economics as if people mattered*. New York: Harper Trade.

Schütz, A. (1973) *The structures of the life-world*. Translated by R. M. Zaner and H. Tristram Engelhardt, Jr. Evanston: Northwestern University Press.

Schwarz, A. (2004) *The numbers game: baseball's lifelong fascination with statistics*. New York: St Martin's.

Scollon, R. (2001) *Mediated discourse. The nexus of practice*. New York: Routledge.

Scollon, R. (2005) Lighting the stove: why habitus isn't enough for Critical Discourse Analysis, in Wodak, R. and Chilton, P. E. (eds.) *A new agenda in (critical) discourse analysis*. Amsterdam: John Benjamins, 101–17.

Scollon, R. and Scollon, S. W. (2004) *Nexus analysis: discourse and the emerging internet*. New York: Routledge.

Scott, S. V. and Orlikowski, W. J. (2014) Entanglements in practice: performing anonymity through social media, *MIS Quarterly*, 38(3), 873–93.

Searle, J. R. (1969) *Speech acts. An essay in the philosophy of Language*. Cambridge: Cambridge University Press.

Searle, J. R. (1985) *Expression and meaning: studies in the theory of speech acts*. Cambridge: Cambridge University Press.

Seyfert, R. (2011) *Das Leben der Institutionen: Zu einer Allgemeinen Theorie der Institutionalisierung*. Weilerswist: Velbrück.

Shenk, D. (2011) *The genius in all of us: new insights into genetics, talent, and IQ*. New York: Anchor Books.

Shilling, C. (2002) 'The two traditions in the sociology of emotion', in Barbalet, J. (ed.) *Emotions and sociology*. Oxford: Blackwell, 10–32.

Shilling, C. (2003) *The body and social theory*. 2nd edn. London: Sage.

Shotter, J. (2013) 'Reflections on sociomateriality and dialogicality in organization studies: from 'inter-' to 'intra-thinking'... in performing practices', in Carlile, P. R., *et al.* (eds.) *How matter matters: objects, artifacts, and materiality in organization studies*. Oxford: Oxford University Press, 32–57.

Shove, E. (2003) *Comfort, cleanliness and convenience: the social organization of normality*. Oxford/New York: Berg.

Shove, E. (2009) 'Everyday practice and the production and consumption of time', in Shove, E., Trentmann, F. and Wilk, R. (eds.) *Time, consumption and everyday life: practice, materiality and culture*. Oxford: Berg, 17–35.

Shove, E. (2014) 'Linking low carbon policy and social practice', in Strengers, Y. and Maller, C. (eds.) *Social practices, intervention and sustainability: beyond behaviour change*. London: Routledge, 31–44.

Shove, E. (2016) 'Infrastructures and practices: networks beyond the city', in Coutard, O. and Rutherford, J. (eds.) *Beyond the networked city: infrastructure reconfigurations and urban change in the North and South*. Abingdon: Routledge, 242–58.

Shove, E. and Pantzar, M. (2005a) 'Consumers, producers and practices: understanding the invention and reinvention of Nordic walking', *Journal of Consumer Culture*, 5(1), 43–64.

Shove, E. and Pantzar, M. (2005b) 'Fossilisation', *Ethnologia Europaea*, 35(1), 59–63.

Shove, E. and Pantzar, M. (2007) 'Recruitment and reproduction: the careers and carriers of digital photography and floorball', *Human Affairs*, 17(1), 154–67.

Shove, E. and Spurling, N. (eds.) (2013) *Sustainable practices: social theory and climate change*. Abingdon: Routledge.

Shove, E. and Walker, G. (2014) 'What is energy for? Social practice and energy demand', *Theory, Culture & Society*, 31(5), 41–58.

Shove, E. and Warde, A. (2002) 'Inconspicuous consumption: the sociology of consumption, lifestyles and environment', in Dunlap, R. (ed.) *Sociological theory and the environment*. Colorado: Rownan and Littlefield, 230–51.

Shove, E., Pantzar, M. and Watson, M. (2012) *The dynamics of social practice: everyday life and how it changes*. London: Sage.

Shove, E., Walker, G. and Brown, S. (2014) 'Material culture, room temperature and the social organisation of thermal energy', *Journal of Material Culture*, 19(2), 113–24.

Shove, E., Watson, M. and Spurling, N. (2015) 'Conceptualizing connections energy demand, infrastructures and social practices', *European Journal of Social Theory*, 18(3), 274–87.

Shove, E., Watson, M., Hand, M. and Ingram, J. (2007) *The design of everyday life*. Oxford/New York: Berg.

Shusterman, R. (2011) 'Muscle memory and the somaesthetic pathologies of everyday life', *Human Movement*, 12(1), 4–15.

Silvast, A., Hänninen, H. and Hyysalo, S. (2013) 'Guest editorial: energy in society: energy systems and infrastructures in society', *Science and Technology Studies*, 27(1), 3–13.

Sinanan, K. and Milnes, T. (2010) 'Introduction', in Sinanan, K. and Milnes, T. (eds.) *Romanticism, sincerity and authenticity*. London: Palgrave Macmillan.

Skinner, M. K. (2014) 'Environmental stress and epigenetic transgenerational inheritance', *BMC Med*, 12(153), 1–5.

Slessor, C. (2015) 'Building study: Alder Hey Children's Hospital BDP', *The Architect's Journal*, 2 October, 2015. Available at www.architectsjournal.co.uk/buildings/alder-hey-childrens-hospital-by-bdp/8689754.fullarticle (accessed 24 May 2016).

Southerton, D. (2006) 'Analysing the temporal organization of daily life: social constraints, practices and their allocation', *Sociology*, 40(3), 435–54.

Southerton, D. (2009) 'Re-oredering temporal rhythms', in Shove, E., Trentmann, F. and Wilk, R. (eds.) *Time, consumption and everyday life*. Oxford: Berg, 49–66.

Southerton, D., Warde, A. and Hand, M. (2004) 'The limited autonomy of the consumer: implications for sustainable consumption', in Southerton, D., Chappells, H. and Van Vliet, B. *Sustainable consumption: implications of changing infrastructures of provision.* Manchester: Edward Elgar, 32–48.

Sovacool, B. (2015) 'Fuel poverty, affordability, and energy justice in England: policy insights from the Warm Front Program', *Energy*, 93(1), 361–71.

Spurling, N. and McMeekin, A. (2014) 'Sustainable mobility policies in England', in Strengers, Y. and Maller, C. (eds.) *Social practices, intervention and sustainability: beyond behaviour change.* London: Routledge, 78–94.

Spurling, N., McMeekin, A., Shove, E., Southerton, D. and Welch, D. (2013) *Interventions in practice: re-framing policy approaches to consumer behaviour.* Available at www.sprg.ac.uk/uploads/sprg-report-sept-2013.pdf (accessed 31 May 2016).

Star, S. L. and Griesemer, J. R. (1989) 'Institutional ecology, "translations" and boundary objects: amateurs and professionals in Berkeley's Museum of Vertebrate Zoology', *Social Studies of Science*, 19(3), 387–420.

Staron, R. S., Leonardi, M. J., Karapondo, D. L., Malicky, E. S., Falkel, J. E., Hagerman, F. C. and Hikida, R. S. (1991) 'Strength and skeletal muscle adaptations in heavy-resistance-trained women after detraining and retraining', *Journal of Applied Physiology*, 70(2), 631–40.

Strasser, S. (1999) *Waste and want: a social history of trash.* New York: Metropolitan Books.

Strati, A. (1999) *Organization and aesthetics.* London: Sage.

Strati, A. (2000) *Theory and method in organization studies: paradigms and choices.* London: Sage.

Strengers, Y. and Maller, C. (2014) *Social practices, intervention and sustainability: beyond behaviour change.* London: Routledge.

Suchman, L. (1987) *Plans and situated actions: the problem of human-machine communication.* Cambridge: Cambridge University Press.

Suchman, L. (2007a) 'Feminist STS and the sciences of the artificial', in Hackett, E., *et al.* (eds.) *The handbook of science and technology studies.* 3rd edn. Cambridge: MIT Press, 139–63.

Suchman, L. (2007b) *Human-machine reconfigurations: plans and situated actions.* 2nd edn. Cambridge: Cambridge University Press.

Suchman, L. (2011) 'Subject objects', *Feminist Theory*, 12(2), 119–45.

Swidler, A. (1986) 'Culture in action: symbols and strategies', *American Journal of Sociology*, 51(2), 273–86.

Swidler, A. (2001) 'What anchors cultural practices?', in Schatzki, T. R., Knorr Cetina, K. and Von Savigny, E. (eds.) *The practice turn in contemporary theory.* London: Routledge.

Szmigin, I. and Canning, L. (2015) 'Sociological ambivalence and funeral consumption', *Sociology*, 49(4), 748–63.

Tammen, S. A., Friso, S. and Choi, S. (2013) 'Epigenetics: the link between nature and nurture', *Molecular Aspects of Medicine*, 34(4), 753–64.

Taylor, C. (1985a) 'Interpretation and the sciences of man', in *Philosophy and the human sciences: philosophical papers 2.* Cambridge: Cambridge University Press, 15–58.

Taylor, C. (1985b) 'Social theory as practice', in *Philosophy and the human sciences: philosophical papers 2.* Cambridge: Cambridge University Press, 91–115.

Taylor, C. (1989) *Sources of the self: the making of modern identity.* Cambridge: Harvard University Press.

Taylor, C. (2002) 'Modern social imaginaries', *Public Culture*, 14(1), 91–124.

Taylor, C. (2004) *Modern social imaginaries.* Durham: Duke University Press.

Thrift, N. (2007) *Non-representational theory: space, politics, affect.* London: Routledge.

Tondl, L. (1974) 'On the concept of 'technology' and 'technological sciences', in Rapp, F. (ed.) *Contributions to a philosophy of technology: studies in the structure of thinking in the technological sciences.* New York: Springer Science & Business Media, 1–18.

Torpey, J. (2000) *The invention of the passport: surveillance, citizenship, and the state*. Cambridge: Cambridge University Press.

Tracey, R., Manikkam, M., Guerrero-Bosagna, C. and Skinner, M. K. (2013) 'Hydrocarbons (jet fuel JP-8) induce epigenetic transgenerational inheritance of obesity, reproductive disease and sperm epimutations', *Reproductive Toxicology*, 36(0), 104–16.

Trilling, L. (1972) *Sincerity and authenticity*. Cambridge: Harvard University Press.

Tuana, N. (2008) 'Viscous porosity: witnessing Katrina', in Alaimo, S. and Hekman, S. *Material feminism*. Bloomington: Indiana University Press, 188–213.

Tuana, N. and Sullivan, S. (2006) 'Feminist epistemologies of ignorance', *Hypathia*, 19(1), vii–ix.

Tukker, A. and Dietzenbacher, E. (2013) 'Global multiregional input-output frameworks: an introduction and outlook', *Economic Systems Research*, 25(1), 1–19.

Tuma, R. (2015) *Vernacular Video Analysis: Zur Vielfalt der kommunikativen Video-Rekonstruktion*. Dissertation. Fakultät Planen, Bauen, Umwelt of the Technische Universität Berlin.

Turnbaugh, P. J., Ley, R., Hamady, M., Fraser-Liggett, C., Knight, R. and Gordon, J. I. (2007) 'The human microbiome project: exploring the microbial part of ourselves in a changing world', *Nature*, 449(7164), 804–10.

United Nations Conference on Trade and Development (2014) 'Executive Summary', *Review of Martime Transport*. Available at http://unctad.org/en/PublicationsLibrary/rmt2014_en.pdf (accessed 2 January 2016).

Urry, J. (2004) 'The "system" of automobility', *Theory, Culture & Society*, 21(4–5), 25–39.

Vaisey, S. (2009) 'Motivation and justification: a dual-process model of culture in action', *American Journal of Sociology*, 114(6), 1675–715.

Verbeek, P. (2005) *What things do: philosophical reflections on technology, agency, and design*. University Park: Pennsylvania State University Press.

Volbers, J. (2015) 'Theorie und Praxis im Pragmatismus und der Praxistheorie', in Alkemeyer, T., Schürmann, V. and Volbers, J. (eds.) *Praxis denken. Konzepte und Kritik*. Wiesbaden: VS-Verlag, 193–214.

Vormbusch, U. (2004) 'Accounting: Die Macht der Zahlen im gegenwärtigen Kapitalismus', *Berliner Journal für Soziologie*, 11(1), 33–50.

Wacquant, L. (1992) 'The social logic of boxing in black Chicago: toward a sociology of pugilism', *Sociology of Sport Journal*, 9(3), 221–54.

Wacquant, L. (1996) 'Auf dem Weg zu einer Sozialpraxeologie. Struktur und Logik der Soziologie Pierre Bourdieus', in Bourdieu, P. and Wacquant, L. *Reflexive Anthropologie*. Frankfurt am Main: Suhrkamp, 17–93.

Wacquant, L. (2004) *Body & soul. Notebooks of an apprentice boxer*. New York: Oxford University Press.

Wainwright, S. P. and Turner, B. S. (2006) '"Just crumbling to bits"? An exploration of the body, ageing, injury and career in classical ballet dancers', *Sociology*, 40(2), 237–55.

Walker, G. (2013) 'Inequality, sustainability and capability: locating justice in social practice', in Shove, E. and Spurling, N. (eds.) *Sustainable practices: social theory and climate change*. Abingdon: Routledge, 181–96.

Wallenborn, G. and Wilhite, H. (2014) 'Rethinking embodied knowledge and household consumption', *Energy Research & Social Science*, 1, 56–64.

Wallenborn, G. (2013) 'Extended bodies and the geometry of practices', Shove, E. and Spurling, N. (eds.) *Sustainable practices: social theory and climate change*. Abingdon: Routledge, 146–64.

Walter, T. (2005) 'Three ways to arrange a funeral: mortuary variation in the modern West', *Mortality*, 10(3), 173–92.

Wang, H. (2004) 'Regulating transnational flows of people: an institutional analysis of passports and visas as a regime of mobility', *Identities: Global Studies in Culture and Power*, 11(3), 351–76.

Wang, S. and Shove, E. (2008) 'How rounders goes around the world', in Thrift, N., *et al. Globalization in practice*. Oxford: Oxford University Press, 202–6.

Warde, A. (2005) 'Consumption and theories of practice', *Journal of Consumer Culture*, 5(2), 131–53.

Warde, A. (2015) *The practice of eating*. Cambridge: Polity Press.

Warde, A., Cheng, S.-L., Olsen, W. and Southerton, D. (2007) 'Changes in the practice of eating: a comparative analysis of time-use', *Acta Sociologica*, 50(4), 363–85.

Watson, M. (2012) 'How theories of practice can inform transition to a decarbonised transport system', *Journal of Transport Geography*, 24, 488–96.

Watson, M. and Shove, E. (2008) 'Product, competence, project and practice: DIY and the dynamics of craft consumption', *Journal of Consumer Culture*, 8(1), 69–89.

Welch, D. (2012) *Understanding the commercial field of sustainability communications*. PhD thesis. University of Manchester.

Welch, D. and Warde, A. (2015) 'Theories of practice and sustainable consumption', in Reisch, L. and Thøgersen, J. (eds.) *Handbook of research on sustainable consumption*. Cheltenham, UK: Edward Elgar Publishing, 84–100.

Wenger, E. (1998) *Communities of practice: learning, meaning, and identity*. Cambridge: Cambridge University Press.

Wertsch, J.V. (1998) *Mind in action*. New York: Oxford University Press.

Whitford, J. (2002) 'Pragmatism and the untenable dualism of means and ends: why rational choice theory does not deserve paradigmatic privilege', *Theory & Society*, 31(3), 325–63.

WHO (2015a) *Noncommunicable diseases: fact sheet*. Available at www.who.int/mediacentre/factsheets/fs355/en/ (accessed 31 May 2016).

WHO (2015b) *Obesity and overweight: fact sheet*. Available at www.who.int/mediacentre/factsheets/fs311/en/ (accessed 31 May 2016).

Wilkinson, R. and Marmot, M. (eds.) (2003) *Social determinants of health: the solid facts*. 2nd edn. Copenhagen: World Health Organization.

Winner, L. (1985) 'Do artefacts have politics?', in MacKenzie, D. and Wajcman, J. (eds.) *The social shaping of technology*. London: Open University Press.

Wittgenstein, L. (2009 [1953]) *Philosophical investigations*. Translated by G. E. M. Anscombe, P. M. S. Hacker and J. Schulte. Edited by P. M. S. Hacker and J. Schulte. 4th edn. Oxford: Blackwell.

Yates, L. and Warde, A. (2015) 'The evolving content of meals in Great Britain. Results of a survey in 2012 in comparison with the 1950s', *Appetite*, 84, 299–308.

Zerubavel, E. (1979) *Patterns of time in hospital life: a sociological perspective*. Chicago: University of Chicago Press.

Zucchi, B. (2015) 'Architect's view', *The Architect's Journal*, 2 October 2013. Available at www.architectsjournal.co.uk/buildings/alder-hey-childrens-hospital-by-bdp/8689754.fullarticle (accessed 24 May 2016).

INDEX